T5-COB-742

Let's Go Out!

Interiors and Architecture for Restaurants and Bars

gestalten

Experience New Values

Fritz Dining Room → 48–49

Poison d'Amour → 256–257

Bad times may be bad, but they have their upsides too. They put our feet back on the ground and inspire us to greater heights of creativity. They lead to renewal, including a renewal of values, and the design world is not immune to this recalibration. Today, the design world has a new valuation and vision of luxury, a luxury that delights in diversity and multiplicity.

PREFACE

/ Increasingly, there is a little something for everyone out there—and by "out there," we mean almost anywhere. The joy of going out in style is no longer the exclusive domain of Parisians or New Yorkers or the Milanese. Good design is spreading into the hinterland—cities you can't quite place on the map without being told which countries they're in—to Kfar Saba, Kilkis, Varna, Port Washington, Osnabrück, Trollveggen. It's Utrecht, Wu Xi, and Hiseko as much as Amsterdam, Shanghai, and Tokyo. Girona and Ashford as often as Barcelona and London. The cities you've never heard of are catching up to the international innovators and integrating local styles and visual vernaculars along the way.

And so hospitality and entertainment have become just a bit more democratic: aesthetic experiments are more widespread, venues are more accessible and, much to patrons' delight, they offer greater variety—of sensibilities, people, and food. Interestingly, it is a boom in specialization that gives us an early clue that this is happening: in recent years, monofood eateries dedicated to, say, only grilled cheese sandwiches, lobster rolls, or the peanut butter and jelly sandwich have sprung up around the world. Specialization allows owners to perfect both their place and their product and lets them pamper a constituency that has been underserved or served only en masse in the past: coffee shops that cater to an increasingly java-savvy public, for example, are presenting themselves as laboratories—equipped with sterile-white tiles, grid lighting, stainless steel surfaces, and beaker-like glassware—where coffee becomes a "crafted" comestible that must be prepared with a skillful combination of art and science.

The recent shift in perspective also acknowledges the great value of simple things: time, well-being, and comfort are counted among the greatest luxuries of all, and the spaces we go out into are catering to these changed perspectives. In progressive design, over-the-top glamour is being toned down, decadence of the clichéd sort pushed to a distance. Luxury is signaled less often by the stereotypical precious materials and finishes and increasingly by objects in which we take comfort: objects that suggest the human hand in their surfaces, objects that are textural and tactile, objects that embrace, shelter or blanket us. No wonder then that textiles, ceramics, wallcoverings, upholstery and drapes are more popular and innovative than ever. *Clancy's Fishbar*→22–25 in Perth is nearly incandescent with a mash-up of varicolored fabric "chandeliers," while curtains and seating made from Kvadrat's *Jungle* fabric soften and warm the white brick walls of the subterranean *GMOA Keller*→114–115 dining room.

Our renewed emphasis on simplicity brings ambitions back closer to home, within our range of focus. Sometimes it is a focus on traveling lighter and trusting more in our materials: the most surprising spaces are stripping down instead of dressing up. In Copenhagen, *Noma Lab*→132–133 consists of simple oak surfaces and a series of cylindrical shelving units that give it an organic Scandinavian coolness. In Lisbon, *Poison d'Amour*→256–257 shares a similar "austerity," but renders it in harder materials like marble and stone and white furnishings that contrast sharply with the monolithic black floors.

Ironically, this simple solution is more complex to execute because there are fewer distractions to obscure banality, derivation, cheapness, or flaws. It requires the rare ability to recognize when "blemishes" have value, can add to a space instead of detracting from it: in the Parisian *Coutume Café*→158–159, freshly stained flooring and new furnishings are paired with industrial plastic sheeting partitions, bare bulbs, and construction site-like excavations that reveal historical elements like the shop's original door, without embellishing or finishing them. Similarly, is Mexico City's *Cantina de Comida Mexicana*→168–169 half-demo'ed or half-built? The interior's structure remains exposed after the designers tore down sections of the ceiling and walls so that its bones serve both as a marker of local history and as ornament. In this way, structure is presented as something that can be mined as much as built. By combining this skillfully displayed construction-site rawness with refined finishes, wood furnishings, and polished cement floors, the designers suggest that the past and present can do more than co-exist; they can enrich one another.

In these projects, (apparent) accessibility has increased in comparison to the speakeasy sensibility of recent years with its secret addresses and unmarked doors in lieu of velvet ropes, where queued visitors have been turned away at the door arbitrarily, sometimes for no other reason, according to one restaurateur, than to make the

Trollwall Restaurant→58–61

point publicly that not just anyone can get in. Instead, the new space is relatively relaxed, friendly, open, inviting—if anything, it's attitude they check at the door.

LOOKING INWARD & OUTSIDE

Following recent trends in retail design, successful spaces for eating and drinking take their clients on a journey inward, not just into the viscera, but also into the imagination. Color, graphics, and tactility are food for fantasy and reflection as well as the ingredients of emotion and designers continue to use both to soothe or animate interiors. Perhaps colors appeal to the same synapses that fire in front of candy shop windows, a fact exploited by the designers of Stockholm's *Café Foam*→50–51 where a series of rooms starts in frothed-milk neutrals that are brought to a sudden boil with hot pink walls that draw all eyes irresistibly through the space. At times, even quiet materials can be rendered highly graphical through obsessive repetition or extremely formal treatments: *Niseko Look Out Café*→68–69 is threaded with wooden ribs set on a uniform grid of tiles, taking a traditional Japanese residential architecture detail to the nth degree. It's nearly Op Art, but in a neutral, natural material.

GMOA Keller→114–115

In spite of recent catastrophes and Hollywood's wildly popular natural disaster genre, designers are willfully envisioning Nature as a source of both shelter and inspiration. Nature is effortlessly graphical and seductively haptic: the shape of the Vietnamese *Lam Café* →70-71 building resembles a coconut leaf, while the focal point in San Francisco's *Frjtz Dining Room* →48-49 is a series of framed terrariums embedded flush in gallery-white walls as if they were man-made canvases, the oldest of the Old Masters.

Nature is, of course, the mother of fractal geometry, the earth having given us facets and polygons, crystals and snowflakes, analog elements that on a macro level appear high-tech. Imitating these therefore nicely reconciles our ambition for technological progress with our craving for a peace it has been unable to provide. It is the vast scale and proportion of the faceted walls and ceiling of Abu Dhabi's *Allure* →78-79 nightclub—not the gold leaf and bronze panels—that make for its out-size sumptuousness.

Twister →96-97, a Kiev restaurant slangily named after hurricanes, is both graphical and tactile. The designer has imagined Nature as fierce but protective and then abstracted it: Pendant lights shaped like raindrops never fall, banquettes ripple through the room, pine cone-shaped seating is all cushion and no needles. In Norway, Nature dwarfs man daily and to an extreme with severe weather, pounding waterfalls and unpredictable glaciers. Here the architect of the *Trollwall restaurant* →58-61 and visitor's center echoed his site, perched atop the tallest rock face in Europe, as if suggesting that we needn't view ourselves in opposition to Nature; humans too are a *force majeure*.

REALITY: ESCAPING IT, EMBRACING IT

In hard times, in particular, escape from reality becomes a necessary extravagance. Not long ago, we were escaping into flamboyantly scripted and deeply themed environments. Lately, however, theatrical treatments have become less histrionic. Immersive experience remains more important than flat imagery and logos in the service of branding, but staged interiors are less like opera sets and more like an Elizabethan theater; less visually overwrought and more narrative. Berlin yogurt shop, *EFA's Box* →74-75, consists of a series of *coulisses*: in spots, holes have been punched in the extant architecture and propped open with rough plywood to frame a vignette, elevating ordinary fast food service to a modest performance.

Even toned down, however, scenographic space still delivers top-drawer escapism: At Amsterdam coffee house, *Smoking Club Hi/Lo* →224-227, visitors toke up in spaces kitted out as postmodern heavens and hells, escaping into … their fumes. At *Stationen Uppsala Three* →234-235 in Sweden, period-based interiors allow guests to escape into another time. *Griffins Steakhouse Extraordinaire* →236-241, which is cluttered with objects sketching out the detailed life and characters of two imaginary hosts, lets visitors escape from their own lives into someone else's. At the Juliet Supperclub, where the interior was modeled on abstracted elements from the *1001 Nights*, clubgoers escaped into a fairytale.

Sometimes we just want to feel good to feel good. But at other times, we crave a space where we know that our consumption makes real sense, where we can do good (or not do bad) to feel good. World events have served as a reminder that having a voice and being able to use it is a rare privilege; we have agency. And we can speak with our cash.

Gone entirely are the days when "sustainable style" meant hemp and hippies. Sustainability can look slick today—the US's first LEED-certified nightclub, *The Greenhouse* →280-282, consisted mainly of recycled or recyclable materials though most guests ordering bottle service at glossy tables would never have known it—but it doesn't have to. The naive, repurposed, and handmade is also increasingly appreciated. Today, upcycled materials like salvaged wood are so popular that New England cows may be threatened with homelessness if barns continue to be stripped at the current rate.

Along with flea market finds and DIY objects, upcycling is being put to resourceful and sophisticated use: *Dishoom Chowpatty Beach Bar* →20-21 recreates a vociferously colorful Indian snack shack beside the Thames by using "construction materials" like rolled-up newspapers and reused yogurt tubs. The greatest virtue of some projects is a rough-hewn appearance that is nonetheless sophisticated in its craftsmanship or execution. Self-production is on the rise: the owner of Bakery in the lobby of Vienna's *Hotel Daniel* →210-213 made some of his own furniture, including a silk-covered sofa that he turned into a swing by cutting off its legs and suspending it from a length of old rope.

In an open-air London market, a pop-up kitchen called *Ridley's* →218-219 promoted local business, local agriculture, and what they called "exhibitionist eating": the cooks prepared meals on the ground floor kitchen of a structure made of scaffolding and hoisted it up via pulleys—table and all—to the floor above where it slotted into the center of a large communal dining table. The concept encouraged visitors to patronize the local market stalls: instead of taking cash payment, *Ridley's* accepted market produce in exchange for a cooked meal.

HOME: GOING OUT VS. GOING OUT TO STAY IN

Many venues are tailored to the harried lifestyle of the new century: In recent years, the artisanal food truck has become wildly popular and increasingly high-end, selling anything from handmade ice cream sandwiches to gourmet cupcakes, even winning over Parisians, who have begun to eat boutique burgers and tortillas on the streets and in the *marchés*.

PREFACE

In Portland, Oregon, the *Sip Mobile Lodge* →120 was converted using white paint and lots of wood from a 1969 Dodge Chinook into a juice and cocktail bar inspired by the cozily domestic feel of mountain lodges. As venturesome as we imagine ourselves to be, we do appreciate allusions to home; we just don't want to get stuck there. So we find ways to reconcile the urge to roam with the gratification that "staying in" represents in a world that is becoming ever more overwhelming: we "stay in" by going out.

Kitchain →202–203 gives the dining room table superpowers by turning it into a mobile unit and stowing basic kitchen tools inside, much like a picnic table or camping equipment. Integrated kitchenettes and grills provide DIY cooking and social space (or can be equipped with a chef) so that it becomes a pop-up dining room table, a place where strangers become neighbors even if only for the course of a meal.

Today, just as some of the newest hotel lobbies are becoming neighborhood living rooms, so too are other hospitality spaces working to simultaneously match and counteract our rampant nomadism (virtual, physical or both) by creating domestic environments that momentarily root us and yet sometimes move themselves: the *Otakara Supper Club* →200–201 takes place in a Brooklyn backyard that feels as casual and naïve as its food is refined. With a similarly undesigned look-and-feel, the *Kinfolk Dinner Series* →220–221 toured 12 cities in 12 months. Supper clubs like these make diners feel at home; it's just someone else's home where none of the guests have to do the dishes at the end of the evening.

In the age of social media, the popularity of the supper club should perhaps come as no surprise. Having arrived on a wave of informal food-related events, design, and media, it is partly a response to the need people feel to reconnect in the flesh. Supper club events hinge on the creativity of the chef, and on local food, produce, people, and styles. Most of all, they are meant to mend frayed community ties, serving as nodes where business relationships and creative collaborations can begin eyeball to eyeball.

KNOWING ONE'S PLACE

The supper club emphasis on the local is matched in more commercial settings like *La Bipolar* →44–45 cantina, where the designers took an almost anthropological approach to their research into (and rediscovery of their own) local Mexican culture and the objects of its expression. Restaurants like *Walden* →150–151 in Brooklyn recall late nineteenth and early twentieth century New York with their pressed tin ceilings, wooden bars, marble countertops, globe lighting, and tiled floors.

The design of *Alemagou Beach Bar* →134–135 on Mykonos works with the harsh local climate instead of against it and drew on surrounding Cycladic architectural elements, becoming a perfect creature of its place: whitewashed, stone-walled, and thatched with naturally insulating reed, it marries this familiar vernacular with crisp modern forms.

At the other extreme, it is still one of the pinnacles of indulgence to do extraordinary things in extraordinary places. Electrolux's *The Cube* →86–87 offers one of these once-in-a-lifetime opportunities: in this angular, hypermodern box craned onto the roof of a different major European landmark every three months, guests sit around a Michelin-starred chef's table while taking in views rarely seen by others through the glazed and perforated walls. It is an architectural symbiont that takes unparalleled advantage of location, location, location.

And then there are the places located somewhere between the physical and virtual worlds. *Zebar* →102–103 in Shanghai is a fine formal example. Imagine an immersive environment somewhere between the belly of Jonah's whale and Tron's living room. Its voluptuous black-and-white ribs arc upward, morphing from floor into ceiling. They are actually unique slices drawn in 3D modeling software but cut manually by Chinese workers. As we delight in our virtual tools but become virtually overwhelmed, both terra firma and the ether acquire new significance to us, values that are beginning to show up in a limbo-like space that might be called the "phygital" world.

In the following five chapters, the spaces we go out in are examined from several aesthetic and conceptual points of view. We start with "Playfull" spaces, celebrations of the emotion generated by color, graphics, form, composition and contrasts, of pop cultural objects and icons, and of cultures ranging from Indian to urban street art and coffee that have acquired a new dynamism thanks to this design approach. "Sophisticated" mines the sculptural, highly graphical, and sometimes layered design schemes that spring from a focus on structure and construction, where the skeleton often becomes the skin and the technical and the organic may be fused or confused. "Northern Comfort" could describe the clean, well-lighted, modernist spaces in the next chapter, with their straightforward Scandinavian elegance. Because these are softly minimalist, forthright and, above all, welcoming, they are places to which it is an easy pleasure to return again and again. Comfort is a key word in the following chapter, as well: "Home Sweet Home" describes interiors that are both cozy and charming. They may share a rustic chic style communicated through upcycled or salvaged materials and DIY details. At the opposite extreme, "Showtime" spaces involve the greatest mixes—sometimes dense mixes—of materials, colors, and patterns and don't necessarily rely on the worn out tropes of luxury that gleam a bit tinnily today. They have a unique voice and tell a story that may be true or may be a gorgeous fiction. Each design approach in these pages reflects our shifting values in a fraught era, where values turn out to be one of the most valuable things we possess.

by Shonquis Moreno

PREFACE

Experience New Values

→ 2–5

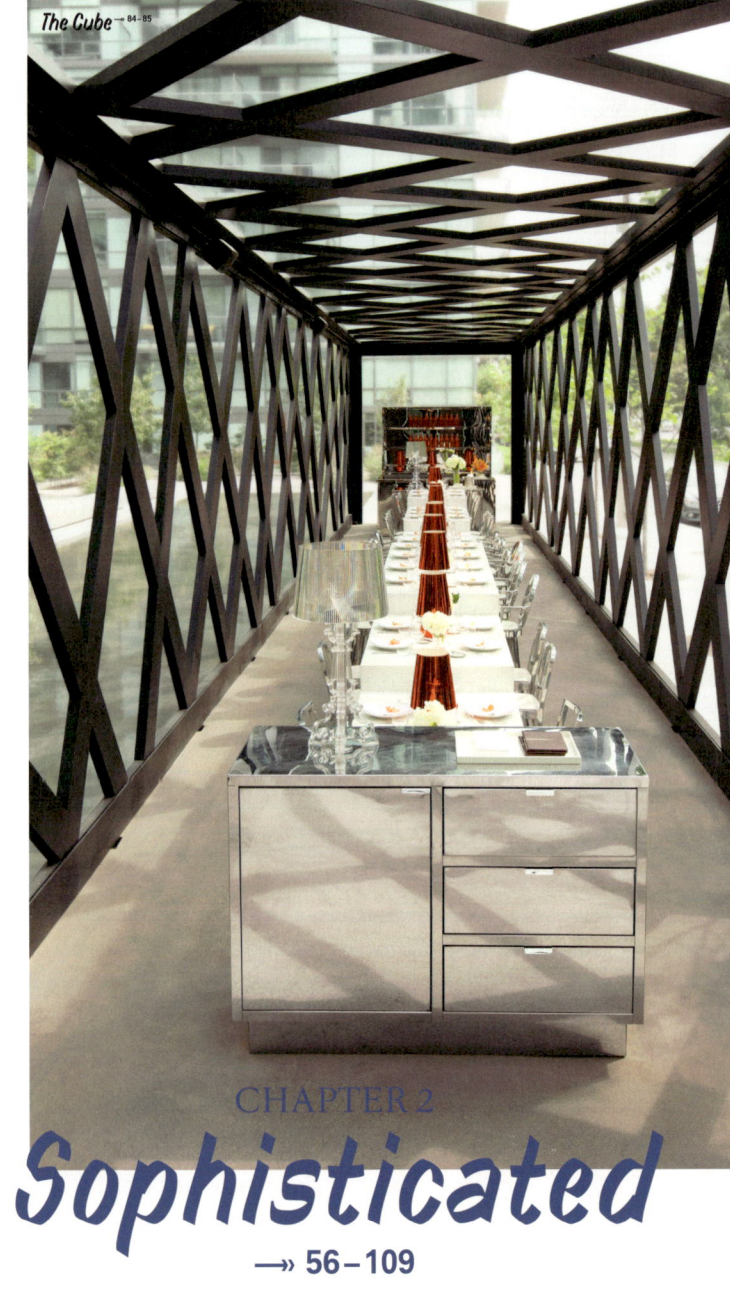

CHAPTER 1

Playful

→ 8–55

CHAPTER 2

Sophisticated

→ 56–109

TABLE OF CONTENTS → 6–7

INDEX → 283–287

IMPRINT → 288

CHAPTER 4
Home Sweet Home
→ 182–221

De Ferme & d'Eau Fraîche — 182–183

CHAPTER 3
Northern Comfort
→ 110–181

The Bridge Room — 122–123

OZONE — 228–233

CHAPTER 5
Showtime
→ 222–282

Cielito Querido Café—16–17

Playful

If eating, drinking, and socializing—if going out—is a celebration of being alive, the spaces we do it in should celebrate and stimulate the senses that let us know we're alive. Designers dress playful environments in whole ensembles of color—gradients, spectrums, or clashing mash-ups—or they use it to accessorize. A whimsical sensibility dramatizes familiar objects and visuals, intensifying their impact through repetition or abstraction, amplifying their graphical qualities, exaggerating form through hue, sharpening the contrast on finishes and materials, or isolating elements that are especially evocative. Sometimes playful spaces glamourize everyday objects of the past or present; others draw on collective fantasies.

Cello Bar →34–35

/ At Düsseldorf-based Toykio →26–27, a shop combining an urban art gallery, designer toy shop, and café, the energy of vibrant seating and rosy-hued, picture-frame cluttered walls is set off by glossy black tiles and dark flooring. The contrast creates a considered balance between the constant visual buzz of the artwork and a calm and composed atmosphere that encourages people to linger.

Sometimes balanced opposites like this—color glowing out of an elegant darkness—are the lure. At other times, balance is gleefully, if thoughtfully, abandoned and diverse objects and color schemes become a celebration in and of themselves, veritable parties of color. Between the tall black beams of the ceiling and wooden floors, Clancy's Fishbar →22–25 is the waterfront proscenium of a café in Perth that is brought to life with off-the-charts colorful furniture in a random range of shades. Some candied pieces—a bench here, a table there, plastic stools, flower-like pendant lights—provide fields of sunny tones. Appropriate to a shoreline eatery, they give the space a casual, antic air without allowing it to slump into laxity; color is used to animate space even before people enter it and then keeps the pitch high and the pace steady.

To an even greater extreme, when the temporary Dishoom Chowpatty Beach Bar →20–21 popped up in London, it re-created the tropical vibrancy of the legendary Bombay beach. Dishoom serves spicy street snacks, like *pau bhaji*, and the space was designed with a nod to the spirit of creative improvisation known as *jugaad* in Hindi. Styled as a shorefront shack set adrift in the great metropolis, its designers made it a febrile collage of repurposed and utterly banal materials, to which it pays vociferous homage: newspapers were rolled into tight tubes to form walls, plastic yogurt tubs were piled up into a counter. This warm visual chaos encourages patrons to let their hair down.

Playful space isn't just pure liberation, a design "wilding": sometimes it is a controlled synthesis of visuals and inspirations. Katrin Greiling's temporary bar and lounge at the Stockholm Furniture Fair was inspired by place just as much as Dishoom. But Greiling rendered her many geographical references in a restrained manner, interleaving multiple personal impressions of travel within a minimalist, abstracted environment as if she had worked in a layered Photoshop document and then flattened those visual layers into a jpeg. Within the fair's high-ceilinged pavilion, she punctuated a light-filled area with crisp fields of color, fabricating a cheerful welcome for footweary, bleary-eyed visitors.

Sometimes playful environments date themselves and, in fact, are intended to contain their own expiration dates: pop-up shops often capture their moment in time like an insect in amber. Other convivial spaces may be tied to a time or place by their look-and-feel, but by enshrining that period's popular character, offer an escape from the here and now. At that point, expiration dates become irrelevant. They are a sophisticated theme park of place or zeitgeist. The genial character of Union Jacks →14–15, a restaurant that takes its customers on a tour of the culinary UK, for example, is communicated through quirky British objects that ornament the interior: knit tea cozies, countertops with graph paper-lined surfaces, classroom stools, and vintage TV screens that let guests observe chefs at work in the kitchen where the cameras are always rolling.

Workaday references, familiar to the mainstream public, can ironically make an interior seem festive. But the designers of Cielito Querido →16–17 captured the spirit of late nineteenth century Mexico City without any literal allusions at all. Instead, they distilled characteristics of regional games, songs, and graphics from that era and infused the space with the exuberance of this reduction. Make no mistake, however: when a playful design scheme visits nostalgia it bespeaks the virtues and pleasures of that past, instead of sorrow at its loss or diversion. These are spaces that turn their drywall backs on the dark aspects of culture and turn up the visual volume on what is jubilant, enduring, dynamic, and emotional. They are a soup of collective optimism that turns the ordinary into a fairytale; while anchoring us to a place or a time, they grant us permission to feel just a little bit bigger than we really are, untethered and free.

Clancy's Fishbar →22–25

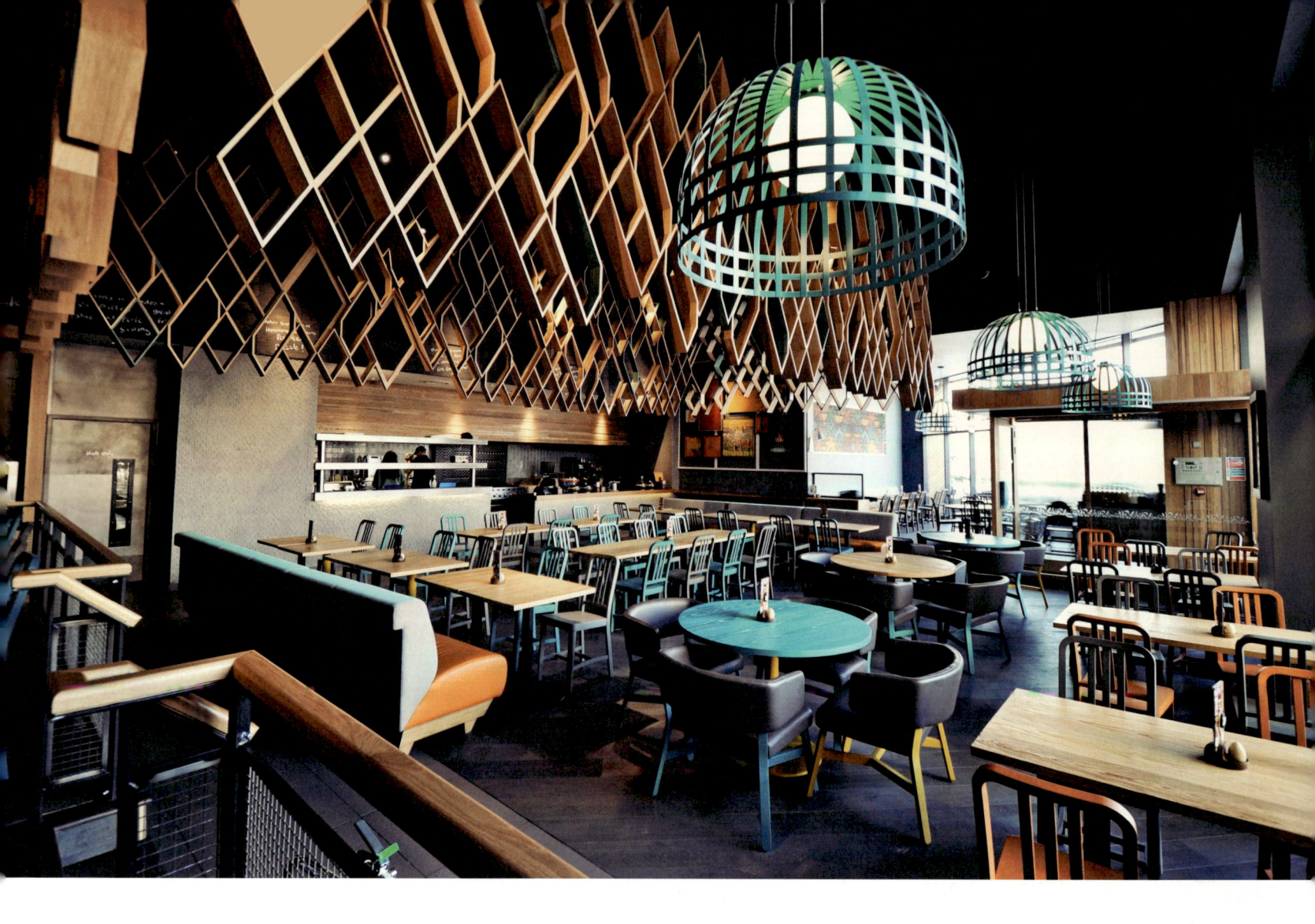

NANDO'S ASHFORD
Ashford, United Kingdom

/ Color and patterns characterize this third refurbishment for a fast-food chicken chain of South African origin by Blacksheep. Departing from the brand's traditional identity to attract a more mid-market customer and exploit the cavernous shell of a former nightclub, the designers lowered the 10-meter ceilings with a suspended wooden lattice and mounted low ceiling lights over a raised dining platform to provide greater intimacy. To create a New York loft sensibility, a combination of wood and metalwork was used sparely and a huge bespoke artwork produced, in the style of the South African Ndebele tribe, with thousands of painted wooden dowels.

/ Design: Blacksheep

/ Material: Floor: timber floor finish, gray porcelain tile, timber effect porcelain tile; Walls: stripped solid oak, distressed metal panels, faceted mosaic tile, wire mesh with hanging artwork, bespoke dowel artwork; Ceiling: lattice work hanging from ceiling

PLAYFUL

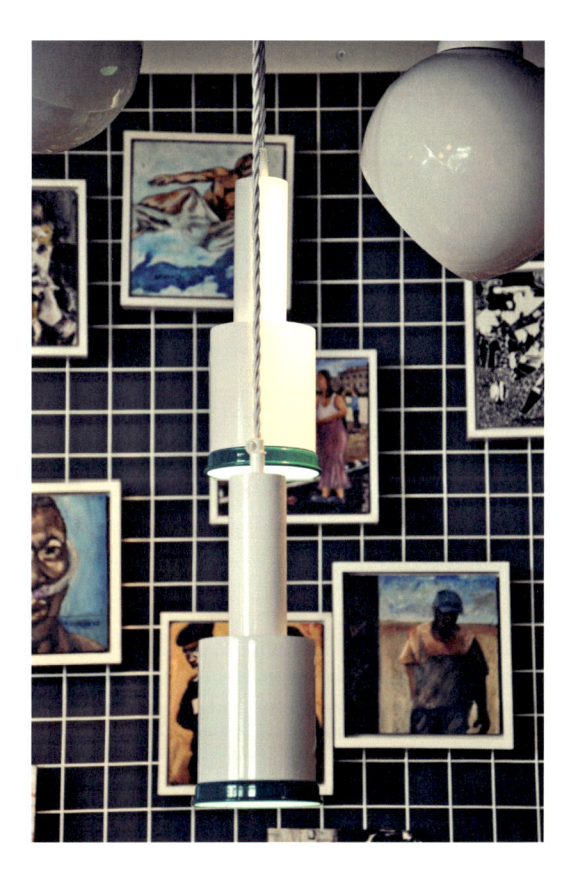

JAMIE ITALIAN WESTFIELD
London, United Kingdom

/ This space for chef Jamie Oliver responded to its high-value retail environment and was inspired by Italian delicatessens and dining, as well as Oliver's "cheeky Britishness." A "Jamie's ice-cream van" announces the eatery to the street, scooter headlights adorn one wall, and the al fresco area is fringed with potted herbs. Bespoke wall and lighting treatments from chandeliers to industrial-style elements ornament the various zones that line the railroad floor plan: a "Market Place" retail section, the "Piazza" main dining area and the less conspicuous and more intimate "Back Room."

/ Design: Blacksheep

/ Material: Reclaimed timber, reclaimed porcelain, bespoke hand carved Italian panels

PLAYFUL

14 / 15

UNION JACKS
London, United Kingdom

/ *Union Jacks* is the sixth project in Blacksheep's series of restaurant concepts for celebrity chef Jamie Oliver. Situated in the legendary Lego building by architect Renzo Piano, the design combines the main elements of the brand—service, food, theater, and ambiance—with an extra nod to British history and flavors and a subtle infusion of post-war nostalgia (including Beryl ware-inspired plates the underside of which reads "Stop looking at my bottom"). Quirky objects are dispersed throughout the interior: knitted 1970s-style tea cozies, countertops with graph paper patterns, stools out of a school science lab, and vintage TV screens linked to cameras in the kitchen that allow diners to watch the chefs at work.

/ Design: Blacksheep

CIELITO QUERIDO CAFÉ
Mexico City, Mexico

/ Named for a late nineteenth century song written by a Mexican composer, pretty *Cielito* is a product of its country's history and draws its vivid colors and ambiance from historical Mexican games, symbolism, and illustrated graphics. The wall-coverings and flooring represent a tapestry of exuberant geometries. The designers sought to establish a graphic language that is uniquely Mexican, but—like Mexico, itself—invites reinvention.

/ Design: Esrawe Studio & CADENA+ASOC.
/ Client: Cielito Querido Café
/ Type of Food/Drinks/Specialties: Coffee, cakes

"Cielito draws its vivid colors and ambiance from historical Mexican games, symbolism, and illustrated graphics."

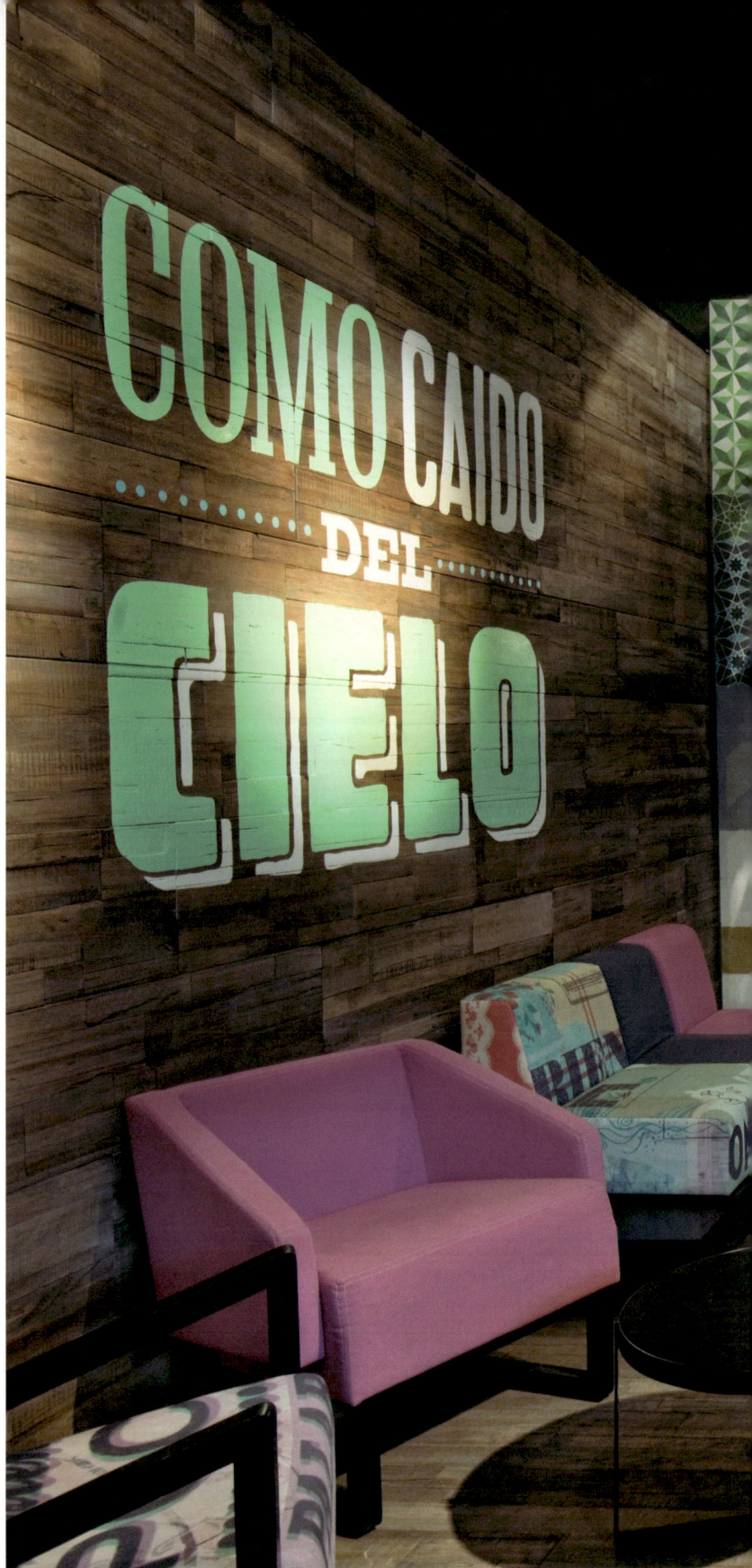

POLVO
HORNEAR
NUEZ
MOSCADA
LECHE
CAFÉ
CHOCOLATE
NUEZ
MOSCADA
CA
NE
LA
CACAO
MIEL

THE KITCHEN
AT THE CIRCUS HOTEL
& APARTMENTS
Berlin, Germany

/ This street level café and lounge by a Lebanese designer adheres to the philosophy of the larger hotel in which it is located and rejects the elitist, aristocratic approach to hospitality established during the late nineteenth century. Instead, it embraces travel as a series of sites that bring different people together on an equal footing no matter their age or wealth. This emphasis on the social aspect of travel made comfort a crucial aspect of the spaces for eating and drinking, and required the designer to establish a strong connection to place and introduce a fresh—in this case sustainable and aware—approach to "luxury."

/ Design: Rani al Rajji

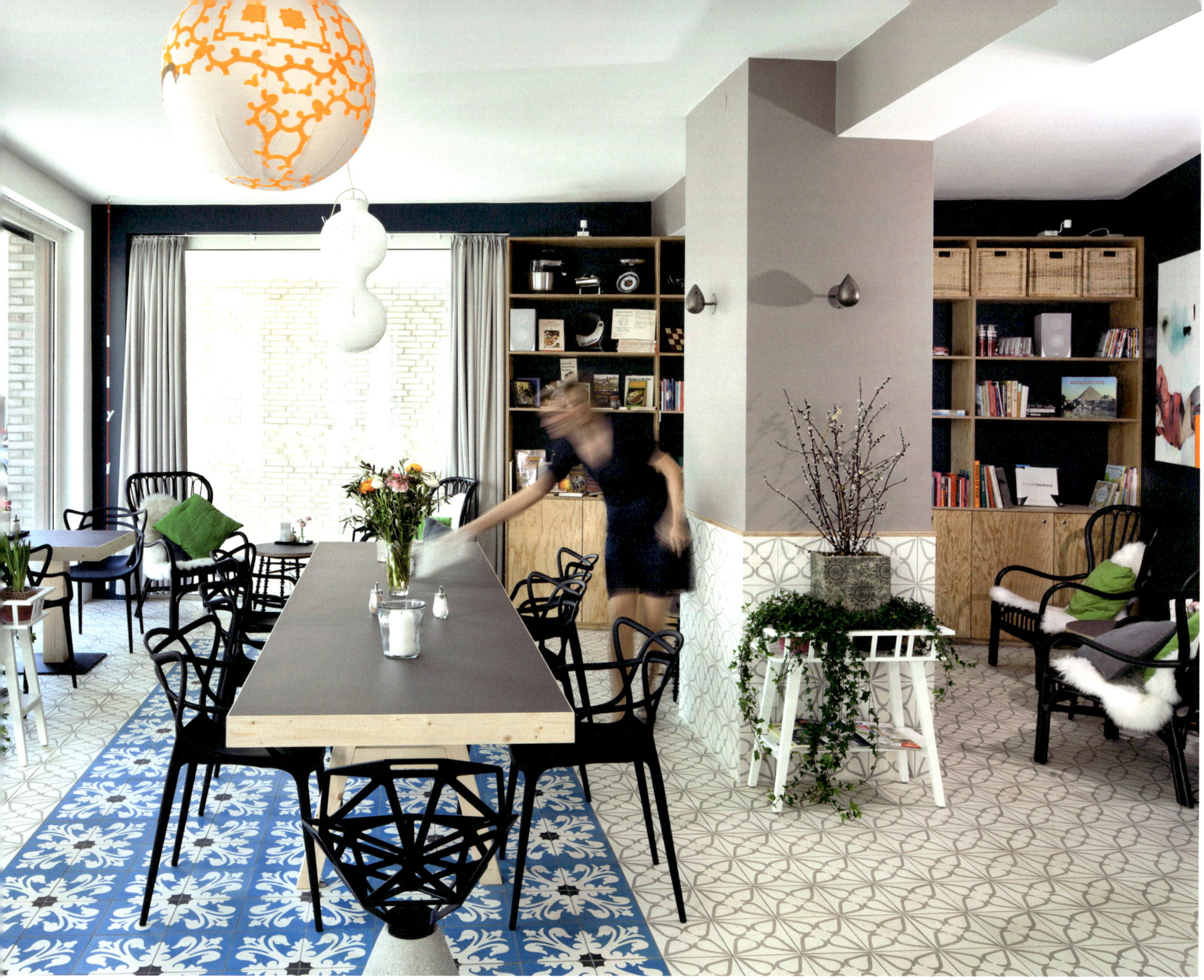

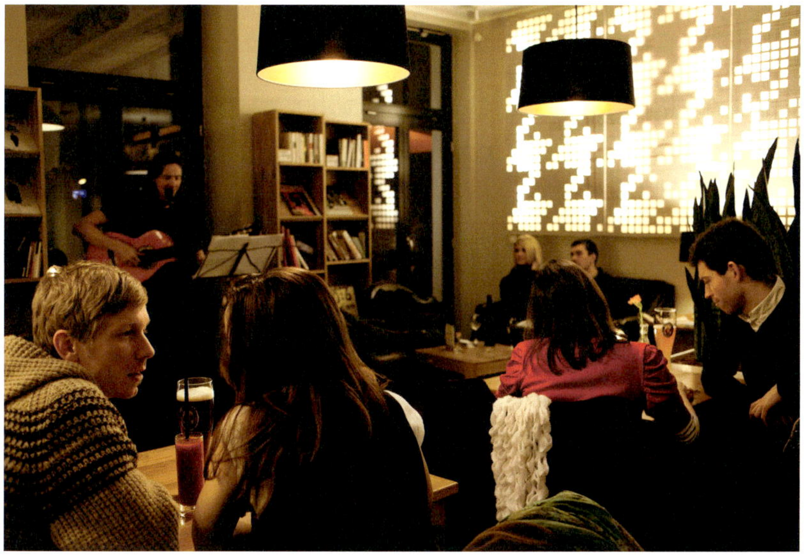

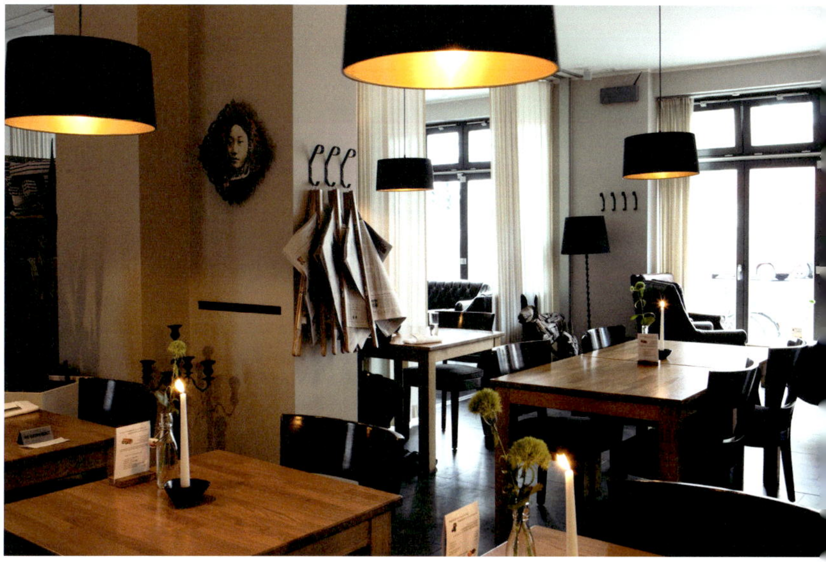

DISHOOM CHOWPATTY BEACH BAR
London, United Kingdom

"Recalling the original Chowpatty Beach in Bombay, Dishoom's candy-colored version offered Indian street snacks to the peckish cosmopolitan crowd."

/ Indians were doing upcycling long before the rest of the world caught on. Recalling the original Chowpatty Beach in Bombay, Dishoom's candy-colored—and temporary—version offered Indian street snacks to the peckish cosmopolitan crowd as much as those homesick for Thums Up soda and *pau bhaji*. Designed in the Indian spirit of creative improvisation known as *jugaad*, the urban beach shack was assembled from salvaged materials, walls of tightly rolled newspapers, a bar of repurposed yoghurt tubs, and sundry plastic containers.

/ Design: Honest Entertainment

/ Client: Dishoom

/ Type of Food/Drinks/Specialties: Bombay street snacks, Naughty golas, Naughty coconuts

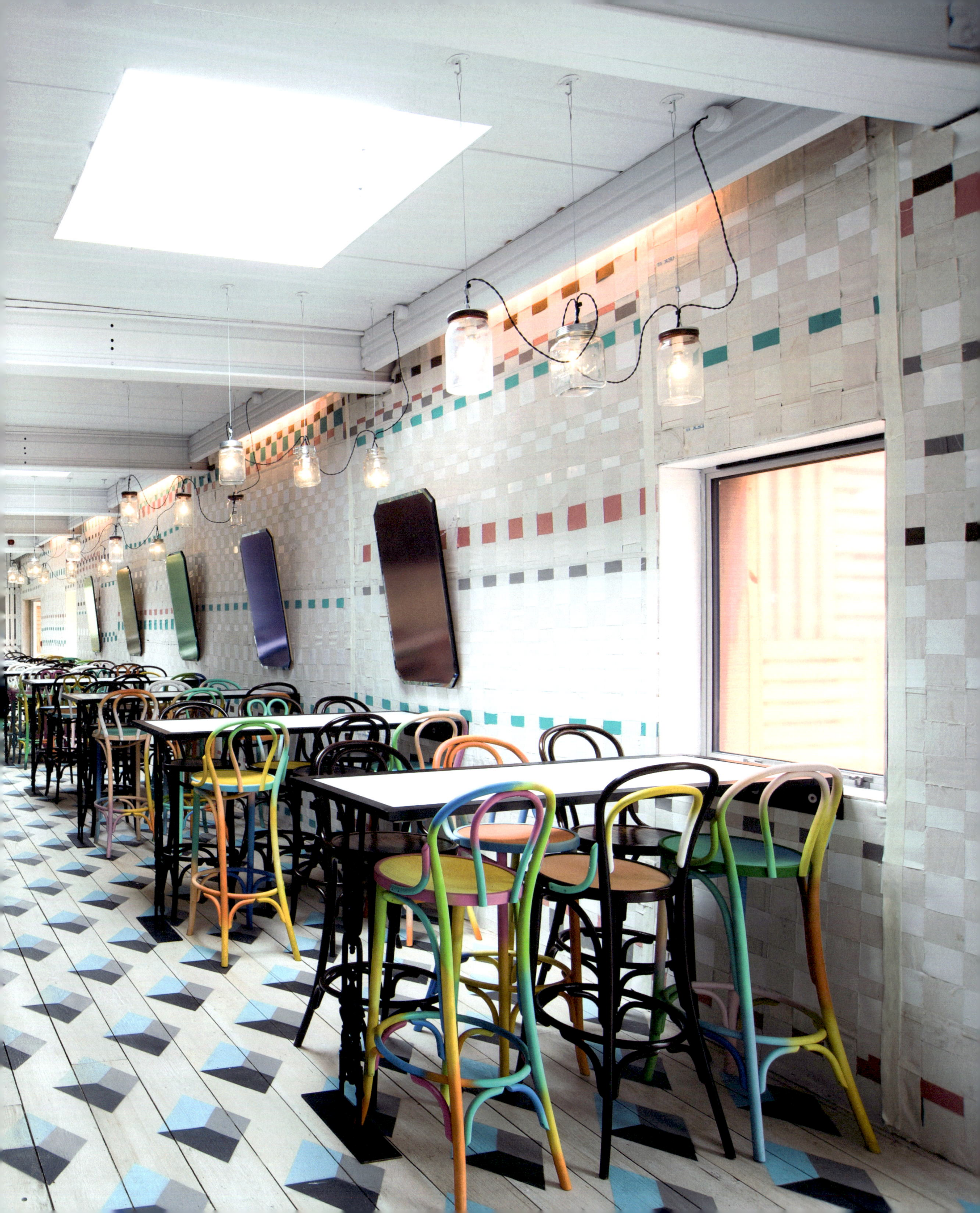

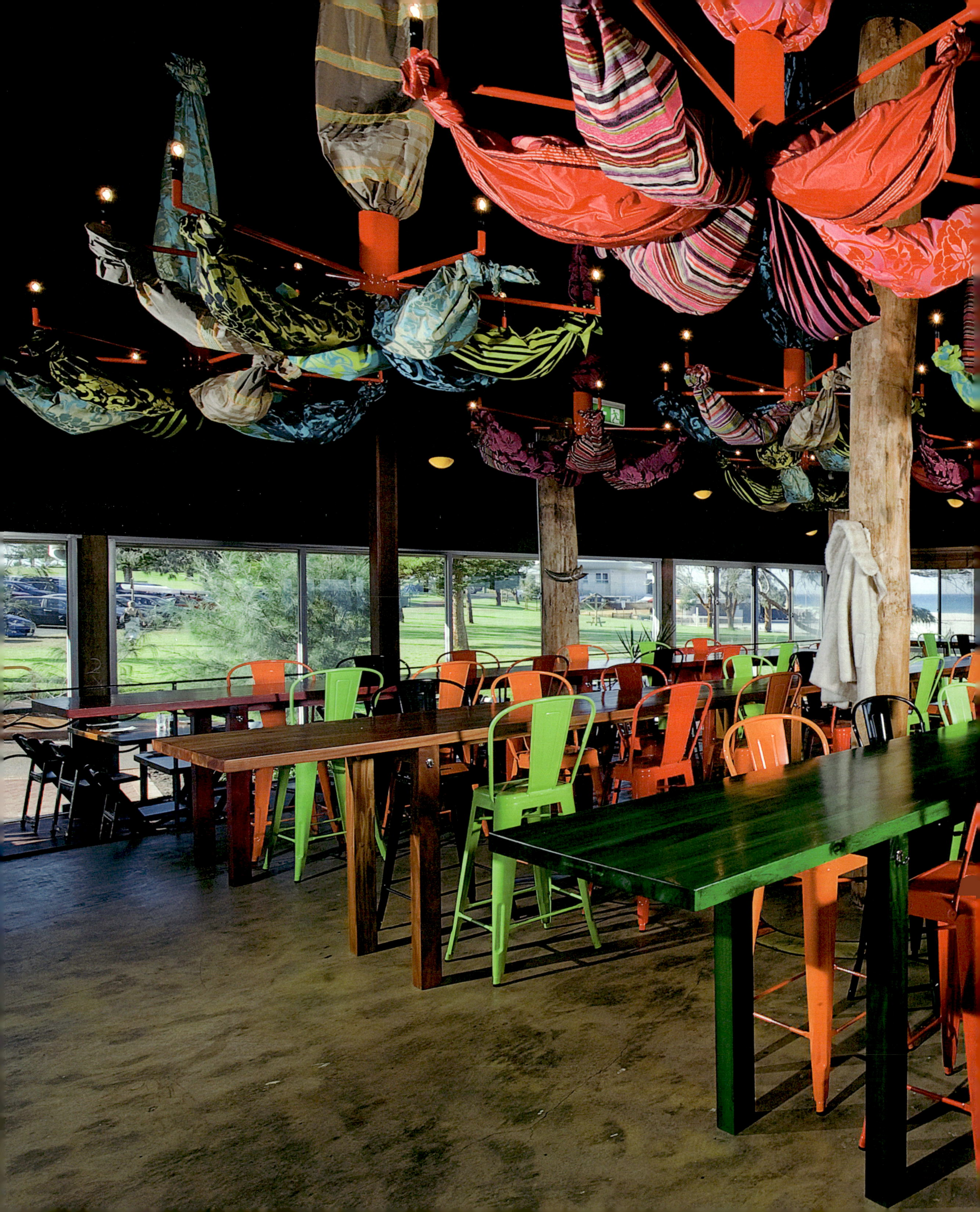

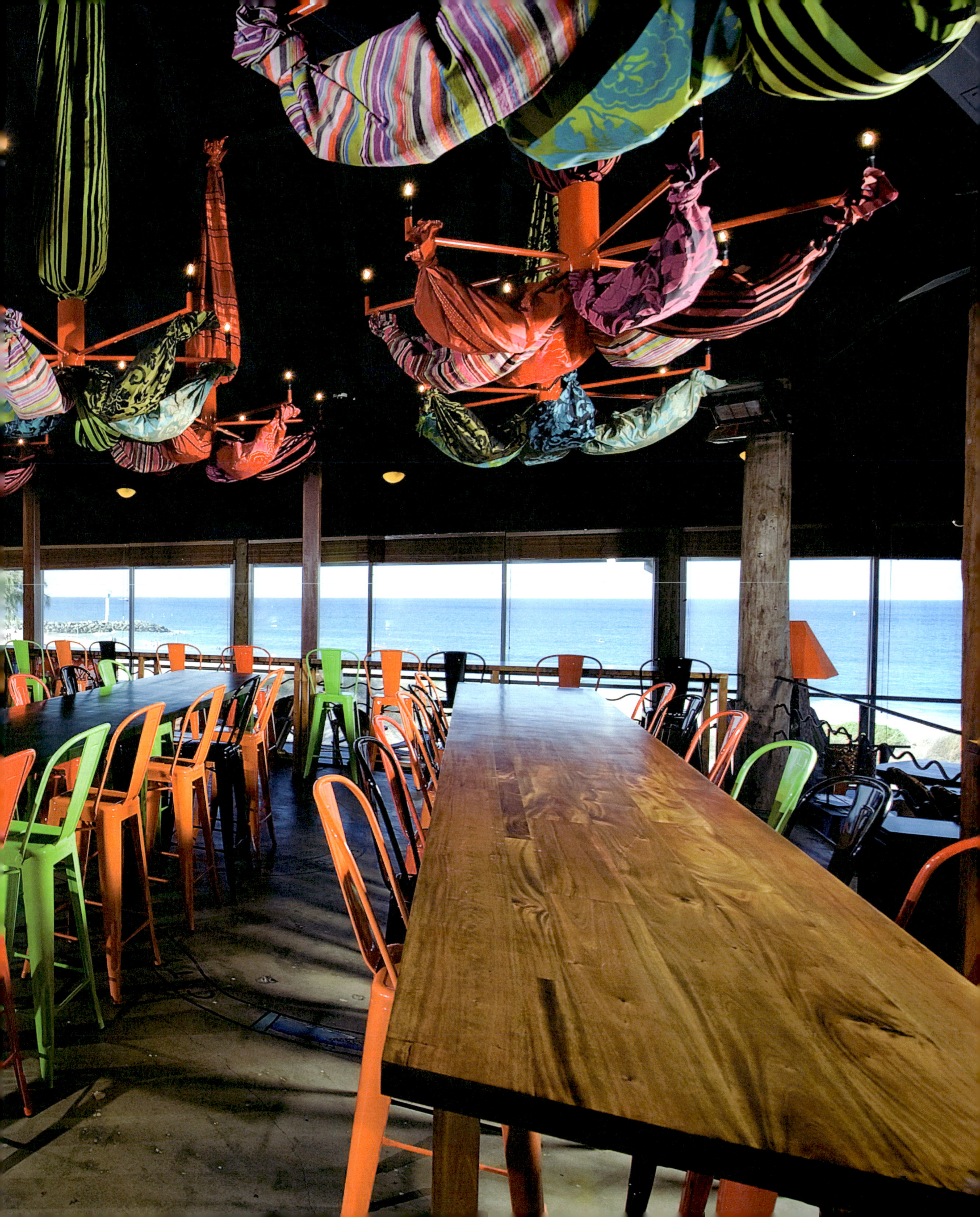

CLANCY'S FISHBAR
Perth, Australia

/ Burnham's re-fit of a shorefront restaurant on City Beach in Perth is both casual and animated with color. Under the high black beams of the roof, stripes and vividly painted wooden slats catch the eye along with bright plastic stools, nest-like pendant lights, patchwork tiling, and chandeliers that resemble the upside-down petals of tropical blooms.

/ Design: Paul Burnham Architect
/ Client: Clancy's Fish Pub
/ Type of Food/Drinks/Specialties: Fish pub

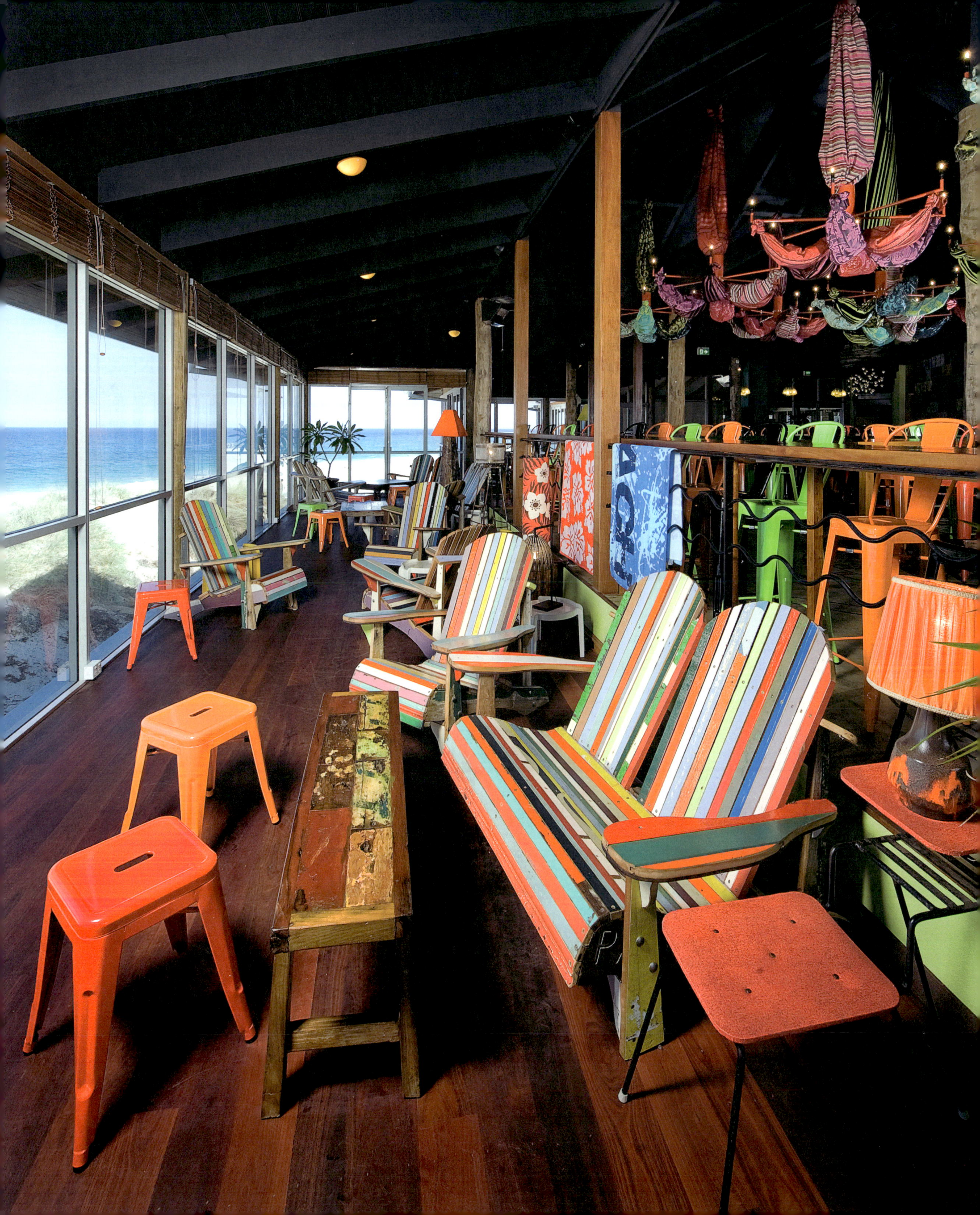

TOYKIO
Düsseldorf, Germany

/ After years as an online store and perennial pop-up, *Toykio* opened this "piece of heaven in the city." It may be heaven for fans of designer toys and urban and lowbrow art, but the frame-cluttered coffee shop and gallery in Düsseldorf's Japantown is embellished with jet black tiles. Thanks to generous window frontage, they don't feel somber though, but provide a stylish backdrop for with the colorful merchandise, which is exploited as the primary element of interior decoration.

/ Design: Toykio

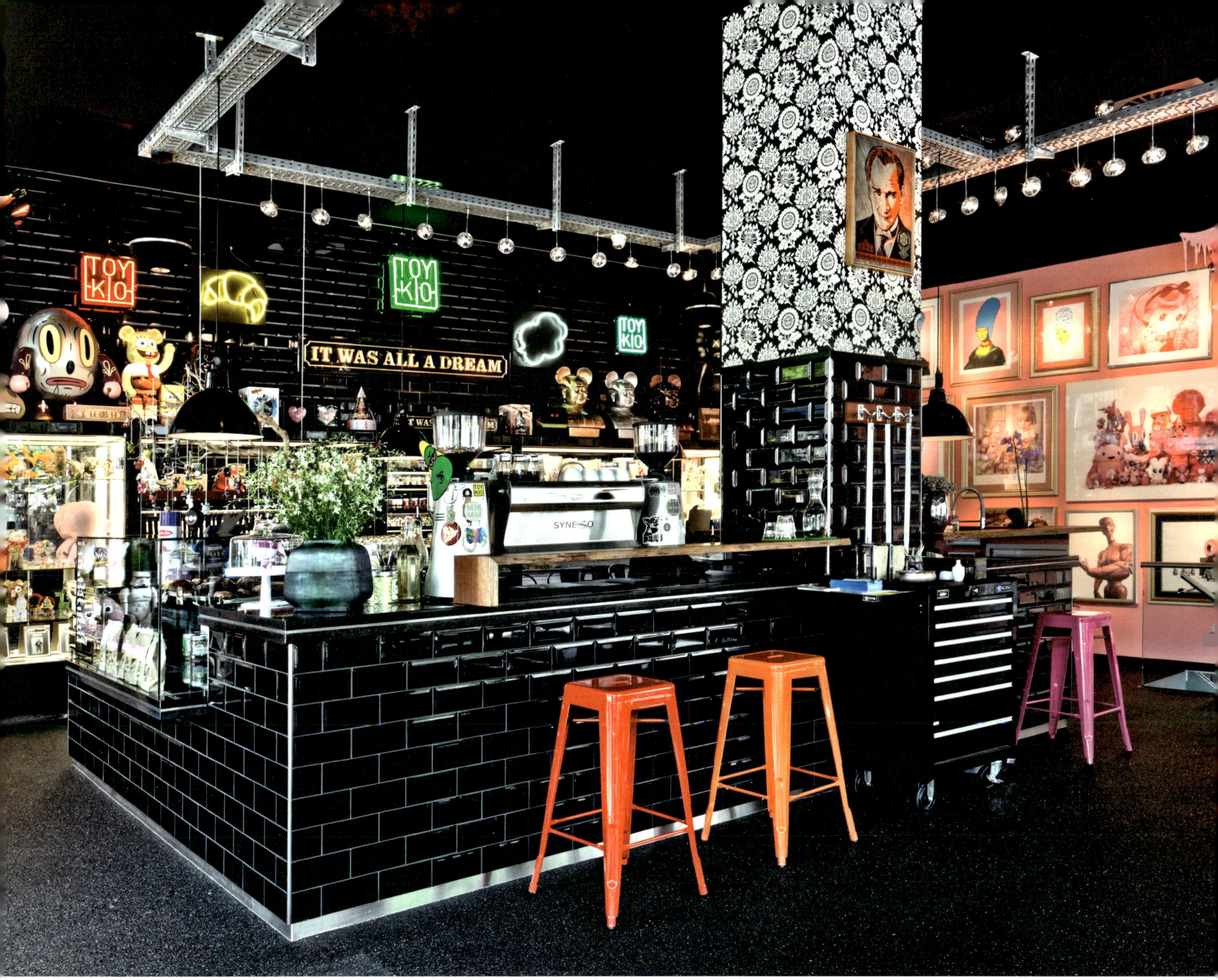
TOY
KIO
IT WAS ALL A DREAM

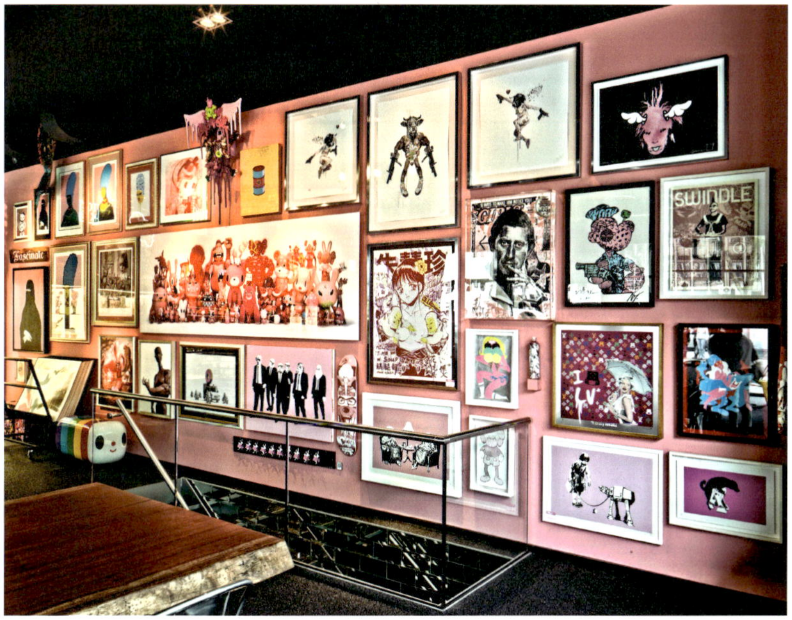
SWINDLE

28 / 29

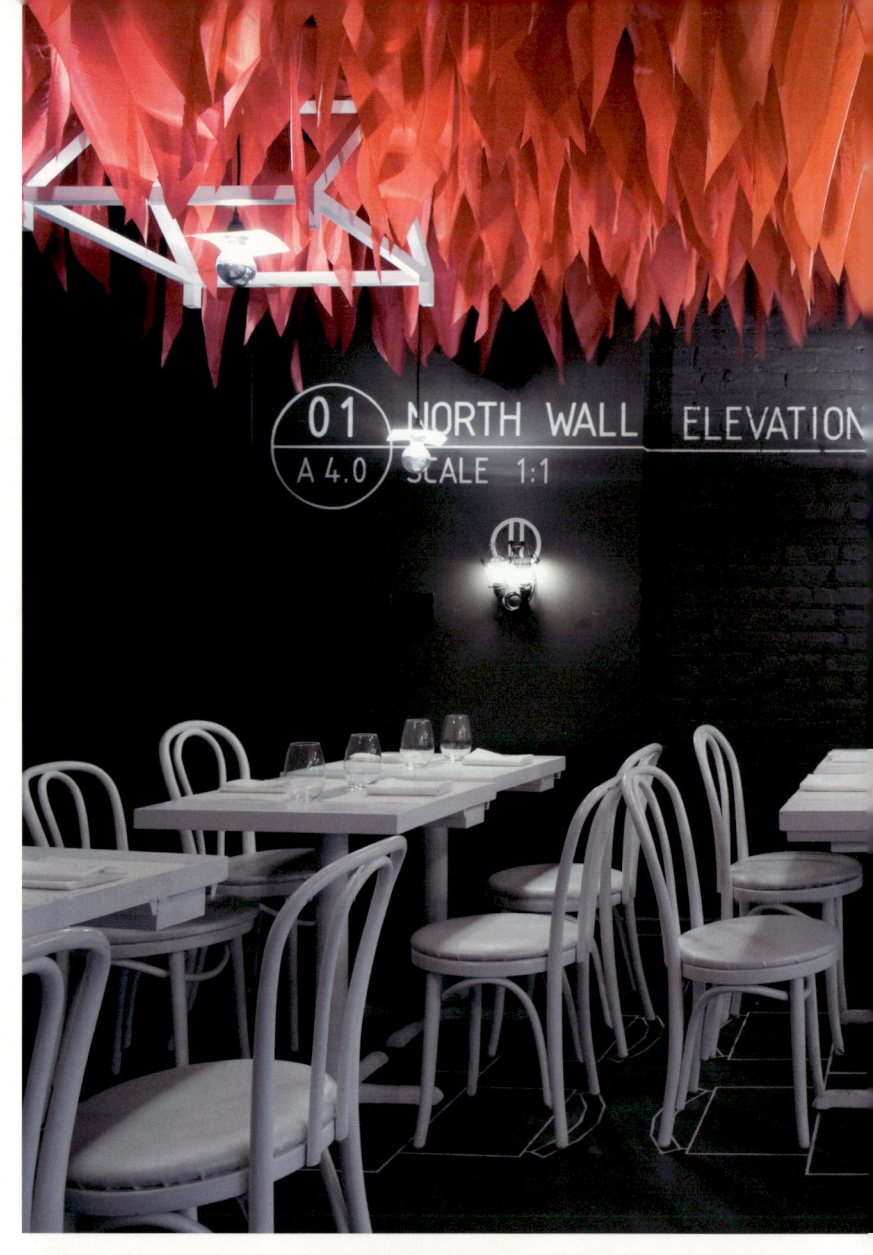

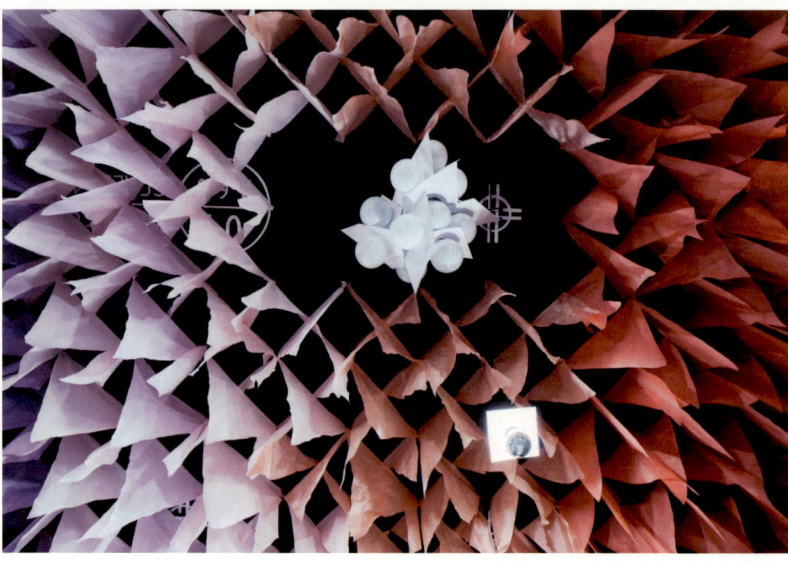

WHAT HAPPENS WHEN
NYC, New York, USA

/ Architecture changing faster than fashion? With a shell reminiscent of a traditional black box theater, the interior of this dark Manhattan boite was designed to transform monthly. To underscore the "work-in-progress" nature of the project and to make the frequent revamps more manageable, designer Elle Kunnos de Voss mounted a grid of hooks to the ceiling. The first monthly look or "movement" was a Scandinavia-inspired, monochromatic landscape of deconstructed volumes and fixtures. The chandeliers were cut-cardboard prisms and the sound installation composed by Micah Silver included recordings of snow falling on plastic foliage and the discordance of orchestras warming up.

The second installment of *What Happens When* was inspired by Sendak's *Where the Wild Things Are*. De Voss played with scale, using over-sized pine needles as room dividers, two moss-laden swings, and miniature landscapes. Animal tracks crossed the floor, walls, and some tables and the lights were made from stapled sheets of bird motif stationery. The music by Geek Squad consisted of calm, synthesizer-based tracks.

/ Design: The Metrics
/ Client: Chef John Fraser
/ Type of Food/Drinks/Specialties: Fine dining, Specialty cocktails

RULES OF THE CAFE

NO SMOKING
NO FIGHTING
NO CREDIT
NO FOOD FROM OUTSIDE
NO TALKING LOUD
NO SPITTING
NO BARGAINING
NO CHEATING
NO WATER TO OUTSIDERS
NO MATCHES
NO GAMBLING
NO COMBING HAIR
ALL CASTES WELCOME

PLAYFUL

DISHOOM BOMBAY CAFÉ
London, United Kingdom

/ A modern Indian food franchise and *Bombay Café's* first UK outpost, Dishoom pays homage to the cafés run by Persian immigrants to (today's) Mumbai during the early twentieth century. Its dark wood, mirrors, and monochrome floor tiles are framed with a subdued color palette of grays, browns, and pale blue. Retro-looking Bollywood posters and low lighting provide plenty of character, but all eyes are drawn to the bustle of the open kitchen. Krassa's careful editing of details—even the toilets feature unique details, including incense and vintage medicine cabinets—take this location out of the realm of chain eateries and give it the feel of a lively brasserie.

/ Design: Afroditi Krassa

/ Client: Dishoom

/ Type of Food/Drinks/Specialties: Modern Indian

CAFÉ KAFKA
Barcelona, Spain

/ Next to the 100-year-old market, Mercat del Born, the two designers remade this interior starting from the remains of two old tables found on the premises of the demolished building that was their site. Paying homage to the past, they filled the space with vintage, often salvaged materials, including lamps from the 1950s, plush velvet settees, square café tables with painted glass surfaces, carbon bulbs, multicolored opaline balloons, and candy-hued stools. The base of the bar comprises elements that recall the old iron-sheet-clad American chimneys while the red and blue fluorescent lights evoke a roadside honky tonk, making the interior a mix of domestic eclecticism, literary café, and Parisian bistro.

/ Design: Yolanda Vilalta and Helena Jaumá

PLAYFUL

CELLO BAR
Kilkis, Greece

/ Lime's design sought to expose and accentuate the height of the space by giving color to the infrastructure anchored to the ceiling. Using polished concrete surfaces, untreated wood, and custom as well as classic contemporary furniture, Lime imbued the interior with a warm, industrial ambiance. Though the eatery, which turns from café to bar as the day wears on, has decorative touches, it remains almost modestly simple.

/ Design: Lime Studio
/ Client: Cello Bar

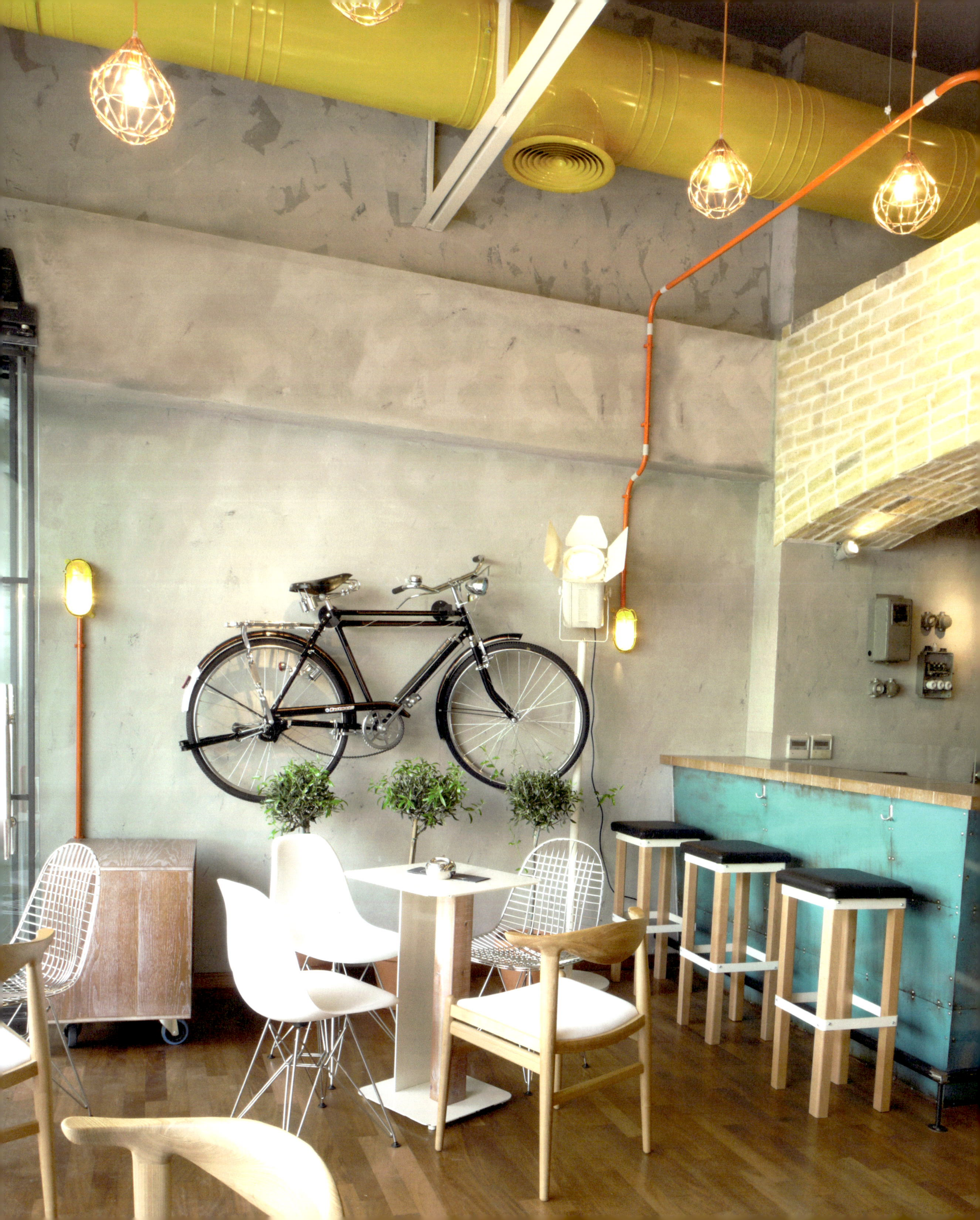

Polpa de fruita fresca
ambsucre i gelatina
2,75€
3,75
Poma de Girona
i sucre negre

PLAYFUL

ROCAMBOLESC
Girona, Spain

/ Every day gelato and its artful accessories are delivered to *Rocambolesc* from the kitchens of the nearby Michelin-starred restaurant that owns the shop. Worthy of the gems scooped out—in six flavors with accompaniments like butter cookie, pop rocks, cotton candy, and fresh fruit—is the whimsical interior of the gelateria, itself. Part laboratory, part Yellow Submarine, and part Santa's workshop, its walls are ranged with Wonka-worthy gauges, tubes, gears, and peppermint-candy-striped ducts. Reflected in staggered walls of mirrors, the confections swallow visitors up in their own fanciful realm, instead of being merely something that is consumed.

/ Design: Sandra Tarruella Interioristas

RESTAURANT STOCK
Amsterdam, Netherlands

/ In the Damrak, at the "entrance to Amsterdam," this café "caters to the paradox of fast living and slow food." Recognizing the modern tendency to embrace healthy and unhealthy indulgences in turn and the robust character of local nightlife, *Stock* serves brunch all day along with simple, good-for-you food. The design was shaped by the need to fit into its host, a hotel, while maintaining its own identity and, not least, by a dearth of space. Everyone also pitched in with the restaurant's development, from builders to investors, had a hand in the interior design by drawing the bird illustrations that tattoo the walls.

/ Design: Ina-Matt

/ Client: Otto Nan and Suzanne Oxenaar (Lloyd Hotel Amsterdam)

/ Material: Hand-made ceramic gold bar, steel powder coated furniture frames in green-grayish colours with a wooden topping, re-used chandeliers in a white varnishing

/ Type of Food/Drinks/Specialties: Breakfast all day, sandwiches and pies, fresh salads and hot soups, coffee and juices

PLAYFUL

DESIGN BAR
Stockholm, Sweden

/ Serving up soups, sandwiches, pastries—and cultural diversity? The design scheme for Katrin Greiling's temporary bar and VIP lounge at the Stockholm Furniture Fair was the product of recent years spent living and working in various far-flung pockets of the Middle East and northern Europe. Rather than create a linear narrative space, Greiling's bright environment became a mosaic of "global impressions" that took visitors out of their comfort zone while making them feel eminently comfortable.

/ Design: Studio Greiling
/ Client: Stockholm Furniture Fair
/ Material: Cardboard, plywood, wood, stretch fabric, metal, diverse furniture
/ Type of Food/Drinks/Specialties: Sandwiches, soups, cakes, danish pastry, alcoholic and non-alcoholic beverages

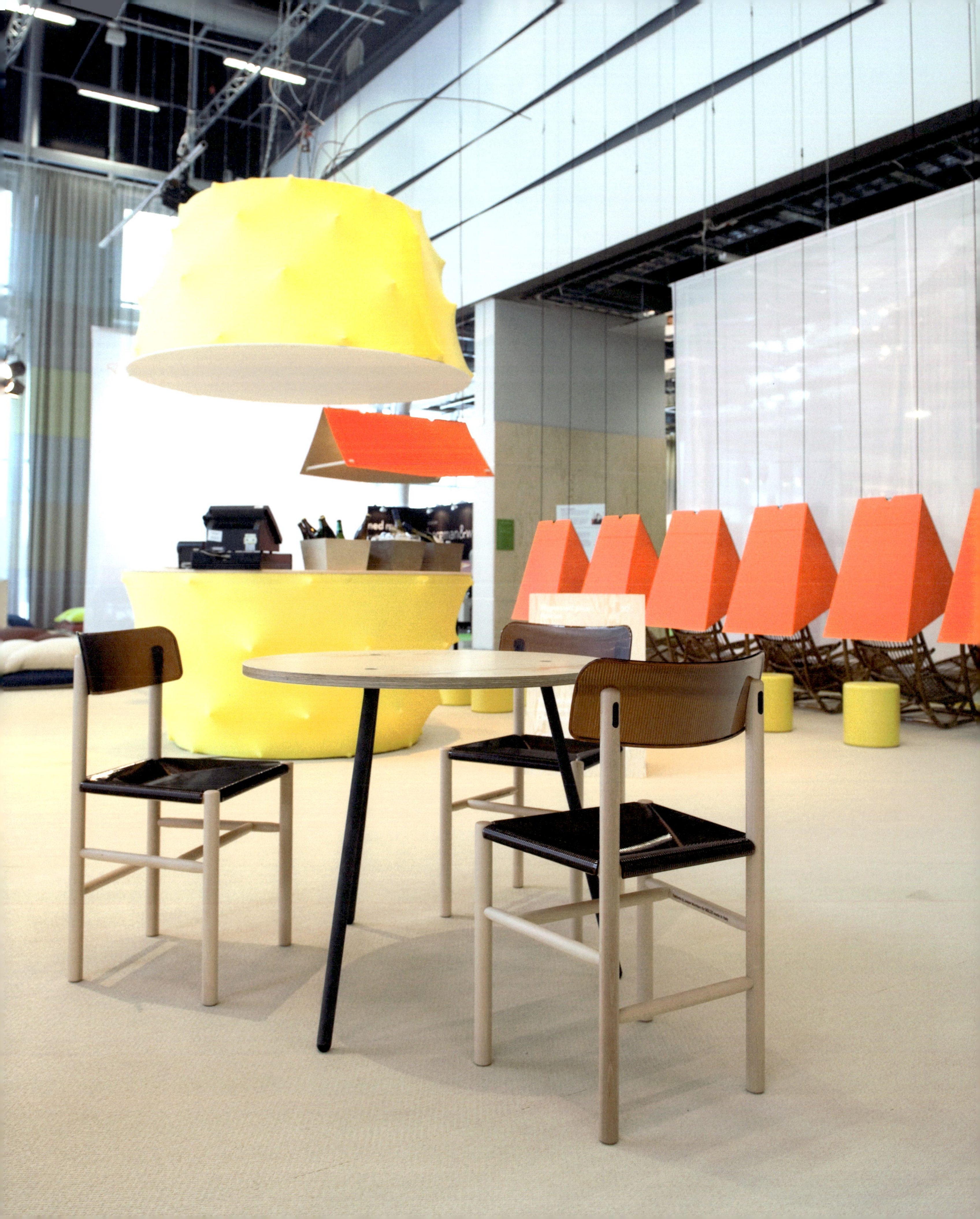

FOOD FOR THOUGHT
London, United Kingdom

/ The Willesden Windows project paired designers with shopkeepers in an effort to revive the business district. Howie worked with the owner of the Food for Thought café, a traditional English café with Italian leanings. Inspired by Rodin's sculpture *The Thinker* and the name of the eatery, Howie laser-etched quotations from the likes of Miss Piggy, Charlie Chaplin, and Albert Einstein onto Tom Dixon-designed Offcut stools made from soaped oak. He also created a more flexible seating plan for the café and a window display cum community engagement board featuring changing monthly questions and comments to which customers can add their own.

/ Design: Robin Howie

/ Client: Food for Thought, supported by The Architecture Foundation and the Mayor of London's Outer London fund

/ Type of Food/Drinks/Specialties: Traditional English cafe with an Italian twist

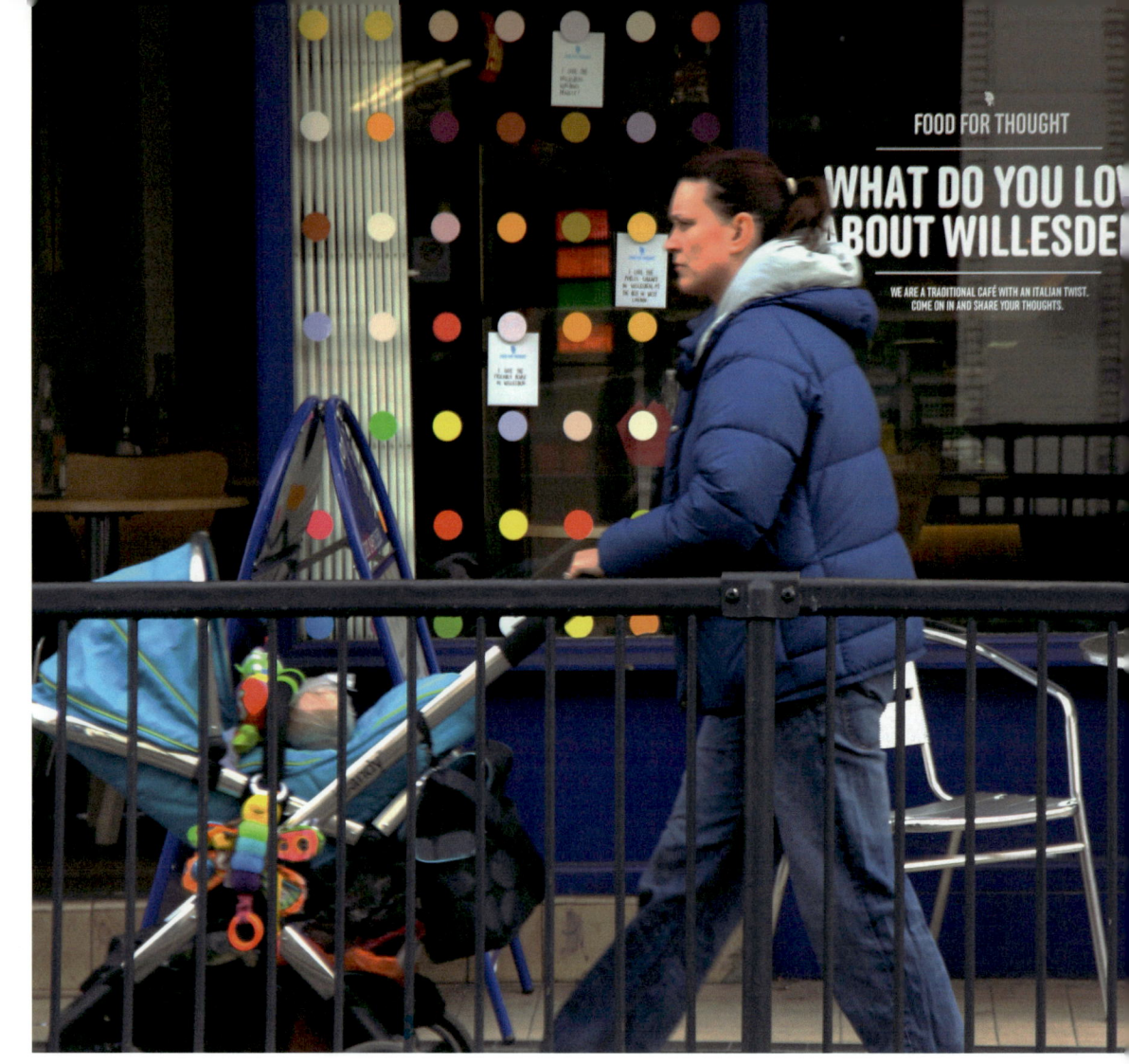

"Howie laser-etched quotations from the likes of Miss Piggy, Charlie Chaplin, and Albert Einstein onto Tom Dixon-designed Offcut stools made from soaped oak."

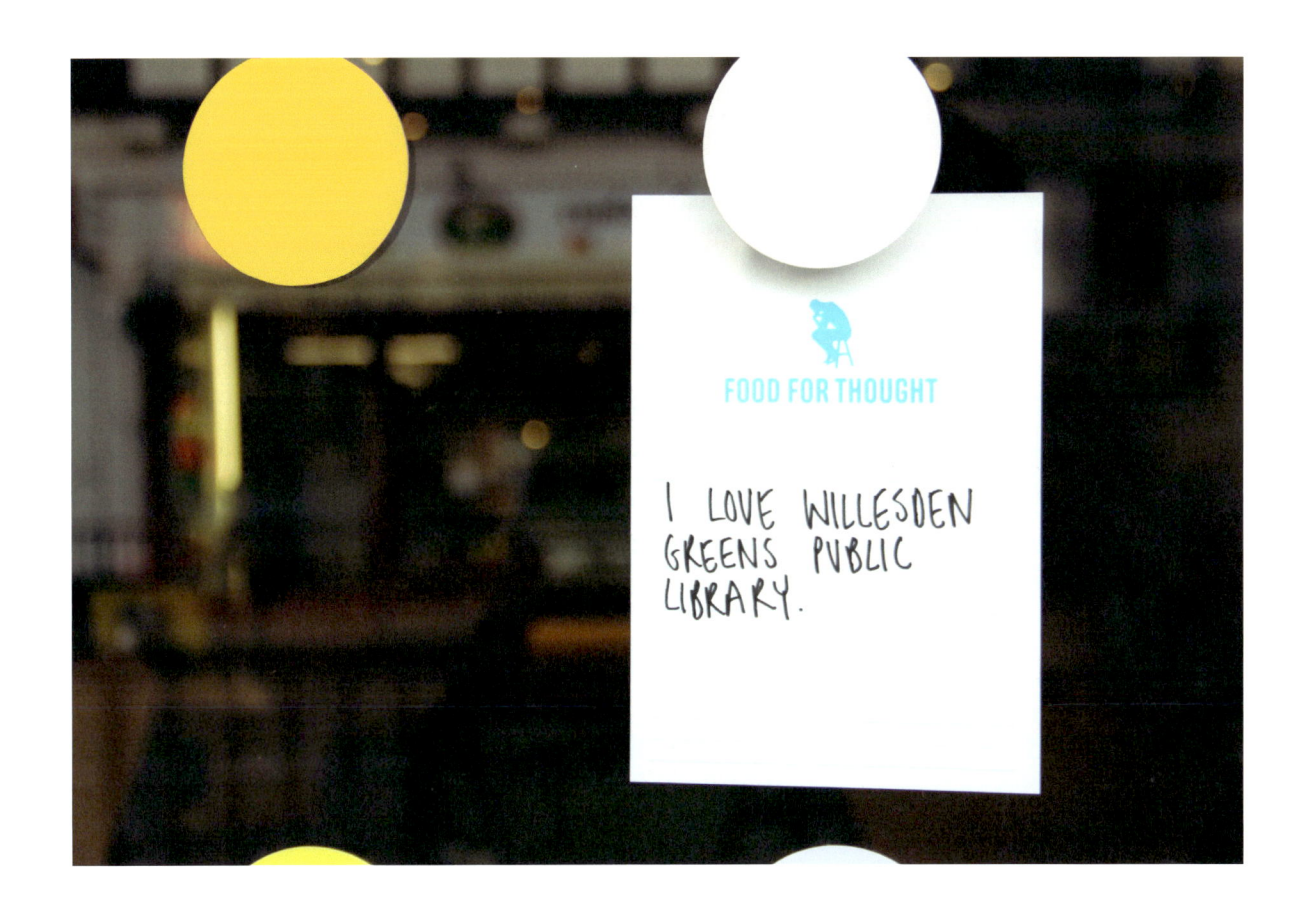

FOOD FOR THOUGHT

I LOVE WILLESDEN GREENS PUBLIC LIBRARY.

NEVER EAT MORE THAN YOU CAN LIFT
— MISS PIGGY, THE MUPPETS

THE SADDEST THING I CAN IMAGINE IS TO GET USED TO LUXURY
— CHARLIE CHAPLIN

IF YOU WANT OTHERS TO BE HAPPY, PRACTISE COMPASSION. IF YOU WANT TO BE HAPPY, PRACTISE COMPASSION
— DALAI LAMA

GRAVITY IS NOT RESPONSIBLE FOR PEOPLE FALLING IN LOVE
— ALBERT EINSTEIN

IF MUSIC BE THE FOOD OF LOVE PLAY ON
— SHAKESPEARE

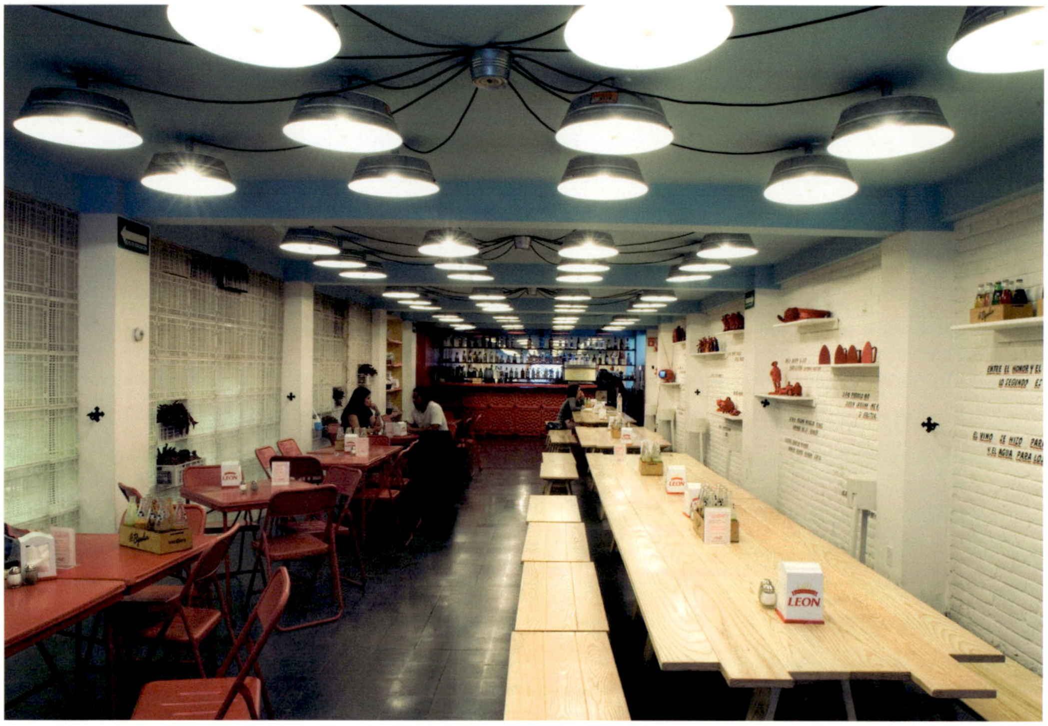
LEON

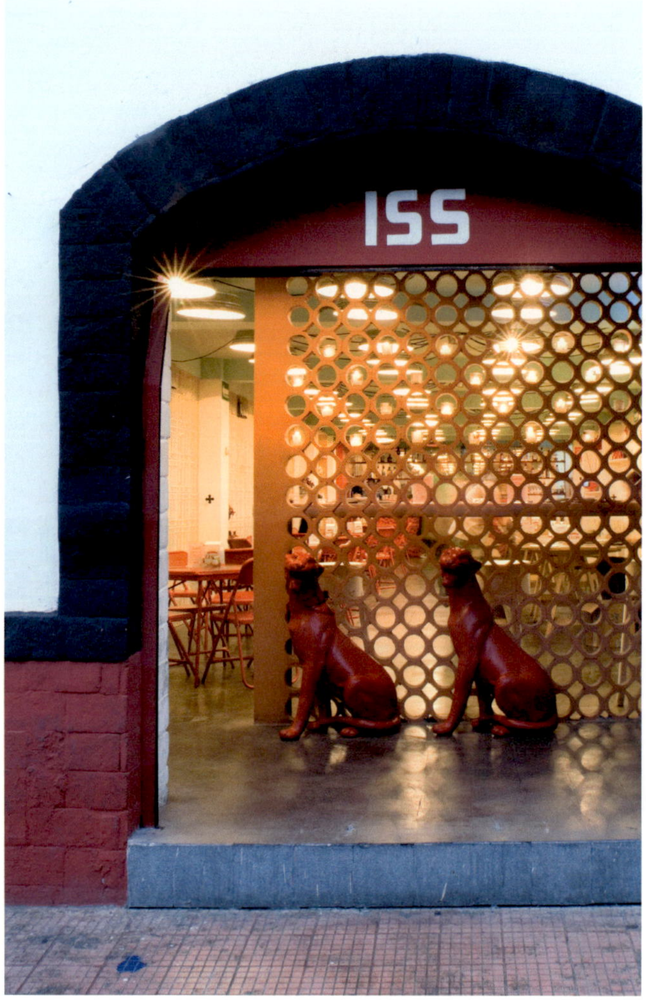
ISS

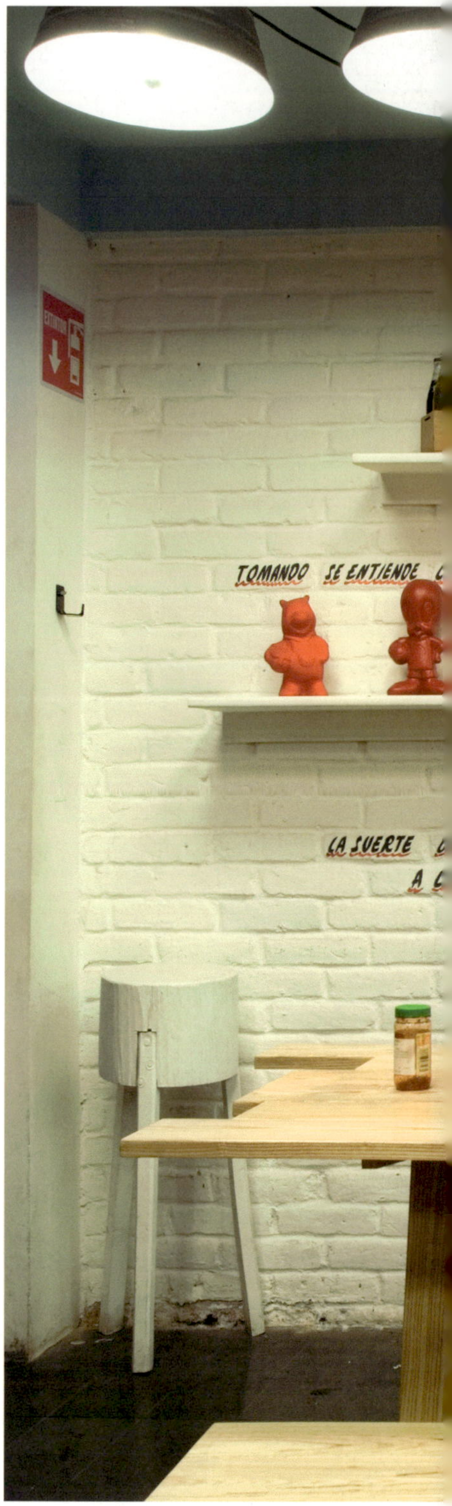
TOMANDO SE ENTIENDE
LA SUERTE

PLAYFUL

LA BIPOLAR
Mexico City, Mexico

/ This project was an exercise in observation, "communion with the essence of the city" and with the culture and identity of Mexico, say the designers. Mdahuar and Esrawe partitioned the 320 sq m space into two zones, with a contemporary "cantina" on the first floor and a bar and performance space on the second. The whitewashed brick walls are lined with irregular shelves holding interesting, colorful everyday objects ranging from milk bottles to a vintage TV, and cement columns are paired with red metal folding chairs and a long communal wooden bench.

/ Design: Mdahuar Diseño with Esrawe Studio

/ Client: NaCo

/ Type of Food/Drinks/Specialties: Mexican cantina

PATRICIA COFFEE
Melbourne, Australia

/ Adele Winteridge was tasked with designing a coffee shop that focuses on bare-bones, quality coffee. The menu is pared-down—black, white, and filter—and so is the seatless space, which the owner envisioned as a bar. Located within the uninspiring confines of an office building, Foolscap focused primarily on functionality, materiality, and detail. The team evoked 1930s New York, pairing dark joinery with brass and marble. Above it all, a neon sign, made in collaboration with graphic designers BTP, reads "sunshine" and white porcelain walls brighten a dark timber newspaper rack.

/ Design: Foolscap Studio
/ Client: Bowen Holden
/ Type of Food/Drinks/Specialties: Coffee

PLAYFUL

BLACK $3.5
WHITE $3.8
FILTER $3.5

FRJTZ DINING ROOM
San Francisco, California, USA

/ Already a hot spot serving up Belgian frites, beer, sweet and savory crepes, a rotating art scene, and the occasional DJ, *Frjtz* was forced to relocate to an adjacent storefront in San Francisco's Hayes Valley neighborhood. When Y.A. studio was tasked with converting a dark concrete shell into a bright, airy café, they started by embedding living terrariums in the walls at eye-level and framing them with chunky blocks of wood. Then they added an indoor garden, grainy wooden backrests for bench seating along the wall, whitewashed dining tables, walls and ceiling, and seating accented with lime green stools and cushions.

/ Design: Y.A. studio
/ Client: Frjtz Café
/ Type of Food/Drinks/Specialties: Belgian fries, sweet and savory crepes

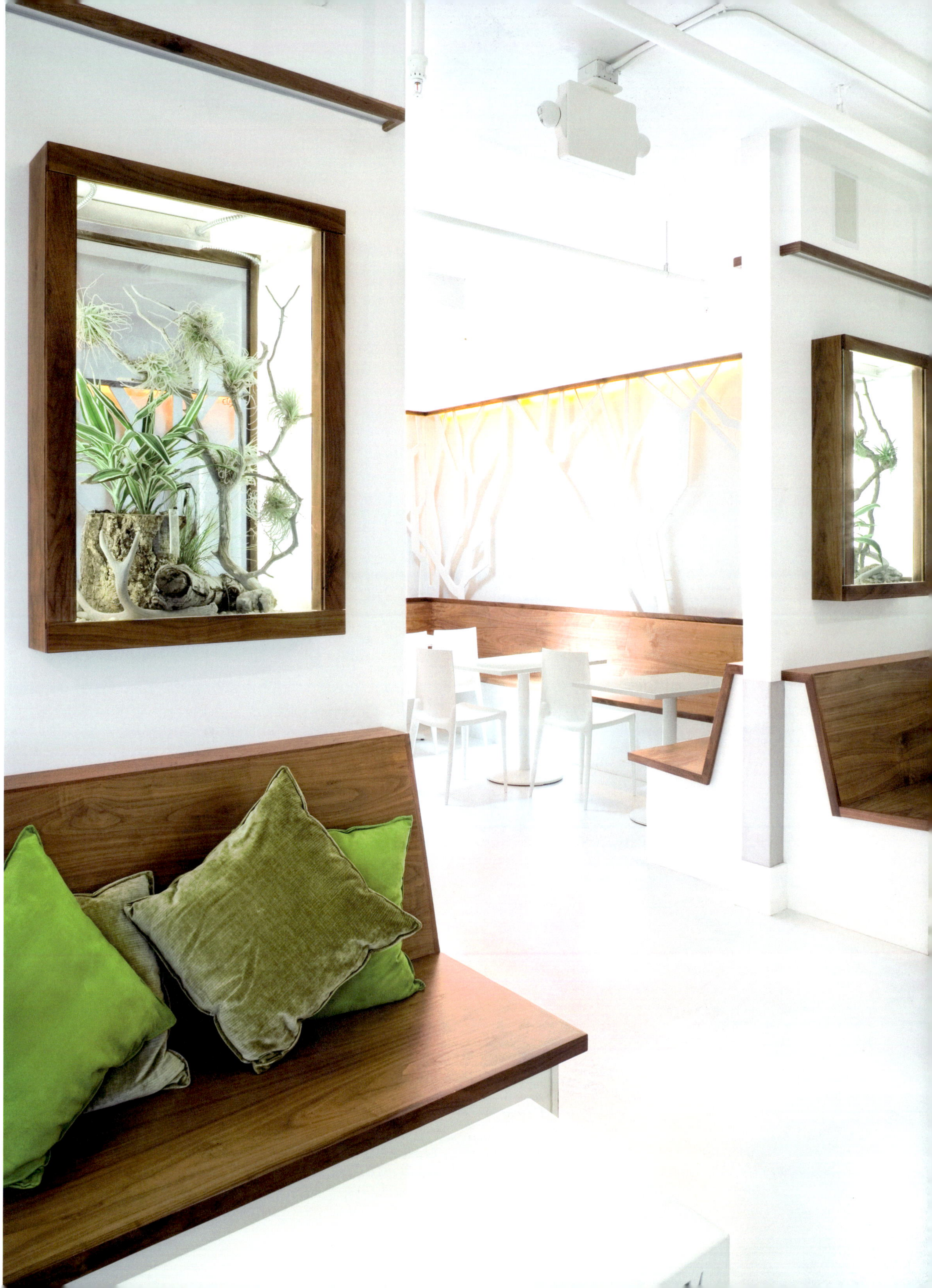

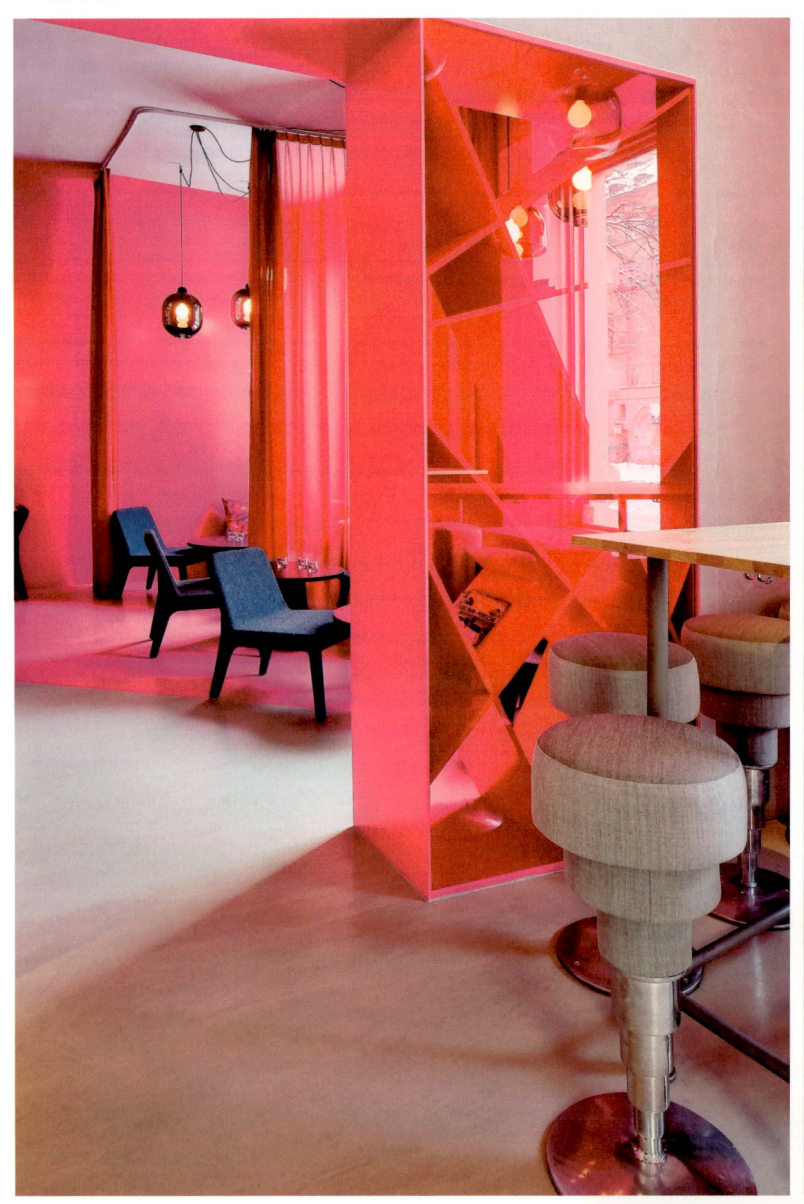

"A hybrid of Spanish heat and Scandinavian coolness."

PLAYFUL

CAFÉ FOAM
Stockholm, Sweden

/ The brief? Create an interior design that guests will either love or hate, but never be indifferent to. Note designers began to search for extreme themes "where passion and hate are equally present," finally settling on of the phenomenon of bullfighting. They were particularly fascinated by the reciprocal movements of the bull and toreador. Along with materials and colors that are common to a stadium, this served as the starting point for the design. The result? A hybrid of Spanish heat and Scandinavian coolness.

/ Design: Note Design Studio
/ Client: Michael Toutongi

ELEVEN INCH PIZZERIA
Melbourne, Australia

/ The interior of this pizzeria makes a playful reference to the traditional takeout joint combined with a robust graphical look. Plywood dresses the surfaces in various modes, punctuated with bursts of chartreuse. The food counter is topped with tilted green aluminium fins while the countertop is lined with stained plywood and routed lines that gently echo the fins above.

/ Design: Zwei Interiors Architecture

/ Client: Eleven Inch

/ Material: Plywood and anodised aluminium

/ Type of Food/Drinks/Specialties: Pizza

Herb Crusted Chicken
Pork & Veal Lasagna
Lamb Kofta with Pumpkin Fritters
Small Coffee $3.50
Large Coffee $4.00
Tea - The Same
Hot Chocolate - Same

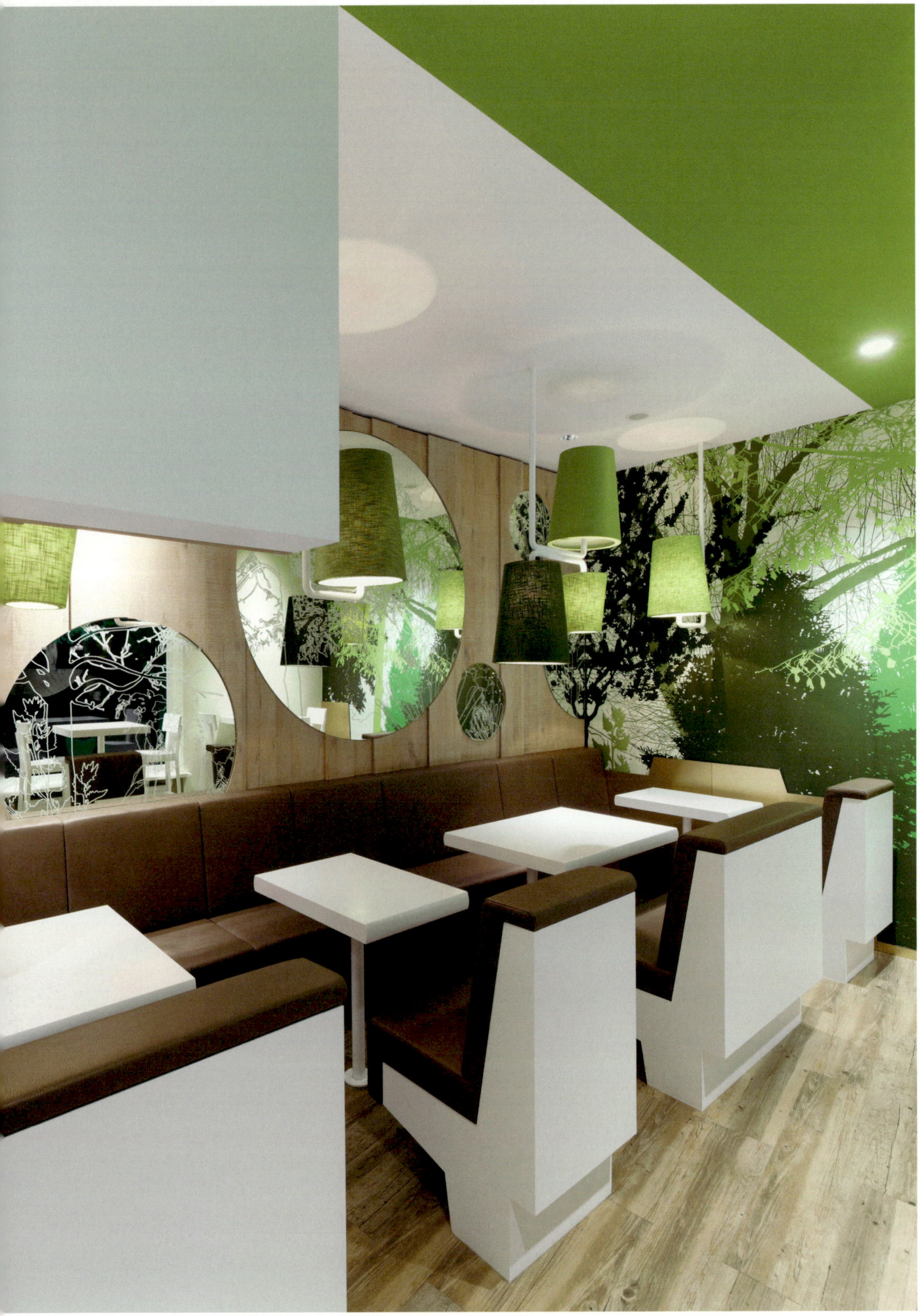

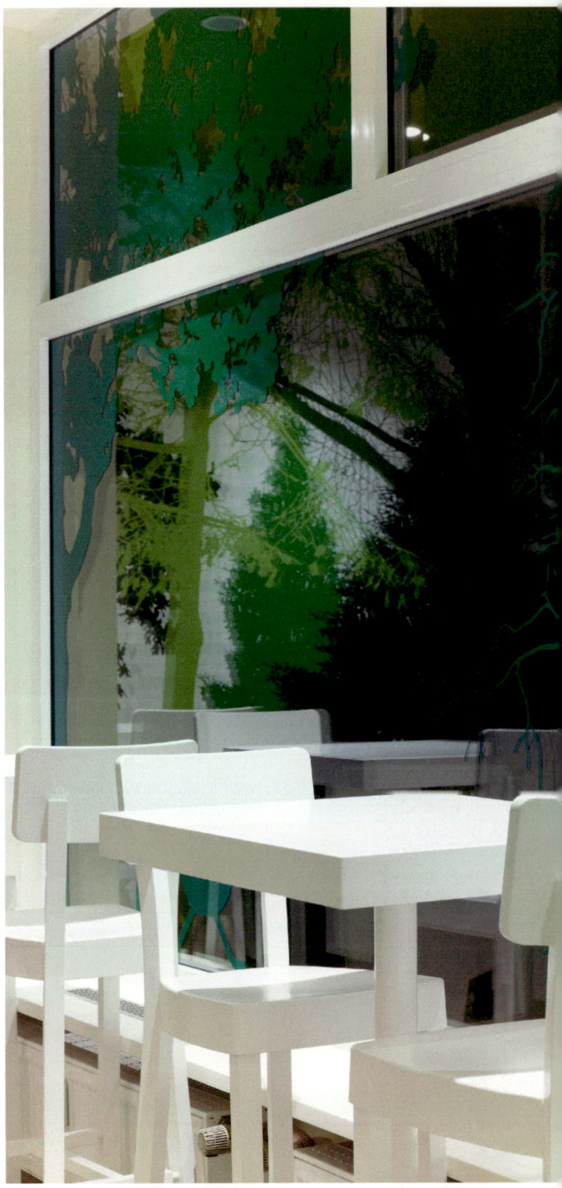

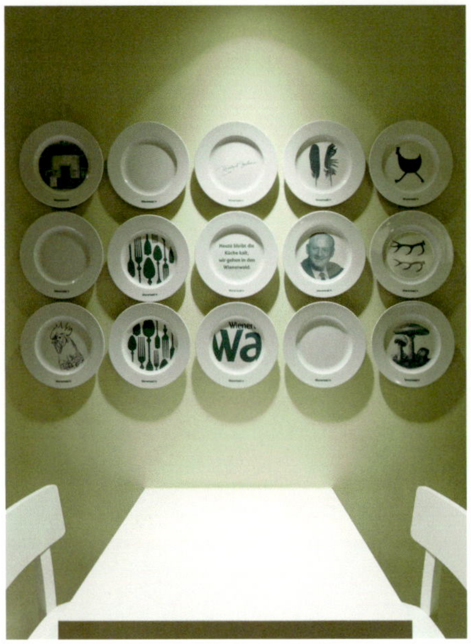

PLAYFUL

WIENERWALD CORPORATE ARCHITECTURE
Munich, Germany

/ *Wienerwald* means Vienna Woods and Ippolito Fleitz rendered this half-century old fast food chicken franchise in greens, browns, and natural wood to reference exactly that. Low-hanging fabric lamp shades, murals depicting silhouetted forest canopies, and soft radiused walls are paired with angular chairs, crisp whites, and mirrors. One wall is tiled with anthracite mosaic stones with embedded frameless stainless steel units. Guests have open sightlines to the food preparation and a range of seating options to suit the amount of time they have to spend.

/ Design: Ippolito Fleitz Group – Identity Architects

/ Client: Wienerwald Franchise

/ Type of Food/Drinks/Specialties:
Fast food, fried chicken

Sophisticated

Der Spiegel Kantine

Sophisticated spaces bare their extraordinary bones. Not just skin deep, they represent design at its most elemental or complex, and usually both. Geometric forms, lines, and layers form the basis of these shells and, by extension, their interiors, which tends to make them highly graphical. But here, ornament is structure and structure is ornament.

SOPHISTICATED

"The shard-like glass and wood roofline thrillingly echoes the surrounding landscape, as if to suggest that, in its small way, our species can walk hand-in-hand with Mother Nature."

TROLLWALL RESTAURANT
Trollveggen, Norway

/ Norwegians, who know better than anyone else on earth how small mankind is beside Nature, tend to opt for plain, modest architecture. Except when they don't. Ramstad's jagged visitors' center and restaurant shears into the sky at the lip of a sheer drop from Europe's tallest vertical rockface. Overhanging the Romsdal Valley, where "birdmen" BASE jump and even birds get queasy with vertigo, the shard-like glass and wood roofline thrillingly echoes the surrounding landscape, as if to suggest that, in its small way, our species can walk hand-in-hand with Mother Nature. You know what they say: If you can't beat 'em, join 'em.

/ Design: Reiulf Ramstad Arkitekter

/ Client: Private

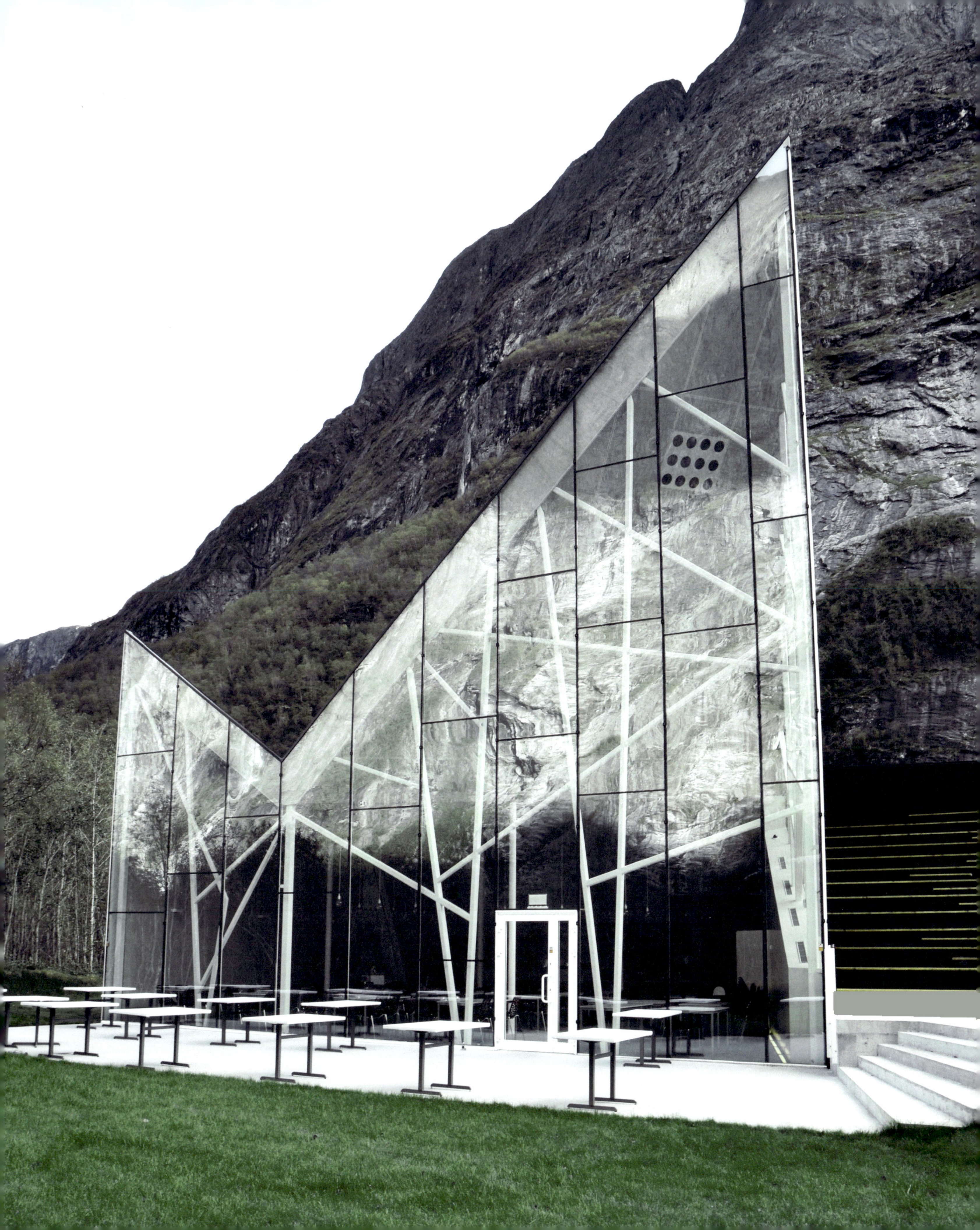

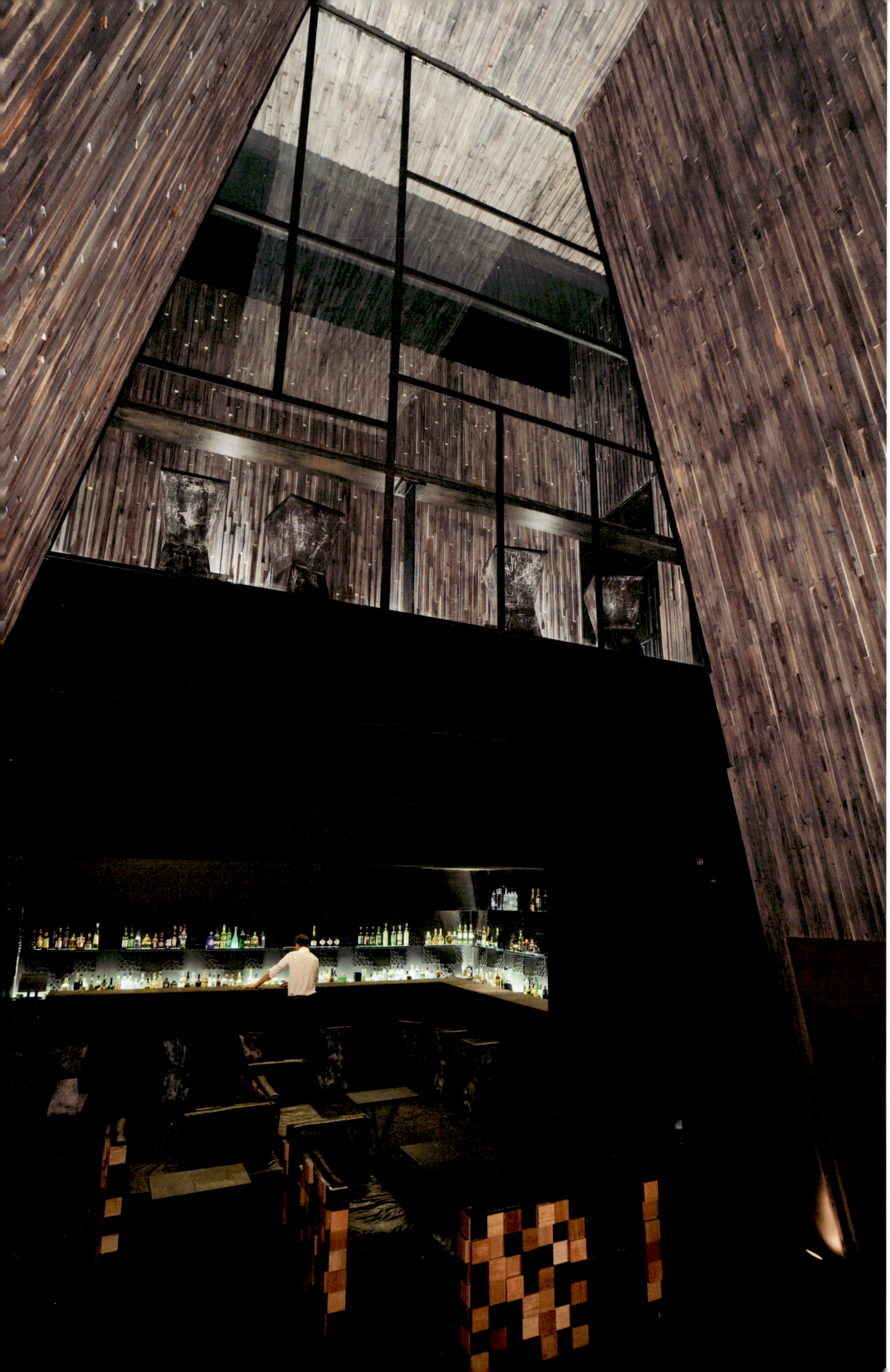

SOPHISTICATED

M. N. ROY
Mexico City, Mexico

/ French architects Emmanuel Picault and Ludwig Godefroy transformed a house once inhabited by Mexican communist party founder M. N. Roy into a nightclub of dramatic scale and proportions, using concrete, stone, and vast accretions of wooden boards. With its ponderous weight, high ceilings, and rough surfaces, the space takes on the dark monumentality of ecclesiastical architecture, which some might find appropriate, and even features glazing on the upper floor divided into irregular panes like a church's stained glass windows, but wiped clear of color.

/ Design: Ludwig Godefroy and Chic by Accident Studio

/ Client: Guayabos del Sur

DIM SUM BAR
Quito, Ecuador

/ The design for this dynamically linear interior for a Chinese dim sum restaurant originated in a set of seique wood tables and chairs purchased by the client. Consisting of white leather cushions and dark wooden frames, the chairs have a densely laddered backrest. Likewise, the bar, lit from within, consists of alternating stripes of light and black granite, a pattern echoed in the horizontality of the glass-fronted floor-to-ceiling rows of wine bottles behind it and CNC milled MDF screens and partitions throughout. Even the storefront is lined with louvered shades.

/ Design: Hou de Sousa

/ Client: Dim Sum Bar

/ Material: Seique wood furniture, CNC cut MDF screen walls, acrylic, one-way mirror, standard mirror, steel rods and bars, black granite bar top

/ Type of Food/Drinks/Specialties: Chinese, dim sum, full bar, wine menu, house cocktails, spicy fish head soup, chili rock shrimp, crispy frog legs, Szechuan lamb chops

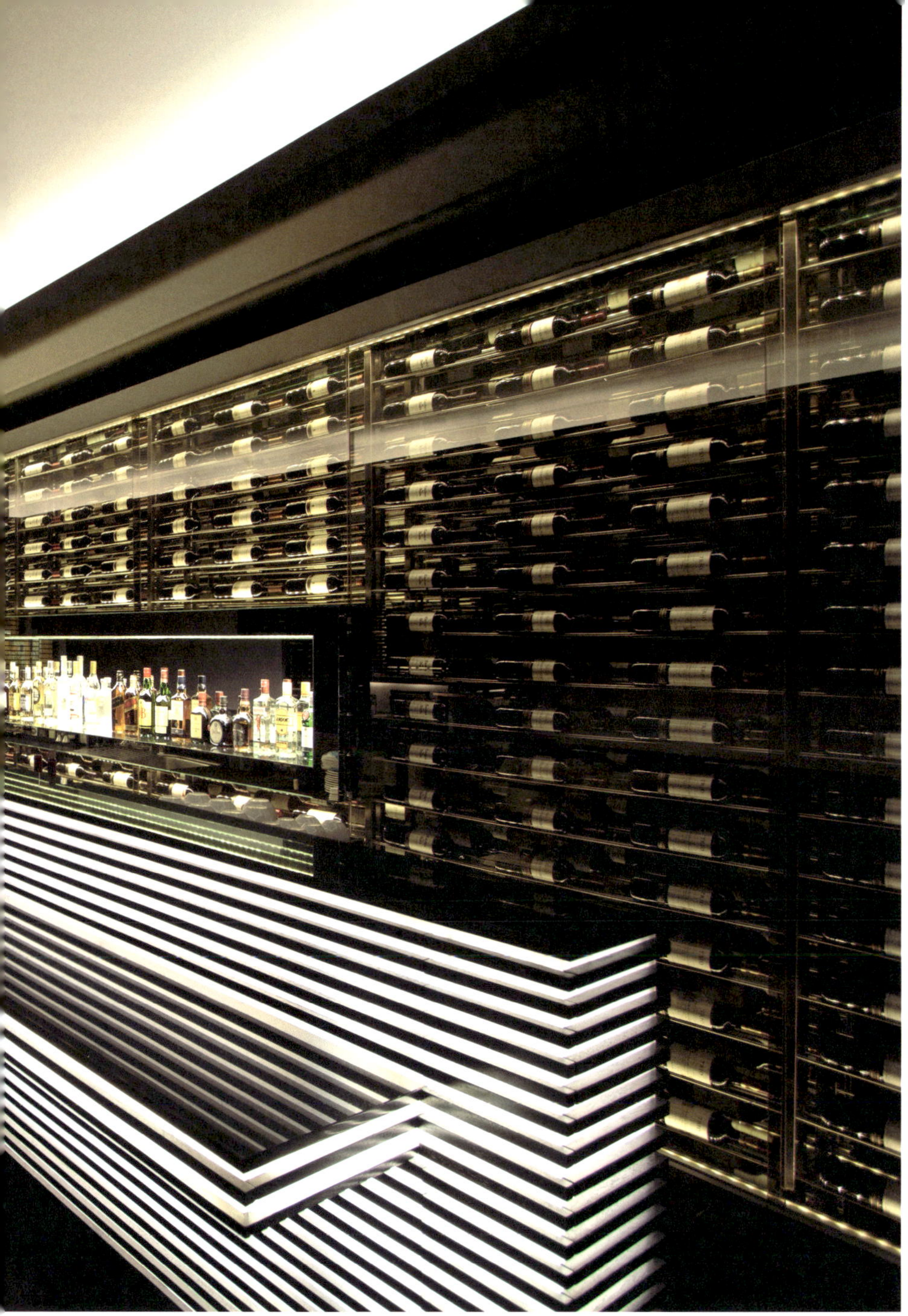

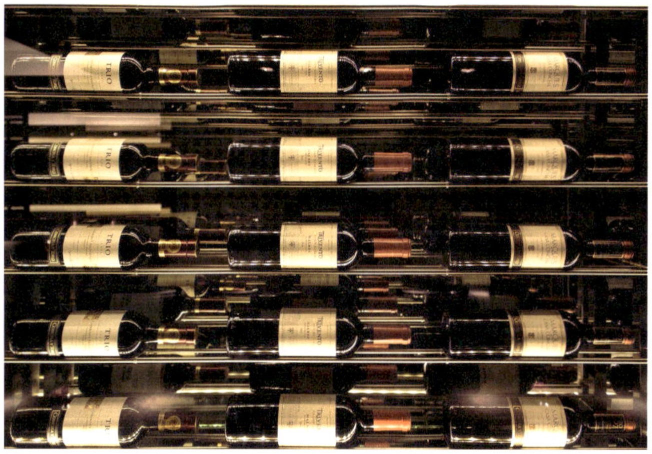

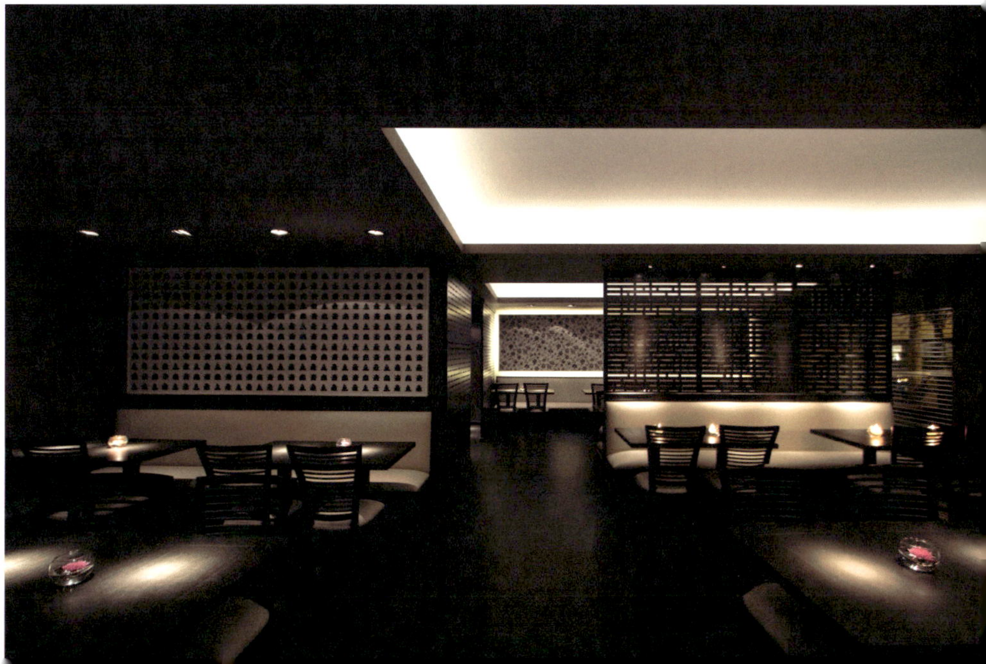

YAKINIKU MASTER JAPANESE RESTAURANT
Shanghai, China

/ The third installment in a chain, this 300 sq m, 130-seater barbecue restaurant was designed by Beijing-based Lee Hsuheng to be both tactile and vaguely narrative. The minimalist space makes references to both Japanese and Southern Chinese architecture. The traditional wood lattices, for example, are typical of Japanese architecture, simultaneously dividing and uniting the interior, while the half-moon-shaped ceiling light fixtures allude to Chinese boats. The seemingly random patches of pebbles are actually meticulously arranged and resemble a feature typical of a Zen garden, while a black-and-white mural behind the bar renders a familiar Chinese roofline. One wall consists of stacked Japanese barbecue coal.

/ Design: Golucci International Design
/ Client: Yakiniku Master

SOPHISTICATED

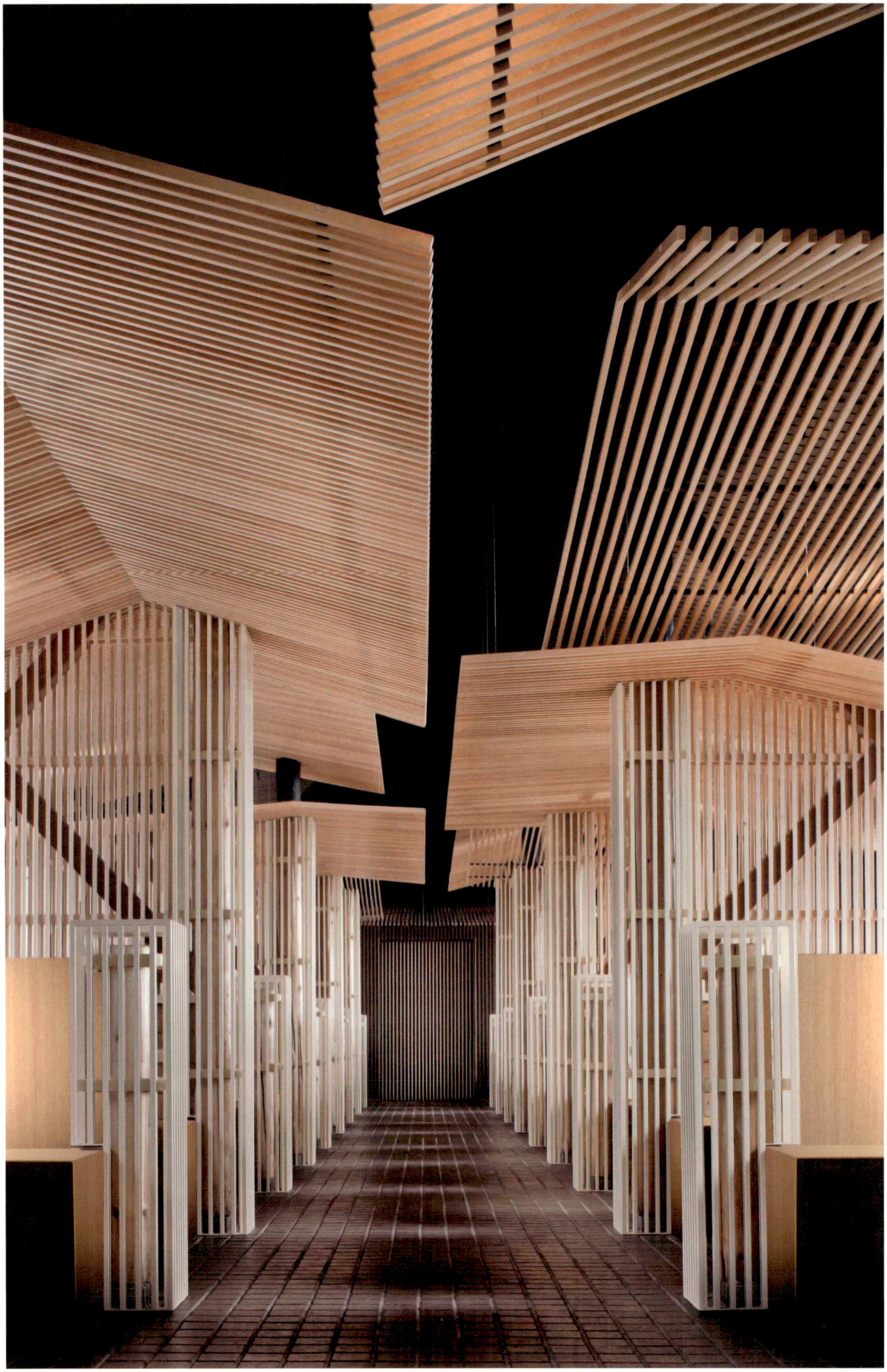

NISEKO LOOK OUT CAFÉ
Niseko, Japan

/ At the top of an island mountain, the *Look Out Café* serves skiers who get there by lift. The architect had little time to renovate the existing building before first snowfall and had to hike to the site which cannot be reached by car or lift during the off-season. He and the workers also faced short winter workdays (4pm sunsets), landslides, and powerful winds. Striving to draw an airy sense of the outdoors inside and wielding a palette of only three materials—wood, paint, and wallpaper—he installed a vertical timber lattice throughout. The extreme repetition of this typically Japanese element gives the space a fine yet strong graphical appearance.

/ Design: design spirits

/ Client: YTL Hotels

/ Material: Floor: existing floor material; Ceiling: existing ceiling painted in black; Roof: spruce louver clear lacquer finishes; Wall: timber plate louver with black paint; Column above roof level: existing column painted in black

/ Type of Food/Drinks/Specialties: Café

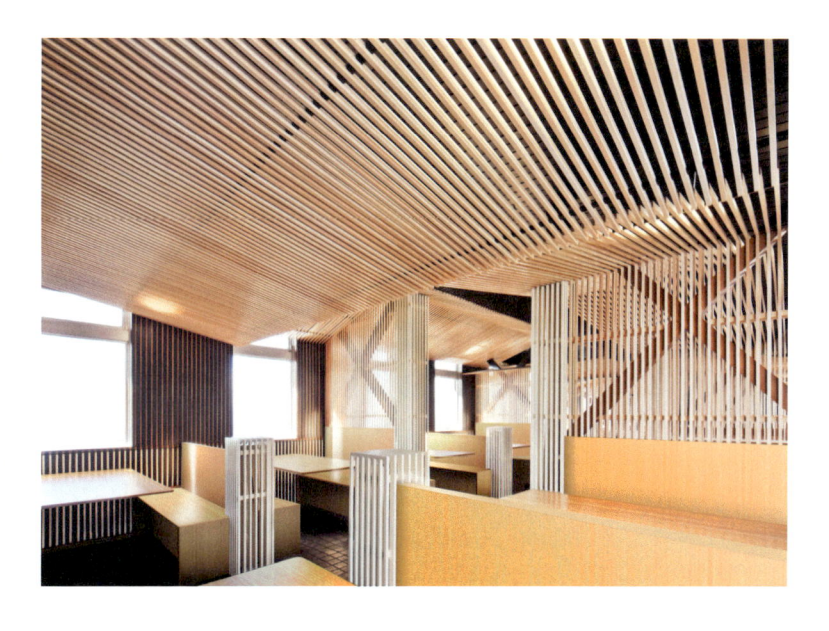

LAM CAFÉ
Nha Trang City, Vietnam

/ A forest in the heart of the city, Lam means "louvers," which describes the structure and architectural concept of this 800 sq m wood and stone eatery in a single word. The monumental roof is shaped like a coconut leaf (ubiquitous in this coastal city) that shears downward at obtuse angles. It consists of three layers—coconut leaves, tile, and fishing net—that generate an interplay of light and shadow throughout the space. The use of wooden slats—aesthetically, as partitions, and as a load-bearing element—made for a quick, low-budget construction that could be easily disassembled while enhancing views through an unattractive residential neighborhood.

/ Design: a21studio

/ Client: Sơn Nguyễn

/ Material: Rock, Sam na wood, coconut leaf, granitoid

/ Type of Food/Drinks/Specialties: Soft drinks, cocktails, spirits, juices, beers, hot drinks, non-alcoholic, martinis

SOPHISTICATED

NOK NOK THAI EATING HOUSE
Sydney, Australia

/ "Nok Nok." "Who's there?" "Not another dark Thai restaurant," according to the brief for this brightly latticed eatery. As airy as a garden gazebo, the fretting and the fig and wisteria trees lend intimacy nonetheless. Giant's Ed Kenny decided that the only architectural archetype not yet exhausted in the panoply of Thai diners was that of the temple, fulgent with white marble and golden mosaics. Kenny used gold and silver mirror to add depth and texture, and gold Alucobond and Corian cladding—perforated with laser-cut lotus leaves—to construct a modern sanctum of Thai cuisine. Even the kitchen is enshrined in a gold-tiled box.

/ Design: Giant Design

/ Client: Thanasarn Thongkhao & Nok Yingprasert

/ Type of Food/Drinks/Specialties: Thai

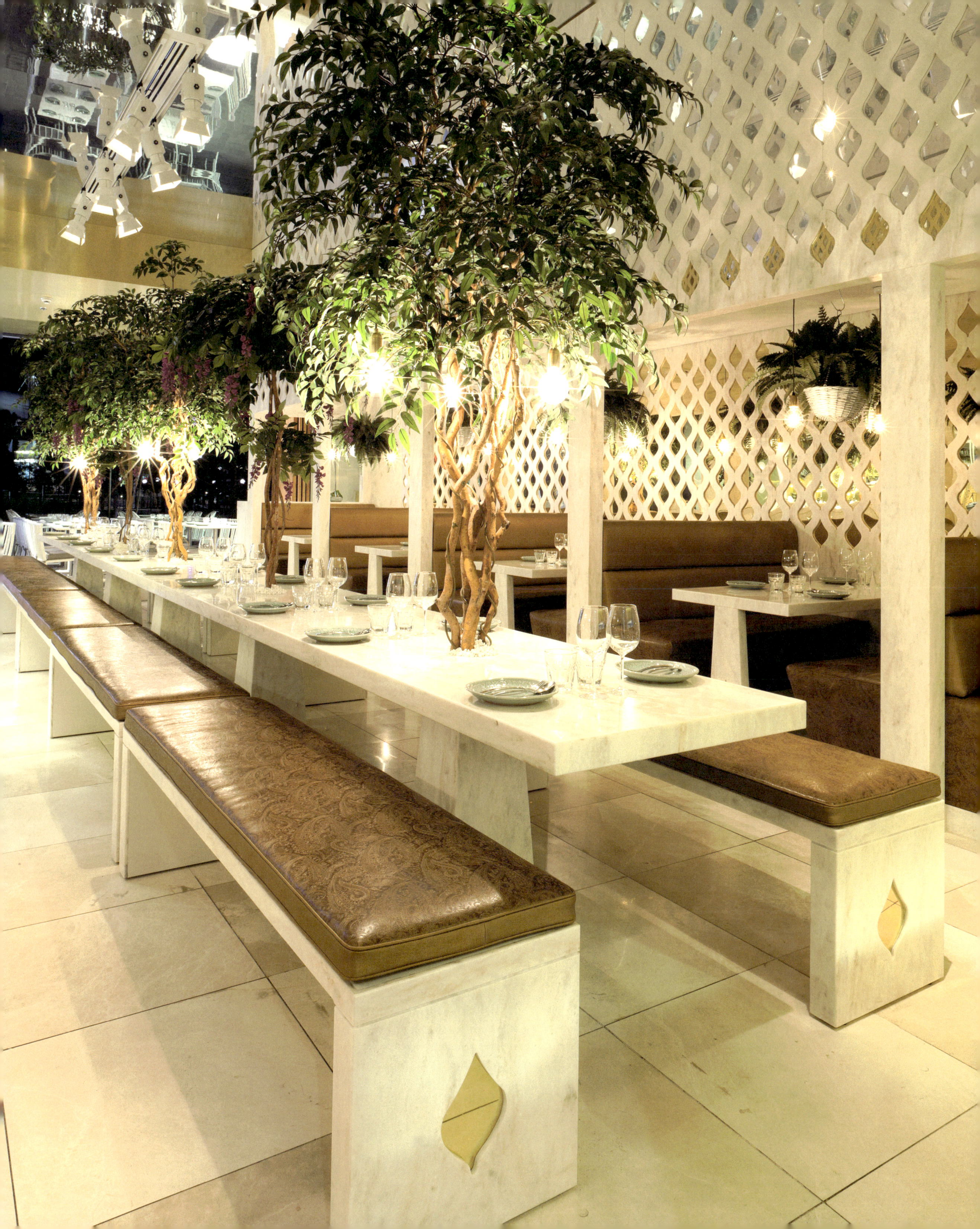

EFA'S BOX
Berlin, Germany

/ Designer Julius G. Kranefuss's re-design of this frozen yogurt store is defined by dichotomy: the brand's history vs. its relaunch and the replacement of the old product, EFA ice cream, with a sustainable and healthier alternative. Kranefuss repeatedly interrupts the existing classical architecture to frame more modern and expressive elements. The interior is consolidated in a box (a room-within-a-room concept that can easily be repeated elsewhere), which is placed inside the store and sliced open to resemble a coulisse.

/ Design: Zweidrei Medienarchitektur
/ Client: EFA Frozen Yogurt
/ Type of Food/Drinks/Specialties: Frozen yogurt

SOPHISTICATED

TORI TORI
Mexico City, Mexico

/ By sculpting this Japanese restaurant's façade to resemble a biomorphic version of extruded sheet metal, architects Michel Rojkind and Gerardo Salinas together with industrial and interior designer Héctor Esrawe gave the popular eatery a striking visual identity while bringing the outdoors in at certain points along the dining room walls. Another richly textured room is boxed with wooden planks, has an indoor vertical garden, and is crowned with a huge skylight, all of which seem to watch over diners at the sunken green zataku tables and their legless zaisu seats.

/ Design: Rojkind Arquitectos and Esrawe Studio

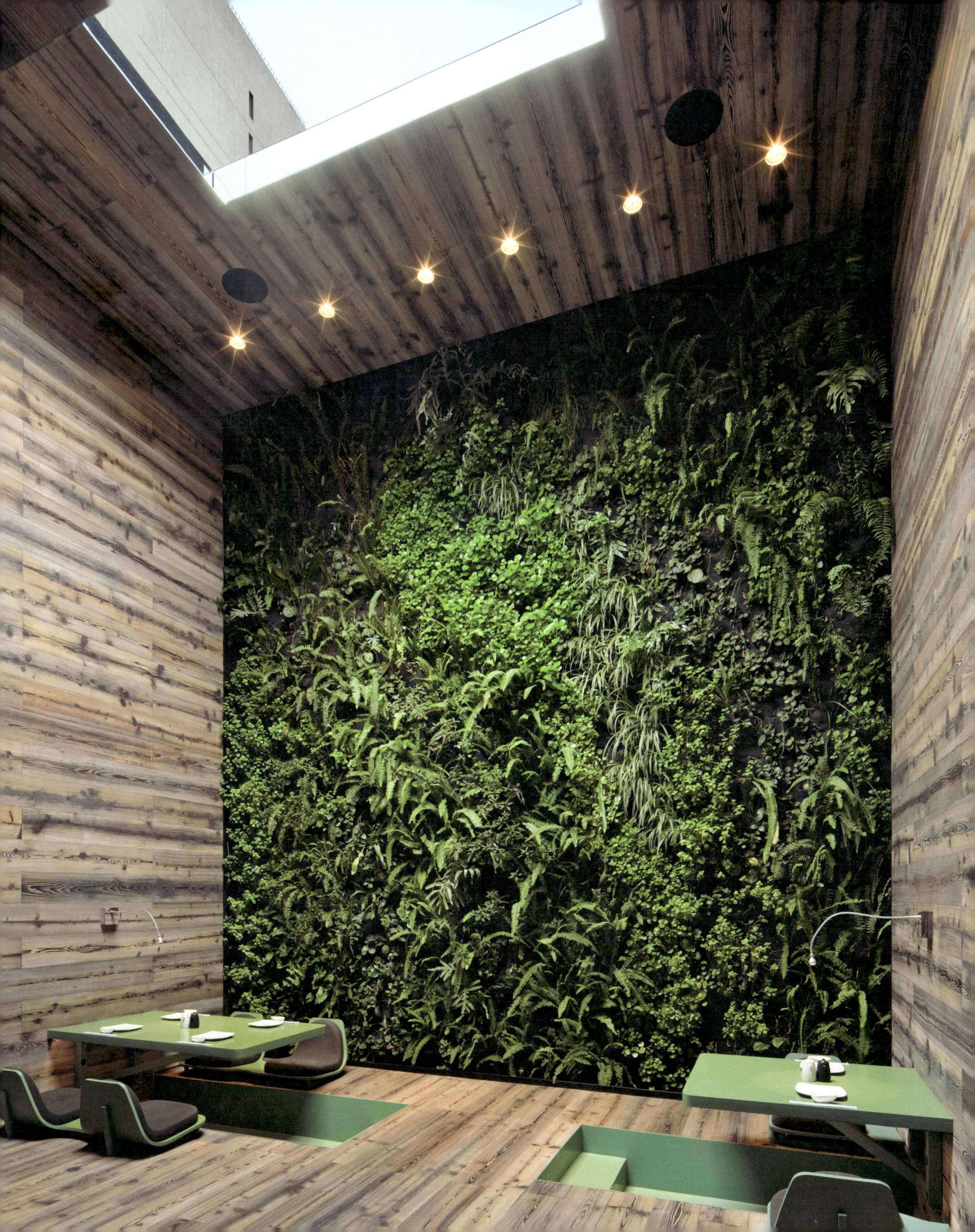

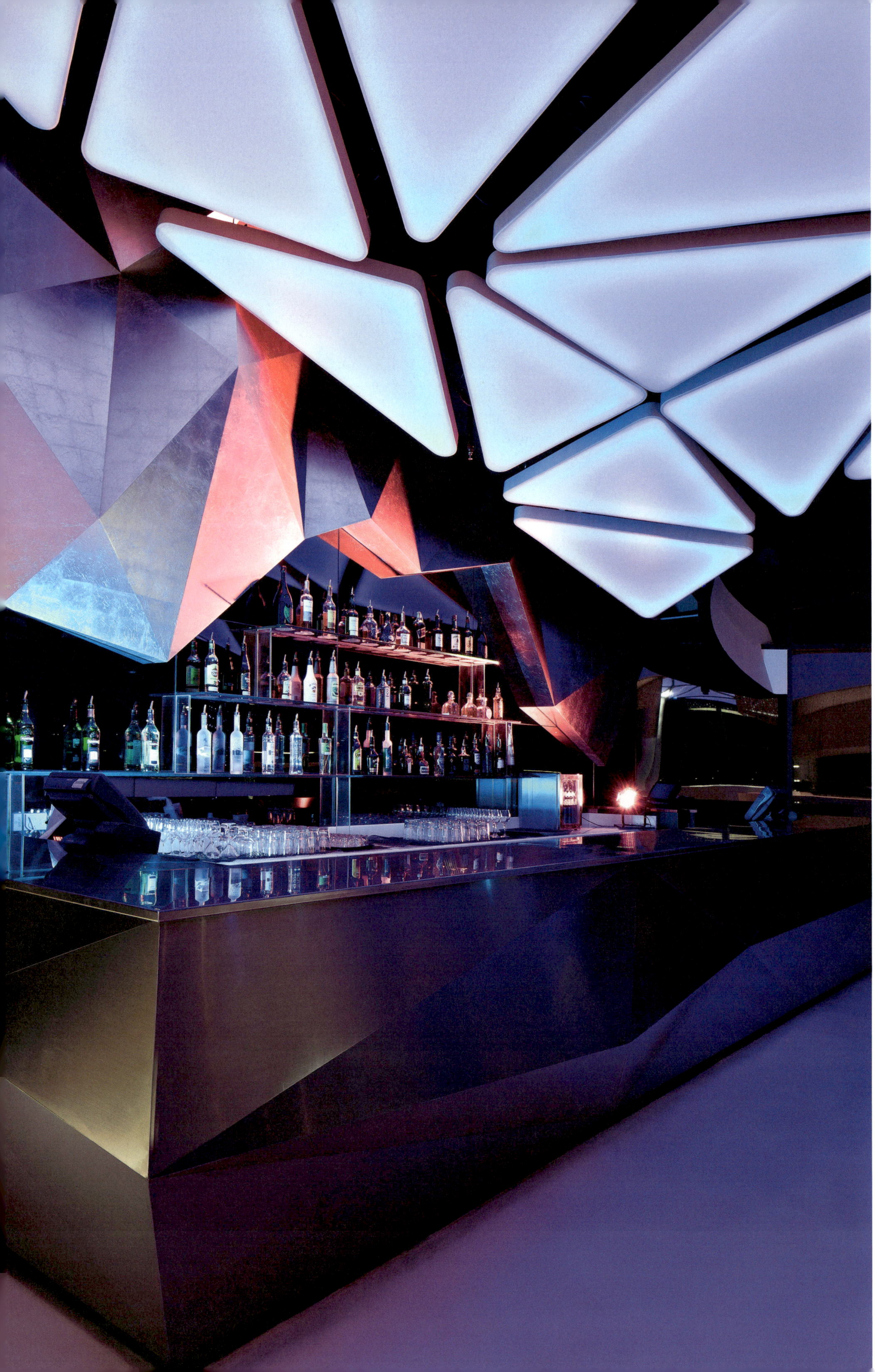

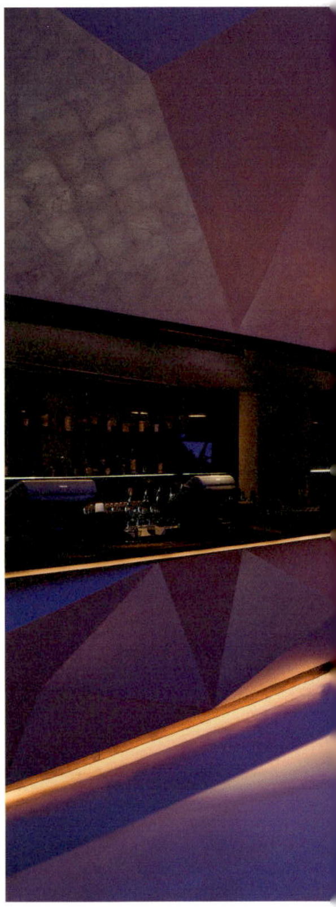

SOPHISTICATED

ALLURE
Yas Marine Island, Abu Dhabi

/ *Allure* is a jaw-droppingly opulent establishment on an exclusive island development and is the first nightclub from the owners of the mythically elite Cipriani restaurants. Orbit designed the space to appeal to the most rarified echelons of the international luxury crowd with views over a Formula One race track, an elevator for VIPs, and a hyperformal plan. It combines yacht-like seating with fractal walls and a ceiling made up of shards of light that sail to the floor and can be illuminated with "infinite color control," provided by mixing red, green, and blue fluorescent lamps. In the main room, radiused corners meet facets while pink gold leaf and bronze cladding step the lavishness up another notch.

/ Design: Orbit Design Studio

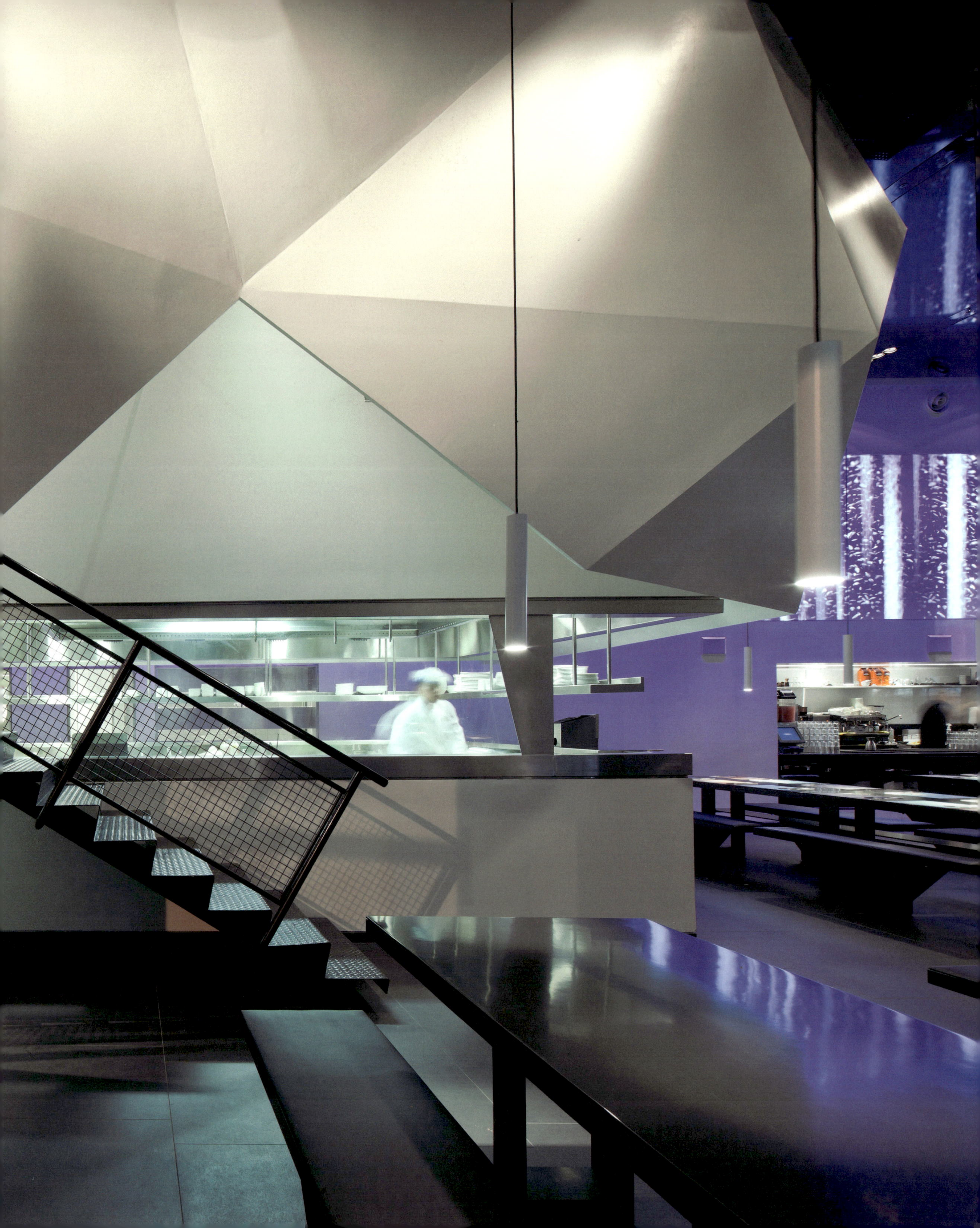

SOPHISTICATED

ZOZOBRA NOODLE BAR
Kfar-Sabba, Israel

/ This rigorously imagined Asian noodle bar—conspicuously *not* located in the major cities of Tel Aviv or Jerusalem—is a mix of studied design and the pop qualities of a fast food joint. A communal eating arrangement undercuts the notion of private eating space, encouraging visitors to mingle under shifting LED lighting and video art that flickers against the walls. The buzzing open kitchen in the center is surrounded by a three-dimensional origami-like structure that is reflected in a dramatic black mirrored ceiling.

/ Design: Baranowitz Kronenberg Architecture
/ Client: Ben Rothschild in partnership with chef Avi Conforty
/ Type of Food/Drinks/Specialties: Asian, fusion food

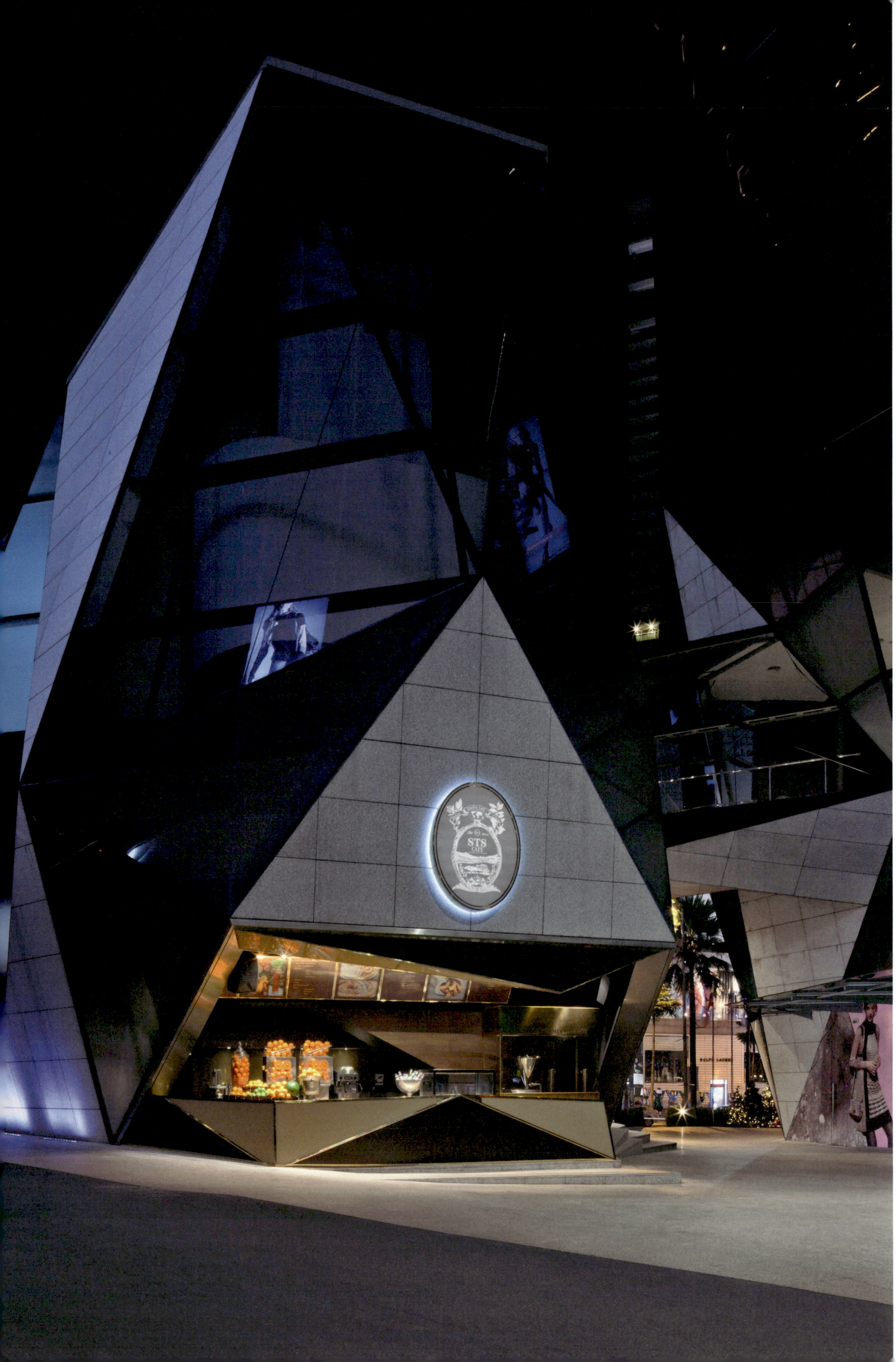

SOPHISTICATED

STS CAFÉ
Kuala Lumpur, Malaysia

/ This kiosk of the Starhill Tea Salon is set outside a shopping center and attached to a two-story polyhedron-shaped building. The structure of *STS Café* works with this polyhedron instead of against it. Indeed, the polyhedron serves as the final "facet" of the café. The designer used colored glass, coated brass, and timber to make it durable in harsh outdoor weather and was able to tailor the new structure to the existing one by pre-cutting panels in a factory and making adjustments to details on-site.

/ Design: design spirits

/ Client: Autodome

/ Material: Floor: homogeneous brown tile; Ceiling, walls, column: as existing; Waist wall: composite timber, walnut color stain, beige color glass, brass flat bar

/ Type of Food/Drinks/Specialties: Café

SCARPETTA
Toronto, Ontario, Canada

/ gh3 created an outdoor dining pavilion for this Italian eatery in Toronto. In a green space in the King West Village arts and design neighborhood surrounded by the Thompson Hotel, residences, and a public park, the design team planted open pergola-like walls made of an oversize latticework of black metal beams that bridges a shallow pool. Inside, the space is accessorized with Kartell lighting and chrome furnishings that provide a deep glow at night.

/ Design: gh3 Architects and Landscape Architects
/ Client: Freed Developments

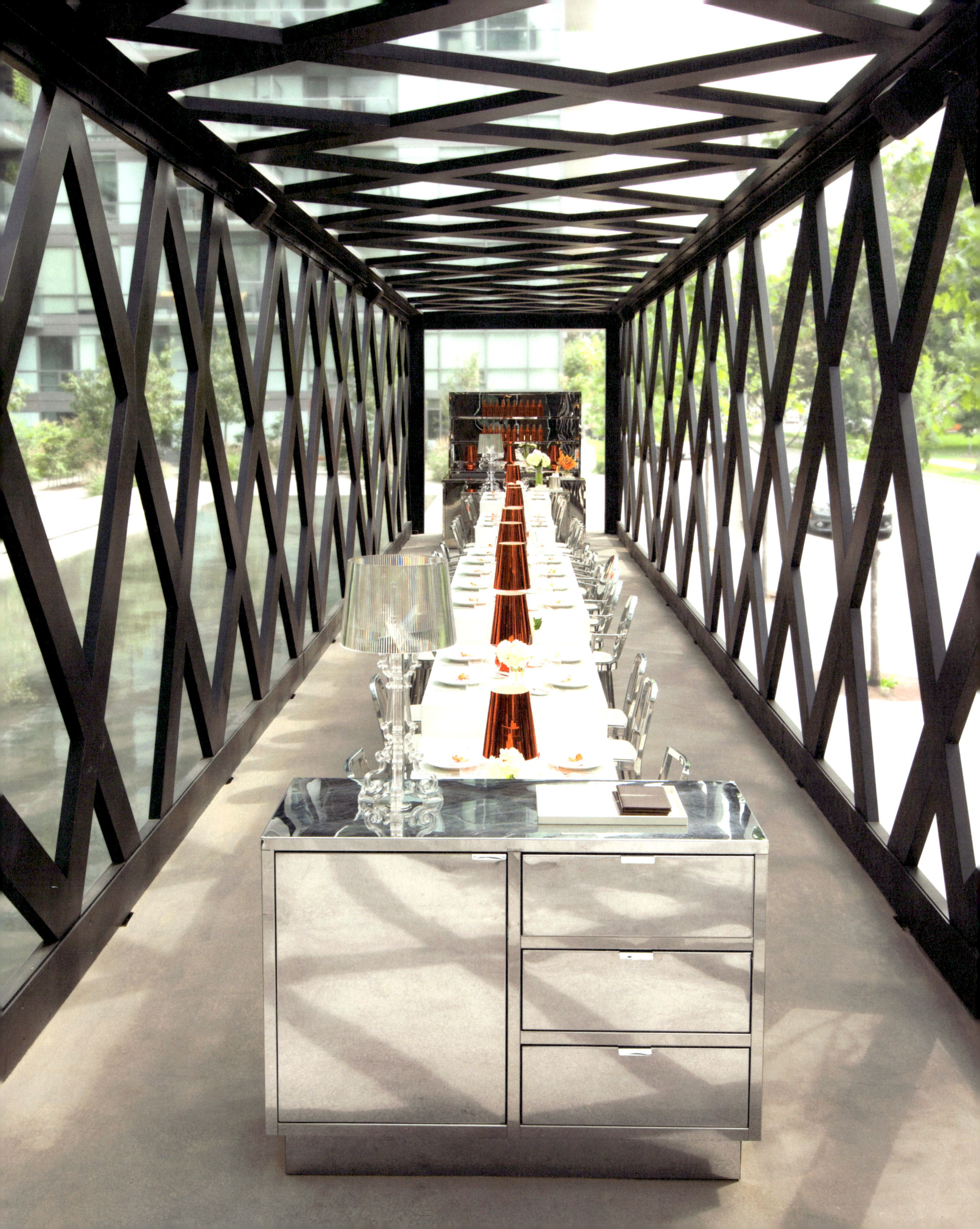

THE CUBE
Multiple Locations

/ This temporary, hypermodern dining room gives new meaning to the term "boite." The faceted and perforated white box is traveling through European cities to be craned onto landmarks, like a gem into its setting. Starting atop Brussels' Parc du Cinquantenaire, it then moved onto the roof of Milan's Rinascente almost within arm's reach of the Duomo before crowning London's Royal Festival Hall. Inside the 140 sq m construction, the open kitchen, staffed with Michelin-starred chefs, is at the center of a twice-daily but once-in-a-lifetime experience. The Cube has porous walls that let in shafts of light, as well as generous glazing and a platform for surveying the views beneath its perch.

/ Design: Electrolux

SOPHISTICATED

"The faceted and perforated white box is traveling through European cities to be craned onto landmarks, like a gem into its setting."

HOLYFIELDS FRANKFURT
Frankfurt, Germany

/ IFG created this modular, scalable concept for a restaurant chain to underscore the brand's commitment to high-end dining at good value for money. Under the strapline "Time to Eat," the franchise boasts a sophisticated, time-saving ordering system ("system gastronomy") that lets customers order via touchscreens and take an electronic device to their seats that signals when the food is ready. Seating is staggered in four tiers and nets of rubber laces separate the booths without impeding sightlines. At the rear, the food counter features a funnel-shaped, floor-to-ceiling copper wall while geometrically patterned holes ensure good acoustics and a pleasing contrast with the raw concrete and floral flooring.

/ Design: Ippolito Fleitz Group – Identity Architects
/ Client: Holyfields Restaurant

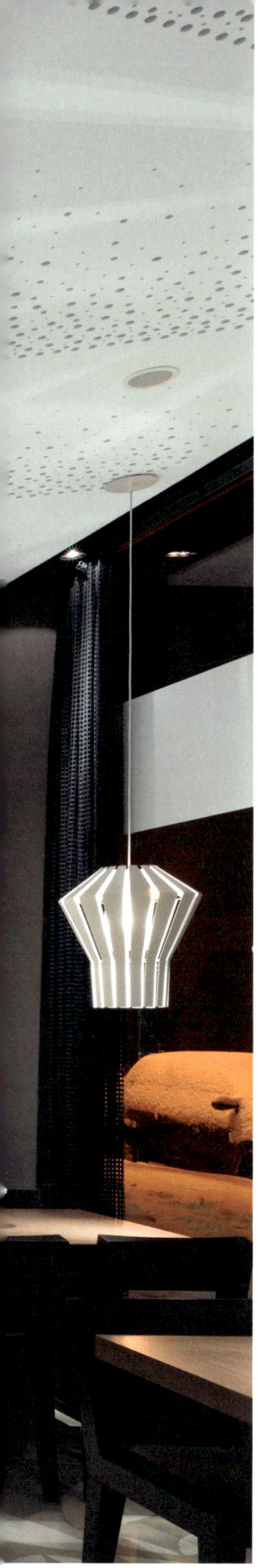

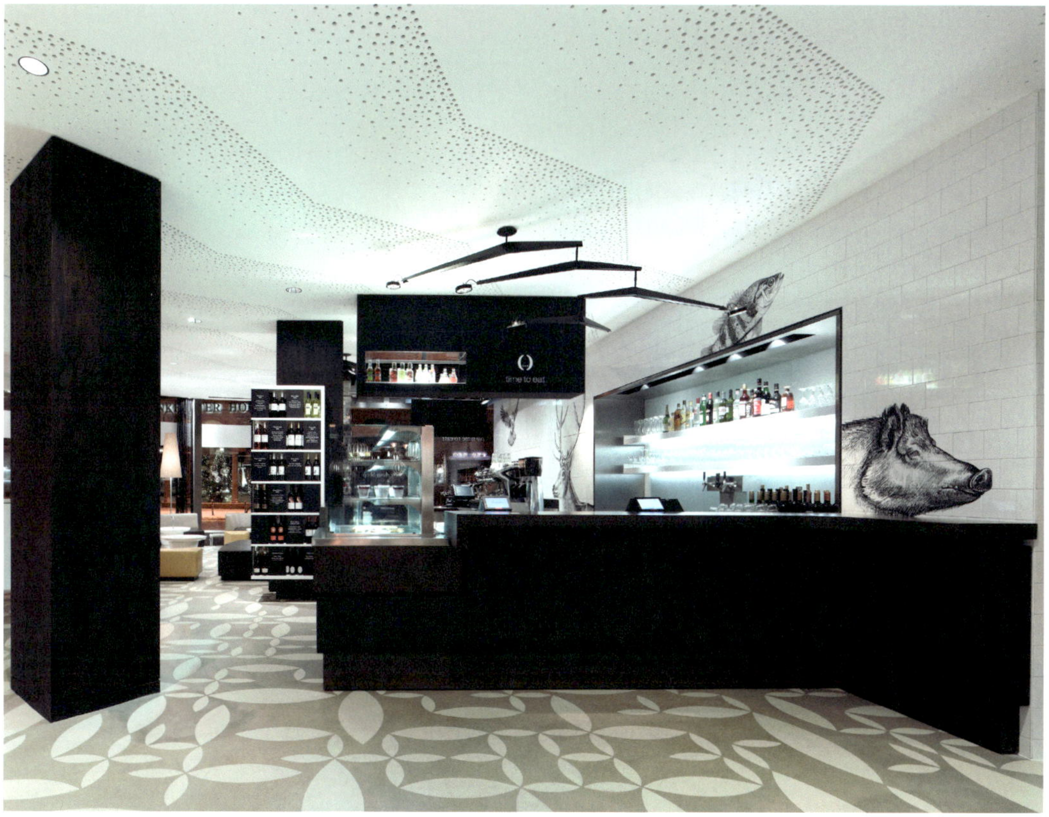

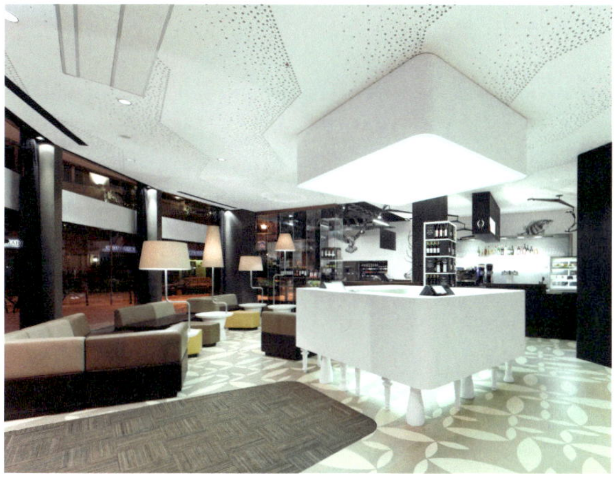

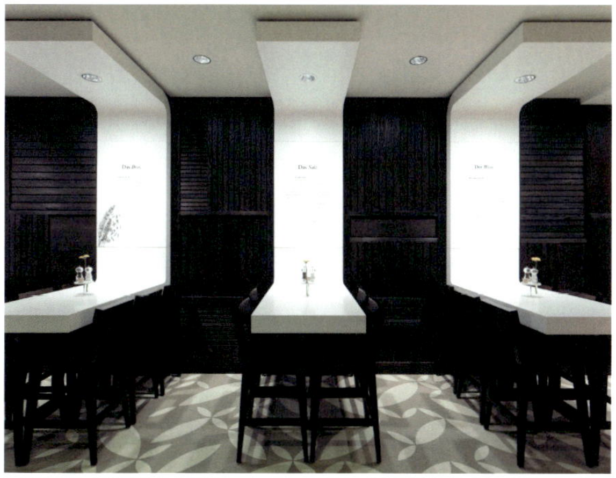

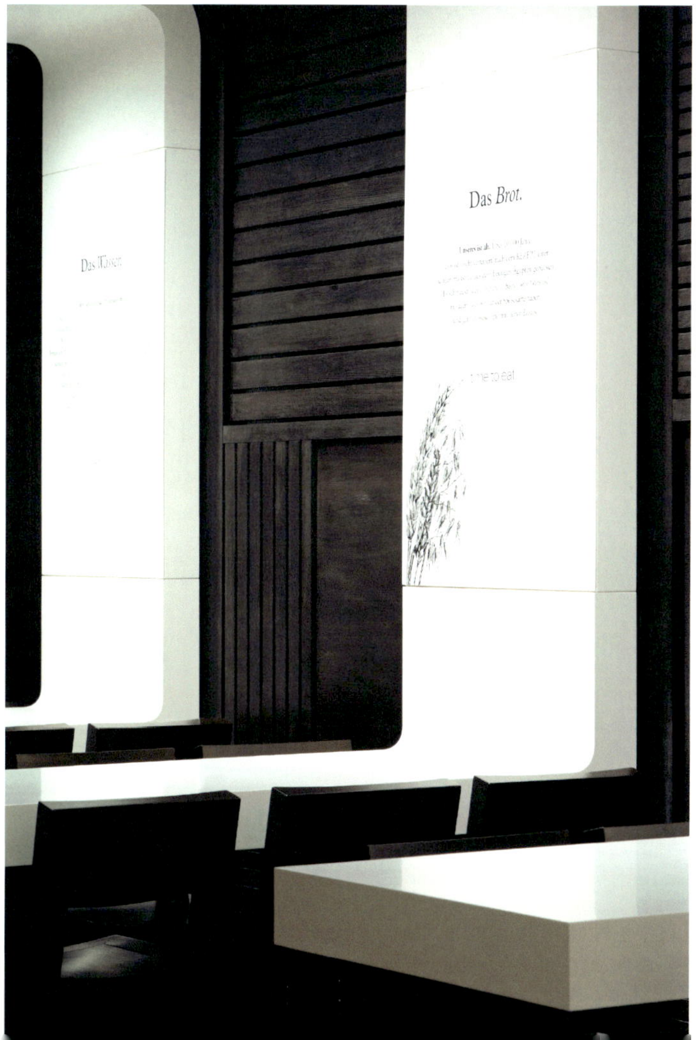
Das Brot.

SPICE SPIRIT RESTAURANT
Shanghai, China

/ Lee Hsuheng's team blends modernity with tradition in this super-textural violet environment. The interior has something of the voluptuousness of a woman's body and is accented with concepts borrowed from Tai Chi: the feminine elements have a counterpoint in the more "masculine" stacked polygonal-brick wall. Three dining areas underscore the juxtaposition of these two aesthetics: either undulating white curves and mirrors or the monumental purple wall that encloses a central dining zone, while dividing the space into more intimate volumes.

/ Design: Golucci International Design

SOPHISTICATED

"An irregular glass façade and 'curtains' of luminous floor-to-ceiling acrylic rods offer discrete dining areas."

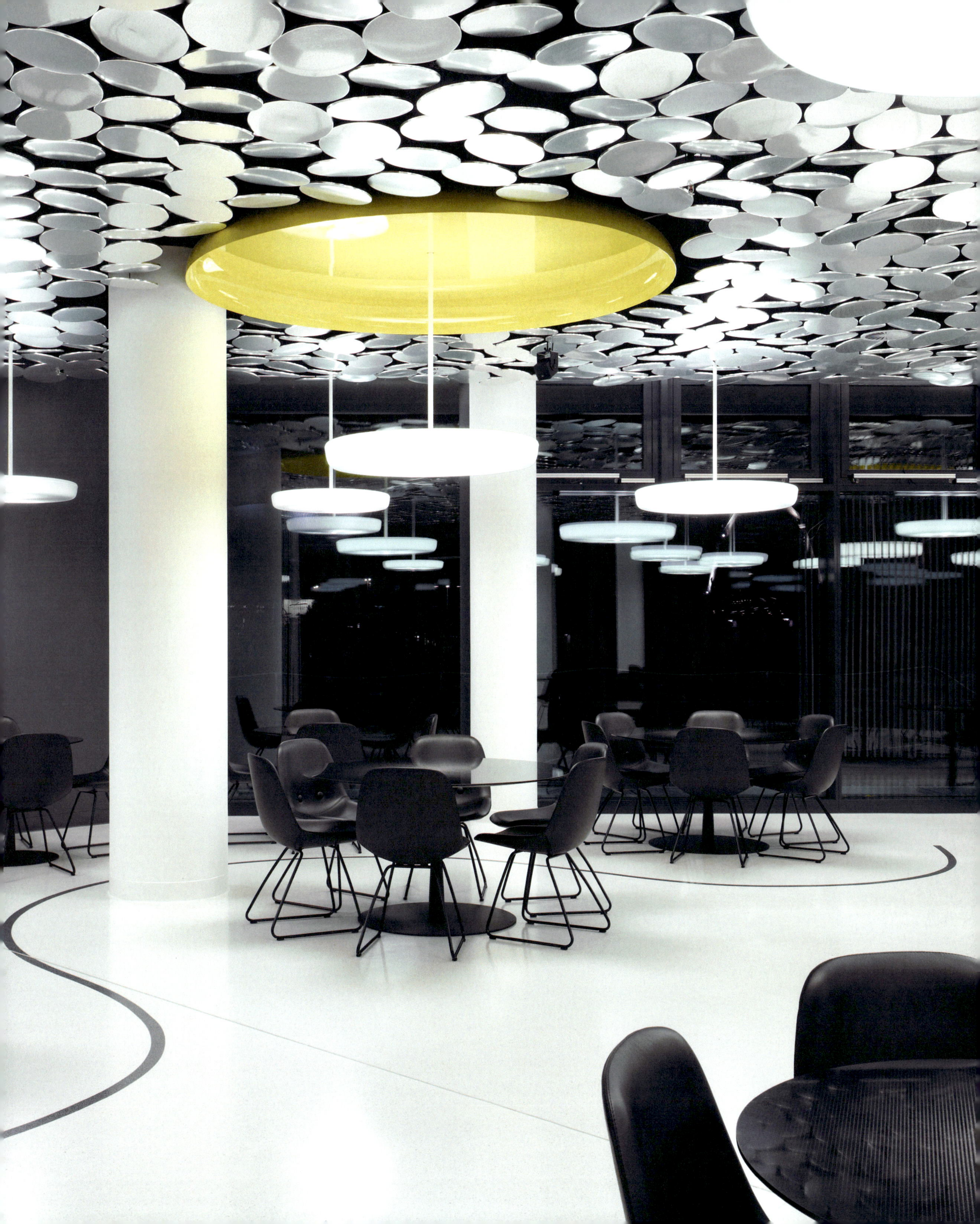

DER SPIEGEL KANTINE
Hamburg, Germany

/ When German publishing house Der Spiegel moved to its new headquarters, it tasked IFG with designing the 520 sq m employees' canteen. The company's old canteen was a famous 1969 design by Verner Panton. Undaunted, the specialists for restaurant interiors came up with a classy solution that represents Spiegel's culture of open communications and free dialogue. The tables are arranged into three loose groups that provide a counterpoint to the polygonal floor plan while niches formed by an irregular glass façade and "curtains" of luminous floor-to-ceiling acrylic rods offer discrete dining areas. IFG sequined the ceiling with 4,230 "paillettes" made of micro-perforated aluminum plates. Facing in slightly different directions, they generate an unusal and dynamic texture and rhythm.

/ Design: Ippolito Fleitz Group – Identity Architects

/ Client: Verlagsgruppe Der SPIEGEL

/ Type of Food/Drinks/Specialties: Canteen

SOPHISTICATED

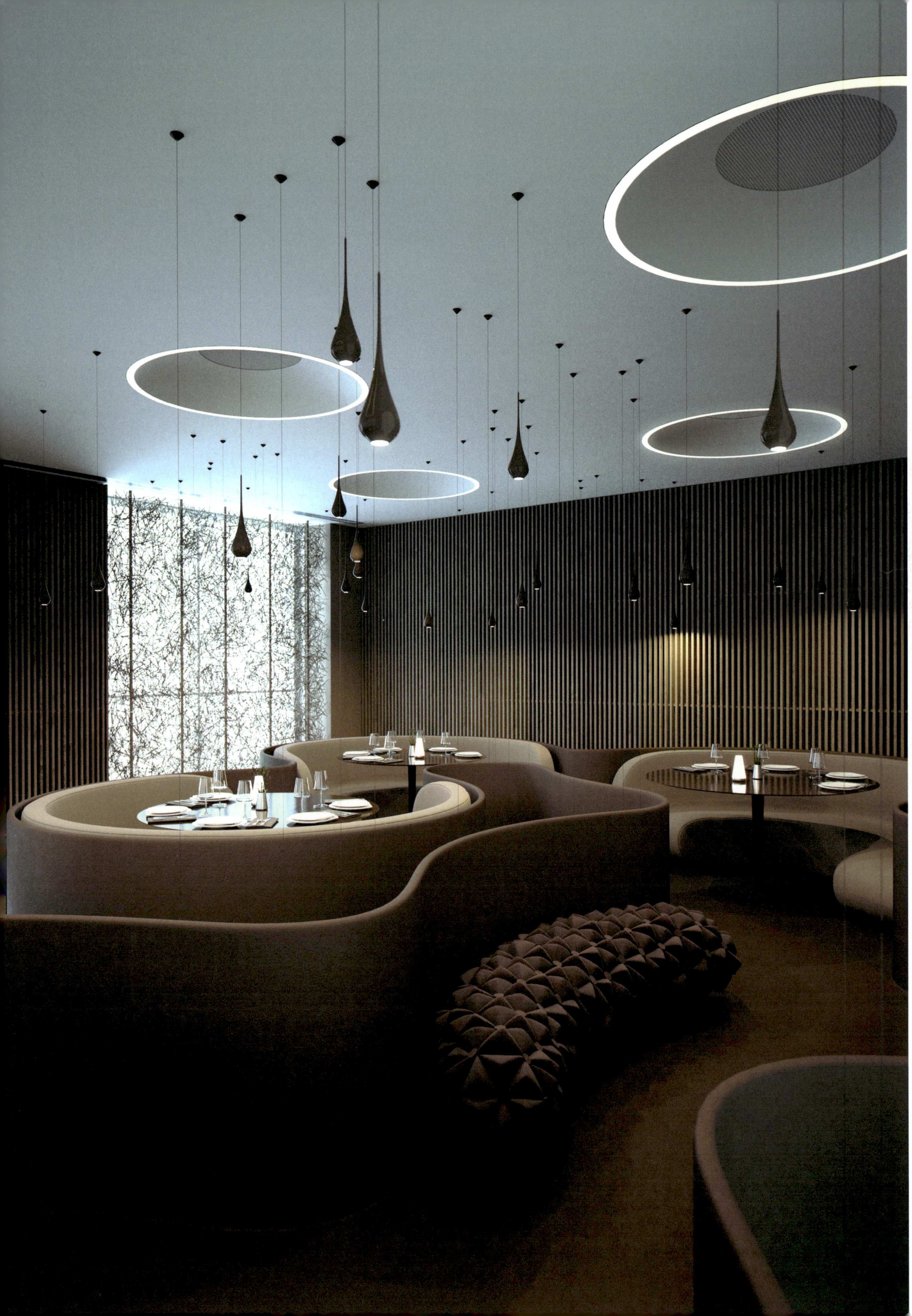
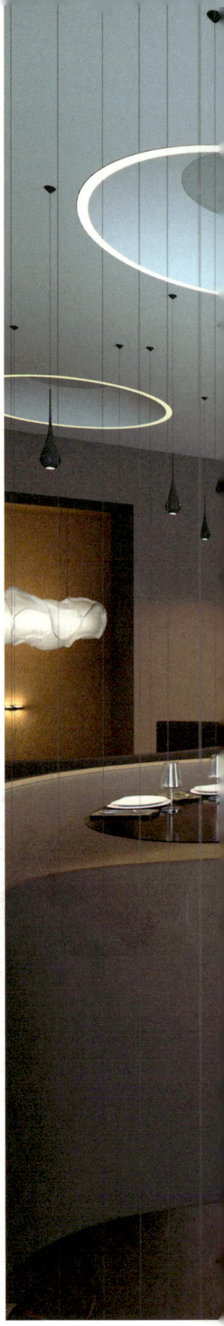

TWISTER
Kiev, Ukraine

/ Sergey Makhno and Vasiliy Butenko's restaurant interior tends to both unleash and tame the forces of Nature. Over two stories, undulating banquettes, armchairs recalling pine cones, ceiling lights that mimic pendulous drops of rain that never fall, and a bar area made of clusters of wooden sticks and resembling an avant-garde bird's nest, represent graphically abstracted natural phenomena that embrace guests instead of lashing them. The two designers used earth tones and wood and stone surfaces to give visitors a sense of remove from the world in the eye of a protective storm.

/ Design: Interior workshop of Sergey Makhno
/ Client: Confidential
/ Material: Wood, concrete, metal, marble, plastic
/ Type of Food/Drinks/Specialties: European cuisine

PHANTOM—RESTAURANT OF THE GARNIER OPERA HOUSE

Paris, France

/ Like the famous phantom, this 90-seat restaurant—with its seamlessly molded plaster-white surfaces and incandescent scarlet furnishings—stalks voluptuously through the historical Opéra Garnier without once touching its walls, columns, or ceiling. Decq made sure that the construction could be removed without damage to the landmark edifice. In the meantime, the lightness of the structure stands in striking visual contrast to the old building in a way that casts both in the finest light.

/ Design: Odile Decq Benoit Cornette Architectes Urbanistes
/ Client: GUMERY

SOPHISTICATED

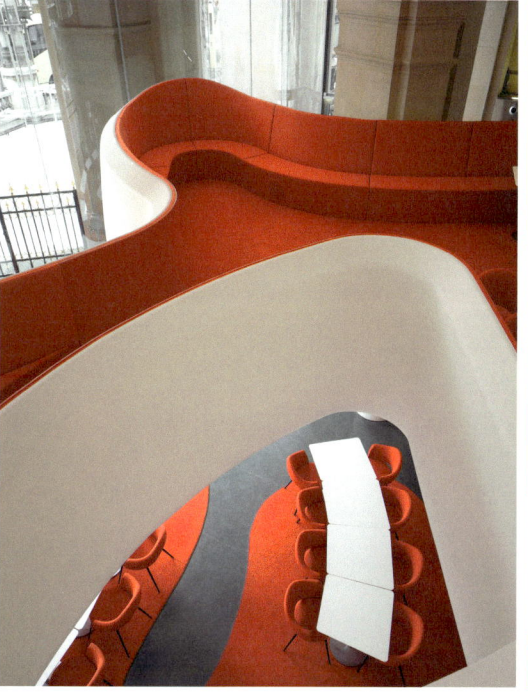

CHAN
Thessaloniki, Greece

/ In this intimate, low-light restaurant and bar, the Australian architect has successfully replaced the exhausted stereotypes of Asian dining with a dark masculine sensibility softened by an under-moonlit-water look-and-feel. Like a river-worn rock, an ellipsoid sculpture sits at the center of the anodized charcoal box of the interior, surrounded by a complex layering of forms that ranges from the illuminated wall panels to open-grid ceilings; the lines that ripple out from around the spot lights are reflected in the minimalist pattern lining the tabletops. In the lounge, tattoo-like illustrations on the upholstery and contemporary interpretations of manga graphics create a cocktail of Asian street culture with distinctly cosmopolitan flavors.

/ Design: Andy Martin Architects

/ Client: Chandris Hotel Group

/ Type of Food/Drinks/Specialties: Asian cuisine, fusion

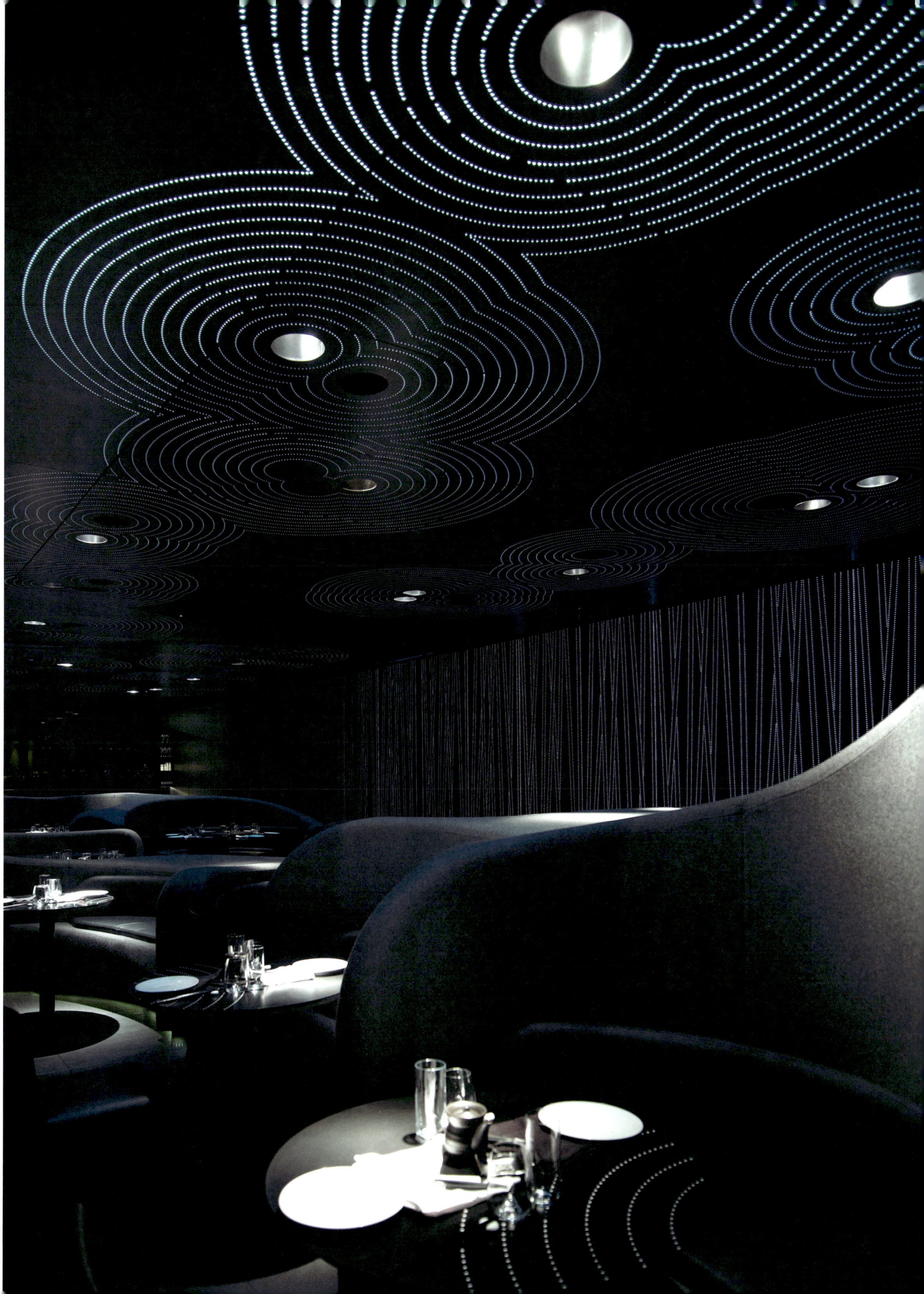

ZEBAR
Shanghai, China

/ Built with white epoxy, black concrete, plywood, plasterboard—and Rhino nurbs, ZeBar is a cave-like space assembled from a digital Boolean subtraction of hundreds of slices extracted from an amorphous blob. The space looks as simple as the technique to construct it sounds complex, but it was a scheme born naturally from the designer's experimentation in digital 3D modeling environments. By giving the digital model to a factory, it could have been easily CNC milled even though each section is different from the next, but instead, the work was done by projecting the sections onto plasterboard and then cutting them manually. The architect calls it "a digital design built into an analog world."

/ Design: 3GATTI China
/ Client: Jim Dandy
/ Material: White epoxy, black concrete, plywood and plasterboard

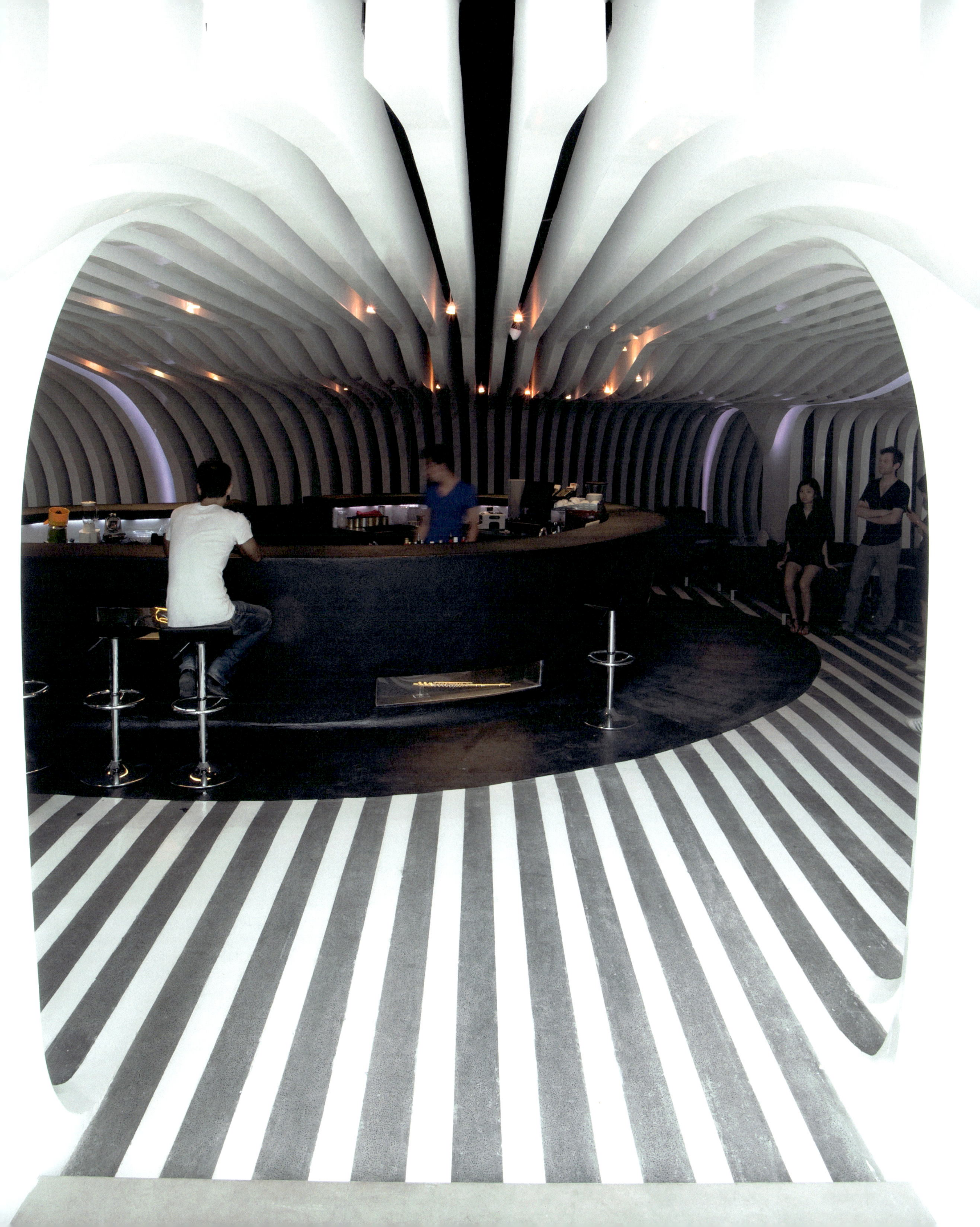

SUSHI CAFÉ AVENIDA
Lisbon, Portugal

/ The design of this molecular Japanese restaurant lets diners discover new textures, colors, and scents throughout the evening. The challenge was to create four distinct bar and dining areas while playing down the T-shaped plan. White dominates in the marble flooring, Corian countertop, and striated surfaces, showing off the super-graphical fiberglass wall panels. Their function determined their form: they morph into steps or serve as a glowing backdrop, and are suffused with varying intensities and colors of light that can radically alter the mood of the space.

/ Design: Saraiva + Associados

/ Client: Kaiten Sushi Restauração

/ Material: Walls in perforated panels, perforated golden plate, wave-like slats, fiberglass strips, white corian (resin)

/ Type of Food/Drinks/Specialties: Molecular Japanese cuisine

SOPHISTICATED

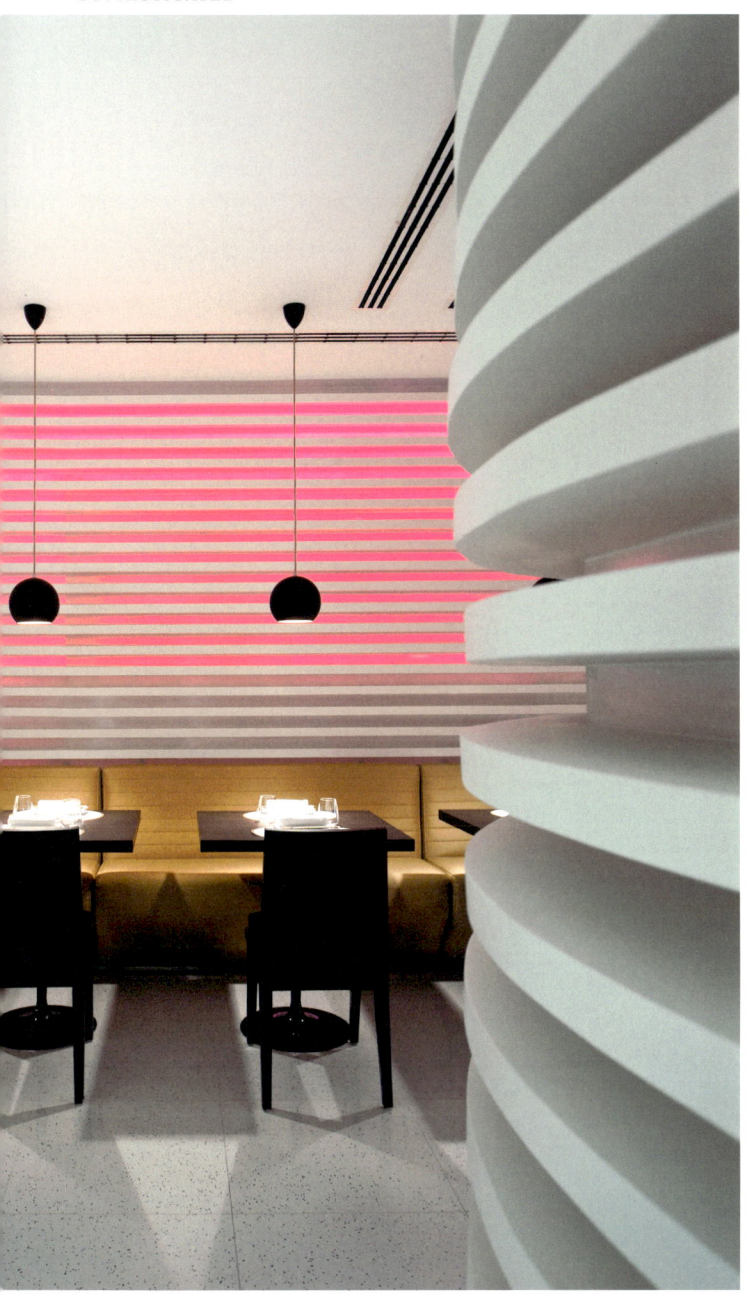

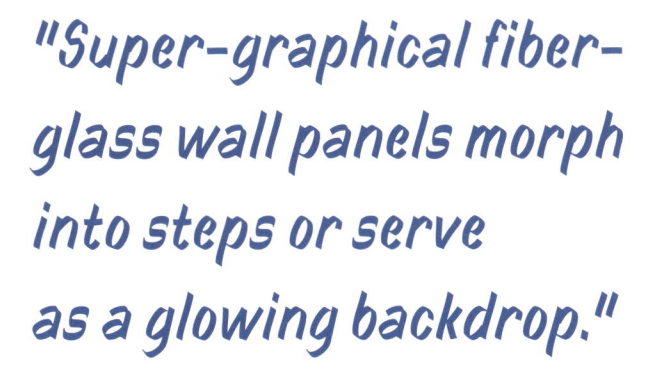

"Super-graphical fiber-
glass wall panels morph
into steps or serve
as a glowing backdrop."

HASHI MORI
Berlin, Germany

/ Construction materials at this Berlin-based Japanese izakaya restaurant included chopsticks, nylon, canvas, and wood. Traditional materials and handcraft are mixed with 3D modeling and computer programming to create an atmospheric space for dining—and by atmospheric we mean meteorological. Affect Studio created a swagging cloud of chopsticks over the 56 sq m ceiling. Like Lewis.Tsurumaki.Lewis' now-closed Manhattan seafood restaurant with its canopy of over 12,000 bamboo skewers, Affect managed, with a single gesture—meaning 13,454 chopsticks, 57,400 knots, over 20 km of nylon thread, a crew of 14 people and three weeks—to create a cozy interior, establish a strong visual identity for the business, and maximize table space.

/ Design: Affect Studio

/ Client: Hashi Japanese Kitchen

/ Material: Chopsticks, nylon, canvas, wood, rice

/ Type of Food/Drinks/Specialties: Japanese Izakaya

"Traditional materials and handcraft are mixed with 3D modeling and computer programming to create an atmospheric space for dining."

CAFFE STREETS
Chicago, Illinois, USA

/ Brent Norsman worked to blend space for a "social" coffeehouse with an active Masters Barista bar designed for craft coffee-making. The 93 sq m interior is lined with marbled bamboo plywood in the form of custom communal tables, chairs, wall paneling, and a striated CNC-sculpted ceiling that was inspired by the complex pouring flourishes "drawn" by baristas in the frothed milk. The designers drew elements of the street into the café, lighting the baristas' workspace with retrofitted Chicago streetlights and connecting the shop to the sidewalk with polished concrete floors and a glassy storefront.

/ Design: Norsman Architects
/ Client: Darko Arandjelovic
/ Material: Custom seating, bamboo plywood, streetlight fixtures, Synessa Hydra espresso machine
/ Type of Food/Drinks/Specialties: Coffee & espresso

SOPHISTICATED

Northern Comfort

Hemingway paid homage to the "clean, well-lighted" places of the world in a 1926 short story and designers are reprising the concept today. Spaces infused with Northern Comfort are as pared-down as the language Hemingway used, and for the same reasons: to give the space and its story clarity, to make it more accessible, inviting, functional, and true to itself. There is no sentiment here to cloud the emotion: the furniture is stripped down and simple, modernist and soft-edged. The spaces are bright, but not bright with color; instead, they rely on neutrals like black, white, gray, and beige. Many of them mix up place or time in ways that feel familiar and freshly discoverable at the same time while others do the opposite: they focus solely on local food, materials, and people. These details make them the easiest, most satisfying kind of places to return to again and again.

Schrannenhalle

NORTHERN COMFORT

/ Venues dressed in Scandinavian chic represent a paradigm of this type of space. The Michelin-starred *NOMA Food Lab* →132–133 in Copenhagen, for instance, is a place where innovative chefs experiment, pushing the limits of Nordic cuisine; they don't need a space that competes or distracts, they need an empty bowl, so to speak, and honest ingredients. Because the designers had to conform to historic area building codes that forbade them to anchor the new construction in any way to the walls or floor, the user-friendly environment also stands—literally—on its own. Four multifunctional shelving towers, containing 500 wooden cubbies that curve around their wide columns, divide the larger room into more intimate zones that contain the Food Lab, a herb garden on wheels, and admin space. Only lightly finished and cleverly plain, like the food itself, the interior uses only regional or local materials.

Ubon →112–113 in Kuwait City represents a more dressed-up, moodier version of the type while remaining simple nonetheless. It consists of planes of poured cement, blackened wood, and mirror that draws in natural light and diffuses it throughout the space, creating counterpoint to the dark walls. Overhead, the matte black surfaces of Tom Dixon pendant lamps are minimal but slivers of hammered copper glow softly from within, an inconspicuous but influential accessory to the design.

Lowkey and softly minimalist the *Red Pif Wine Depot & Garden* →166–167 in Prague is the color of Kraft paper and concrete. *Pif's* designers reclaimed a garbage-filled street corner into a garden shaded with large maple trees and hemmed with a fence made from unplaned boards. The interior features bottle-shaped cabinets and shutters, clean oak surfaces, and a spacious room framed with bottle-lined walls that make the product accessible. All of this renders the space welcoming and comfortable without falling into a saccharine coziness.

Simple, timeless, charming and local—sort of: *Walden* →150–151 restaurant in New York City is built to evoke the story of its place and then interpret it anew: part saloon, part Victorian general store, it has the pressed tin ceilings so common to North America once upon a time, along with tiled floors, wooden bars, marble counters, and brass globe lighting. It bespeaks a local joint for a local crowd, albeit from a loosely defined era that isn't quite now, a gentle confusion that is, ironically, what makes the design so trendy today. Familiar elements are combined with unfamiliar, making it difficult to identify the space with a single period (or, sometimes, place). There is always something to discover here and yet guests feel convinced that they already know the place and belong in it.

Measured doses of detail often frame these spaces: The *GMOA Keller* →114–115 restaurant inhabits a long, windowless cellar whose vaulted brick walls have been brightened with white paint. The white brick becomes a blank canvas for two long clean lines of wood that serve as backrests for bench seating and both upholstery and drapes sewn from a highly graphical fabric by Kvadrat illustrated with a jungle motif. The *Graffiti Café* →116–117 in Bulgaria is another blank canvas filled with bright white surfaces and seating, white floor tiles and columns, but it is accented with slats of blond wood that make stripes up and down the bases of tables, climb up three fat columns and over half of the dining room ceiling, looking for all the world like lathe-turned trees. The trees give the space interest and energy so that the rest of the interior can afford to stick to the basics without boring diners to death.

Its designers didn't try to make *Alemagou* →134–135 restaurant on Mykonos something that it is not. To protect it from driving winds, a relentless sun, and the parched landscape ever encroaching upon it, they borrowed from the vernacular—whitewashing, stone walls and naturally insulating thatched roof—but they gave these elements an updated clarity and cleanness of form. Dignified and elegant but informal, *Alemagou* honors local recipes and ingredients as much as it respects the severe local climate and local architectural traditions. This is the highest virtue of the contemporary Nordic-influenced space: It is true to itself, true to its materials, and true to the people who will return to it again and again.

Cheese Bar →124–125

Mogg & Melzer Delicatessen →154–155

Jaffa →156–157

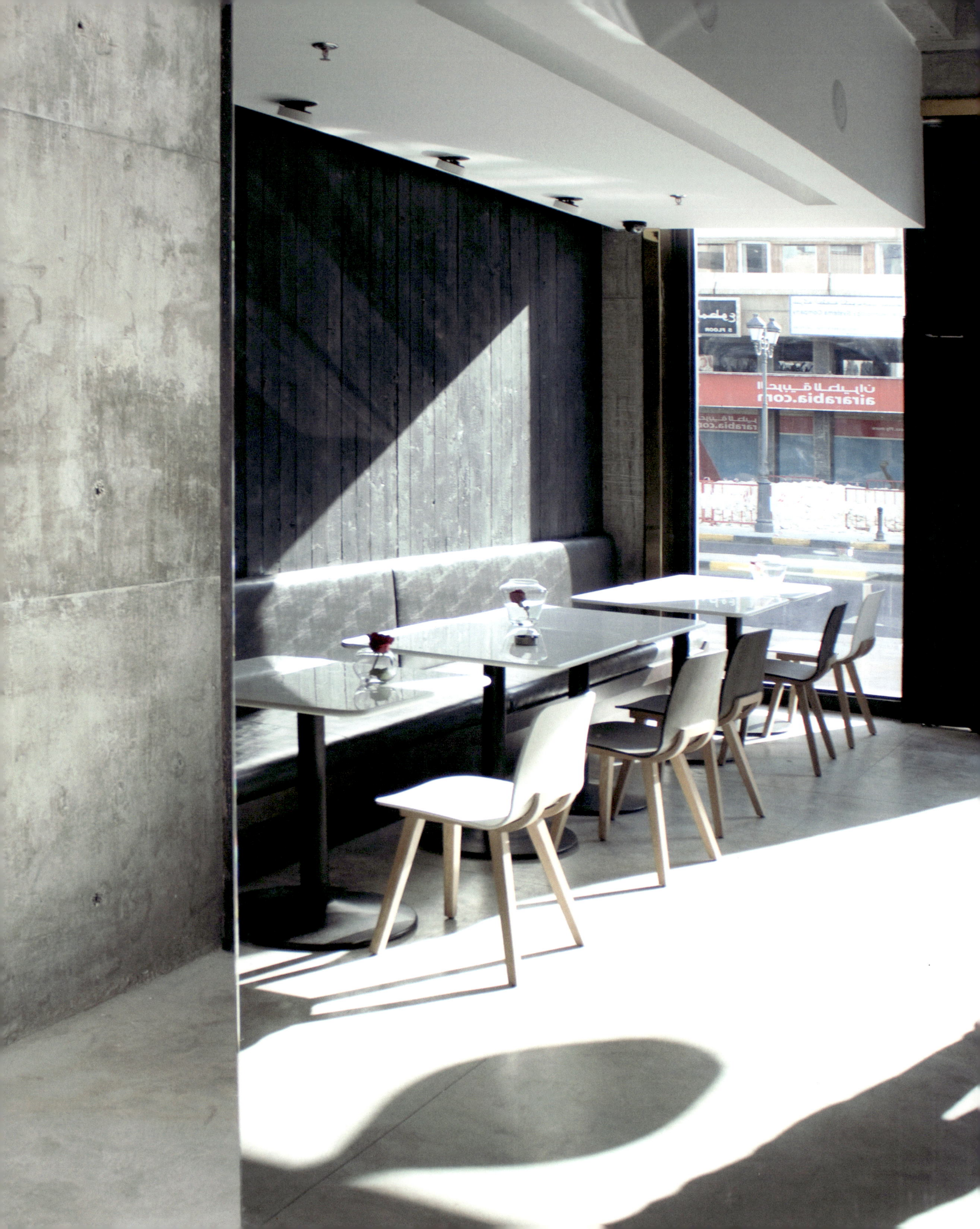
airarabia.com

NORTHERN COMFORT

UBON
Kuwait City, Kuwait

/ The architects of *Ubon* treated the service components of this Thai bistro with great economy only to be all the more generous in the dining room. They used black mirror and burnt wood panels infused with golden copper details to evoke the eatery's Asian spirit and allude to an historical aesthetic that runs strong in the DNA of Thai ornamentation. They added voluptuous pendant lights to make the space more soothing and on the restroom's poured concrete walls left the imprint of wood grain, unifying the contrast in color and material with a common texture.

/ Design: Rashed Alfoudari

/ Client: Ubon Kuwait

/ Material: Concrete floor with matt water sealer, existing raw concrete, burnt wood, black mirror, wood print concrete, existing rib system/gypsum

/ Type of Food/Drinks/Specialties: Contemporary Thai food

"They painted the brick vault white, giving it a superficial uniformity that actually underscores the handsome irregularity of the surfaces."

NORTHERN COMFORT

GMOA KELLER
Vienna, Austria

/ Whitewash, wood, and wilderness are the three elements in the simple materials palette of this 115 sq m eatery. The austere and formal regimen of the cellar furnishings shows off a series of delicious texture/pattern pairings. SUE eschewed the stereotype of the romantic subterranean bistro by avoiding distracting details; instead, they painted the brick vault white, giving it a superficial uniformity that actually underscores the handsome irregularity of the surfaces. They also designed the 60 × 60 cm tables for easy rearrangement, hid ductwork behind Kenzo's distinctive Jungle fabric drapes, and mounted repositionable lighting on the canted belt of dark wood wainscoting to generate an intimacy otherwise difficult to achieve in an open-plan dining room.

/ Design: SUE Architekten
/ Client: GMOA Keller, Sebastian Laskowsky
/ Material: White brick arches
/ Type of Food/Drinks/Specialties: Traditionnal Viennese cuisine

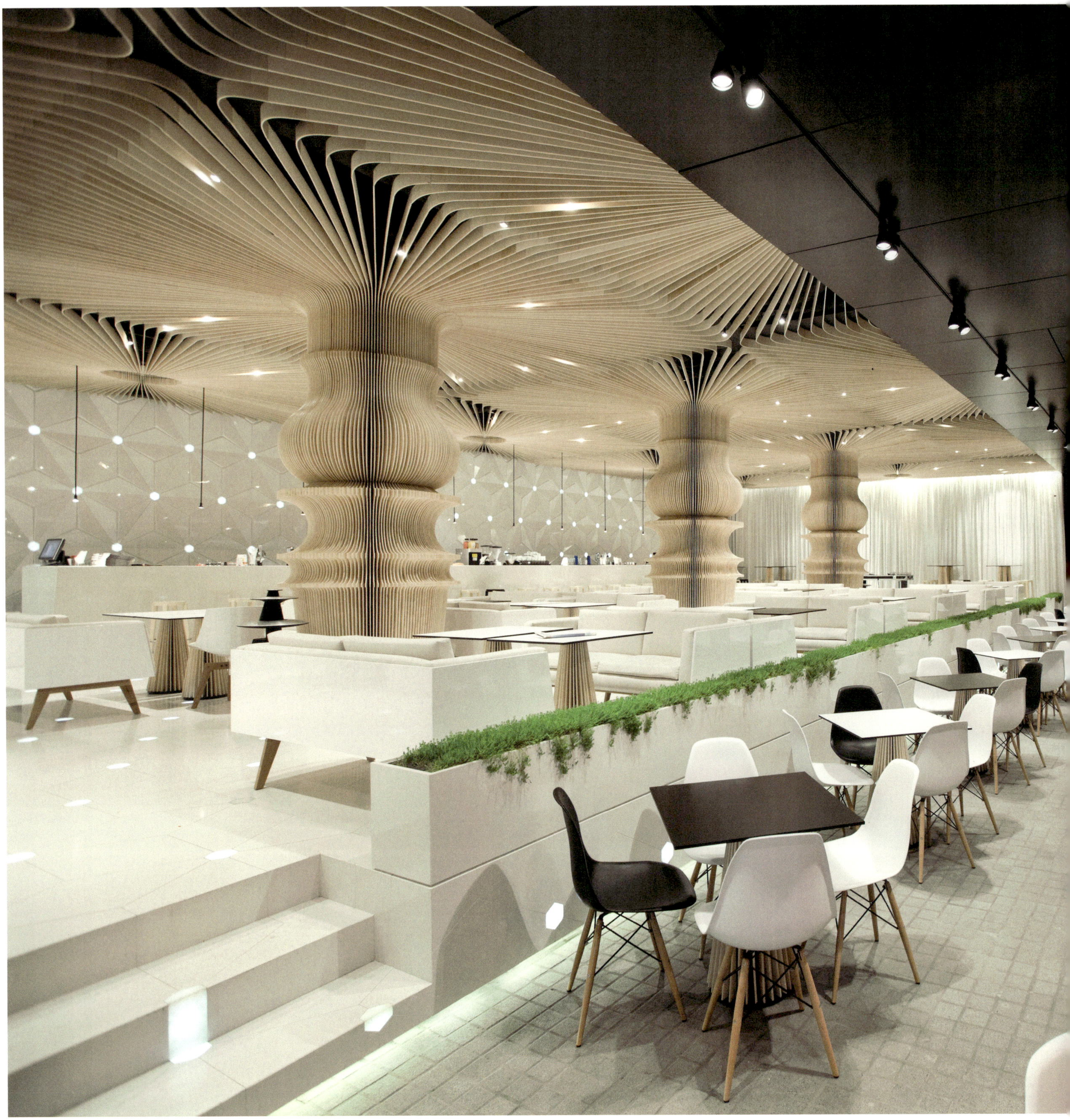

GRAFFITI CAFÉ
Varna, Bulgaria

/ The interior of this café, situated beneath the city's Gallery of Modern Art, is an extension of its architecture. Separated into two zones, the front of the café is integrated into the façade, creating public space, while the rear is divided visually by establishing discrete plans for the floor and roof designs. The makers resolved functional challenges related to ventilation, sound, and acoustics through an interpretation of Escher that incorporated materials sparingly but in an extraordinarily sculptural and textural way.

/ Design: Studio MODE

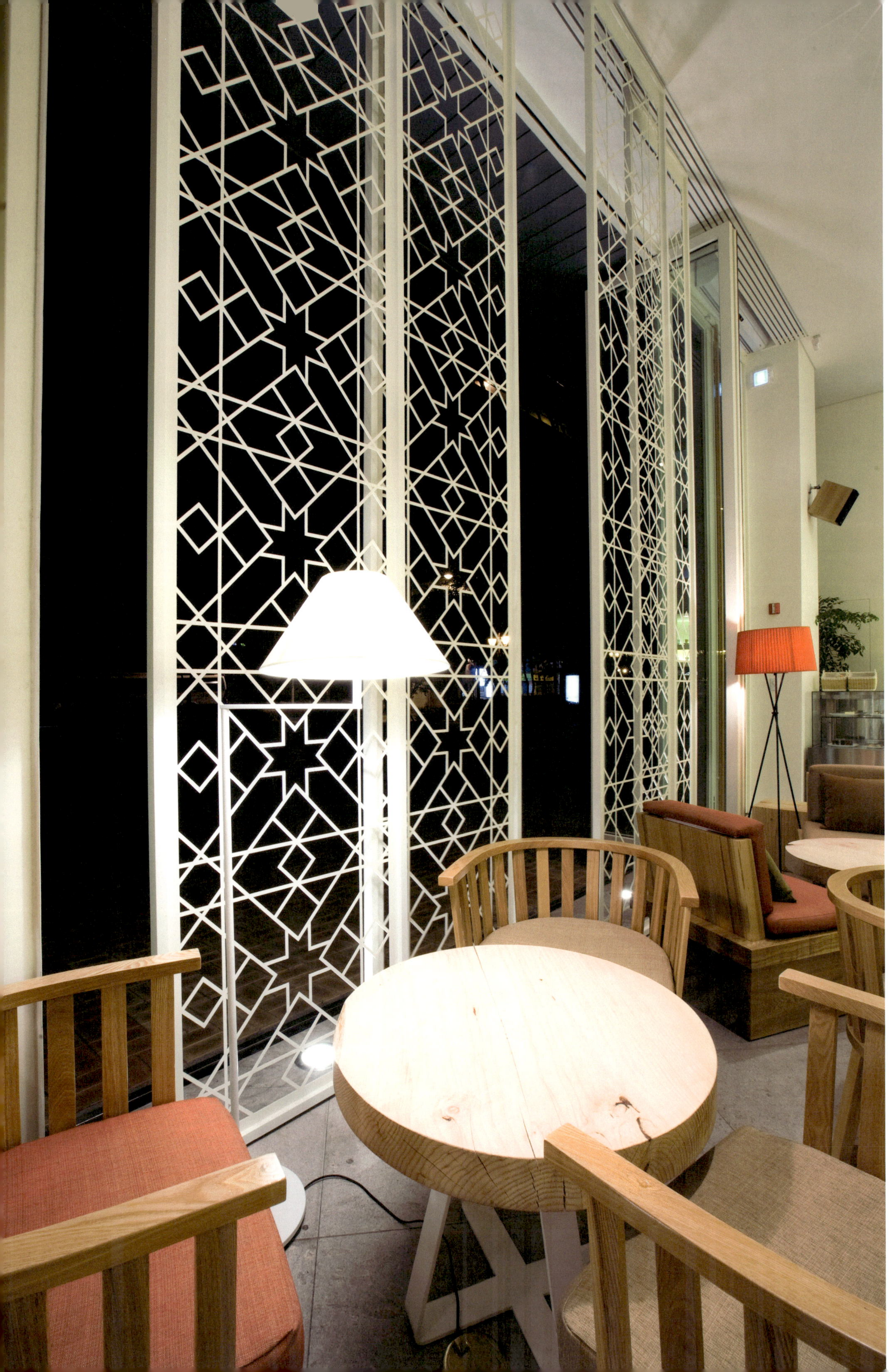

NORTHERN COMFORT

COFFEE THE SOL
Seoul, Korea

/ The designer, who took "a refined natural or supernatural approach," envisioned this coffee shop as a sun-lit void opening up in the midst of the city. The narrow high-ceilinged space inspired the scheme: an abstracted forest. The forest consists of scattered columns and masses that gives the space deep texture and moments of intimacy within the void. Counterintuitively, the height of the highest elements and the narrowness of the narrow elements were exaggerated in order to increase the "tension" of the space, making it not just interesting to look at, but giving customers the odd sensation of discovering something in plain sight.

/ Design: Design Bon_O

SIP MOBILE LODGE
Portland, Oregon, USA

/ This conversion of a 1969 Dodge Chinook Mobile Lodge into a mobile juice and cocktail bar targets Portland's street food-savvy inhabitants. The scheme borrows its aesthetic cues from the vehicle's mid-century vintage and from the cozy, Arcadian mountain lodges of the American Northwest. Architects Dan Anderson, Chris Held, and Brian Pietrowski reconfigured the Chinook's tight quarters into a multi-use environment using white surfaces and blond wood to wed efficient commercial use with traditional comfort.

/ Design: Von Tundra
/ Client: Sip PDX
/ Material: 1969 Dodge Chinook Mobile Lodge
/ Type of Food/Drinks/Specialties: Juices, smoothies, cocktails

NORTHERN COMFORT

FRÜUTE
Los Angeles, California, USA

/ Using the shop interior to brand its business, this fruit tart maker asked for a minimal but natural design to reflect its fresh take on a traditional dessert. At *Früute*, the tart is elevated from its modest, not-quite-a-pie status to edible art—without adding pretension. Owen Gee, Priscilla Jimenez, Ann Kim, Sunjoo Park, and Wendy Thai used clean-lined white display surfaces, natural wood, and humble brown product packaging to strike a balance between chilly and rustic, a solution that allows the colorful confections to shine in their own light.

/ Design: Ferroconcrete

/ Client: Früute

/ Material: Natural materials

/ Type of Food/Drinks/Specialties: Früute: tarts unordinary

three berries

crème brulee

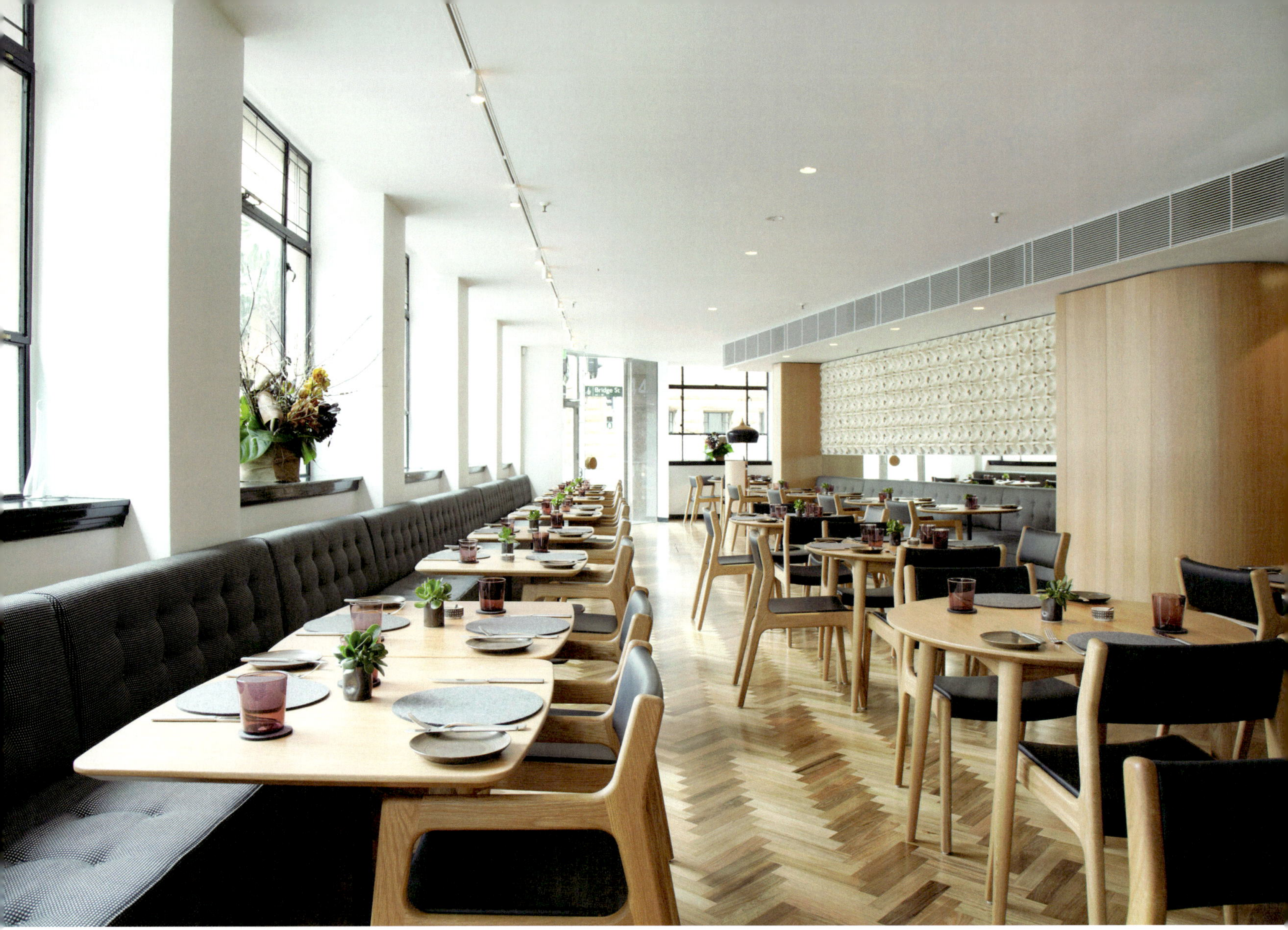

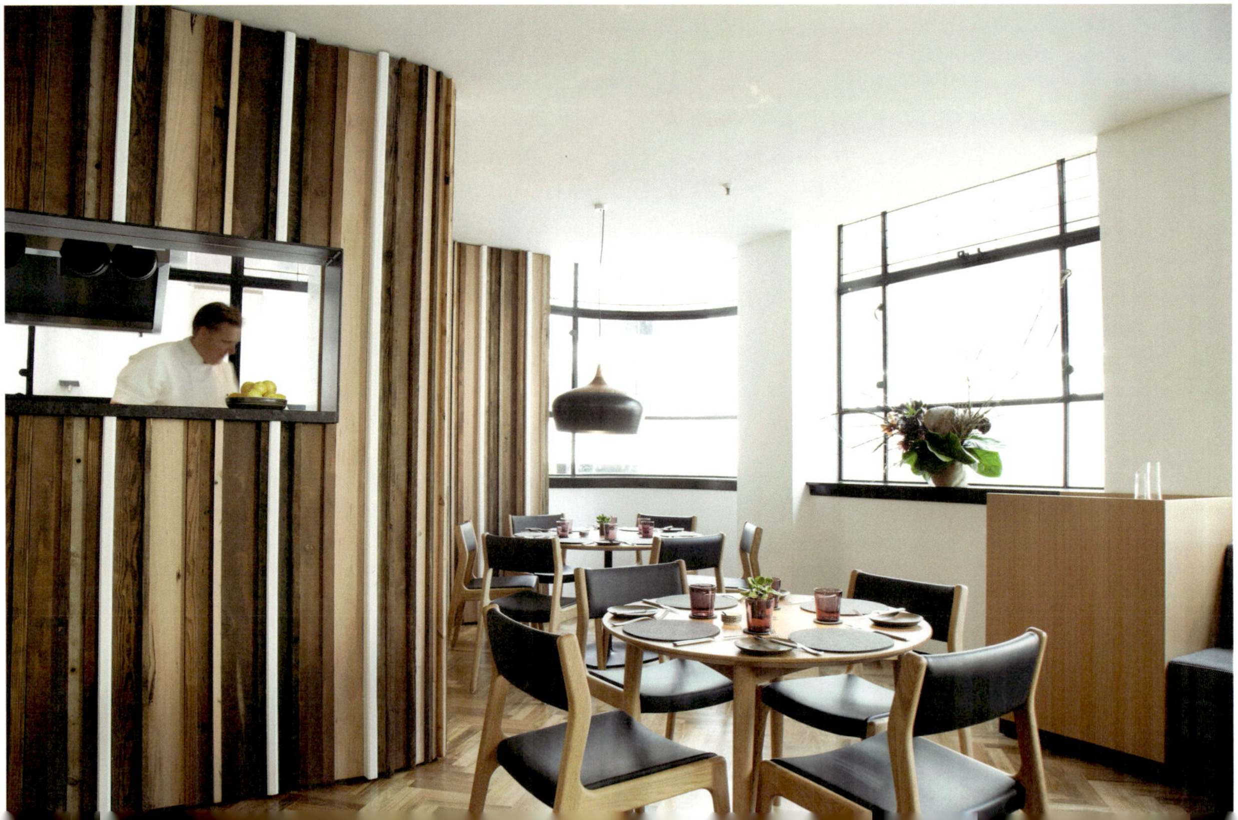

NORTHERN COMFORT

THE BRIDGE ROOM
Sydney, Australia

/ The menu here includes dishes inspired by Europe and Asia, some cooked over charcoal and some slow-smoked in the Japanese robata style. This blend of influences is reflected in a mix of materials. The 60-seat venue sits on the ground level of a low-rise 1930s heritage-listed building and features an open kitchen, hand-made ceramics, solid oak tables, and Turkish studio Autoban's iconic Deer chairs.

/ Design: Tobias Partners

/ Client: Ross and Sunny Lusted, and Fink Group

/ Type of Food/Drinks/Specialties: Seasonal ingredients; Asian and European cuisine, using Japanese robata style slow-smoking and charcoal cooking techniques

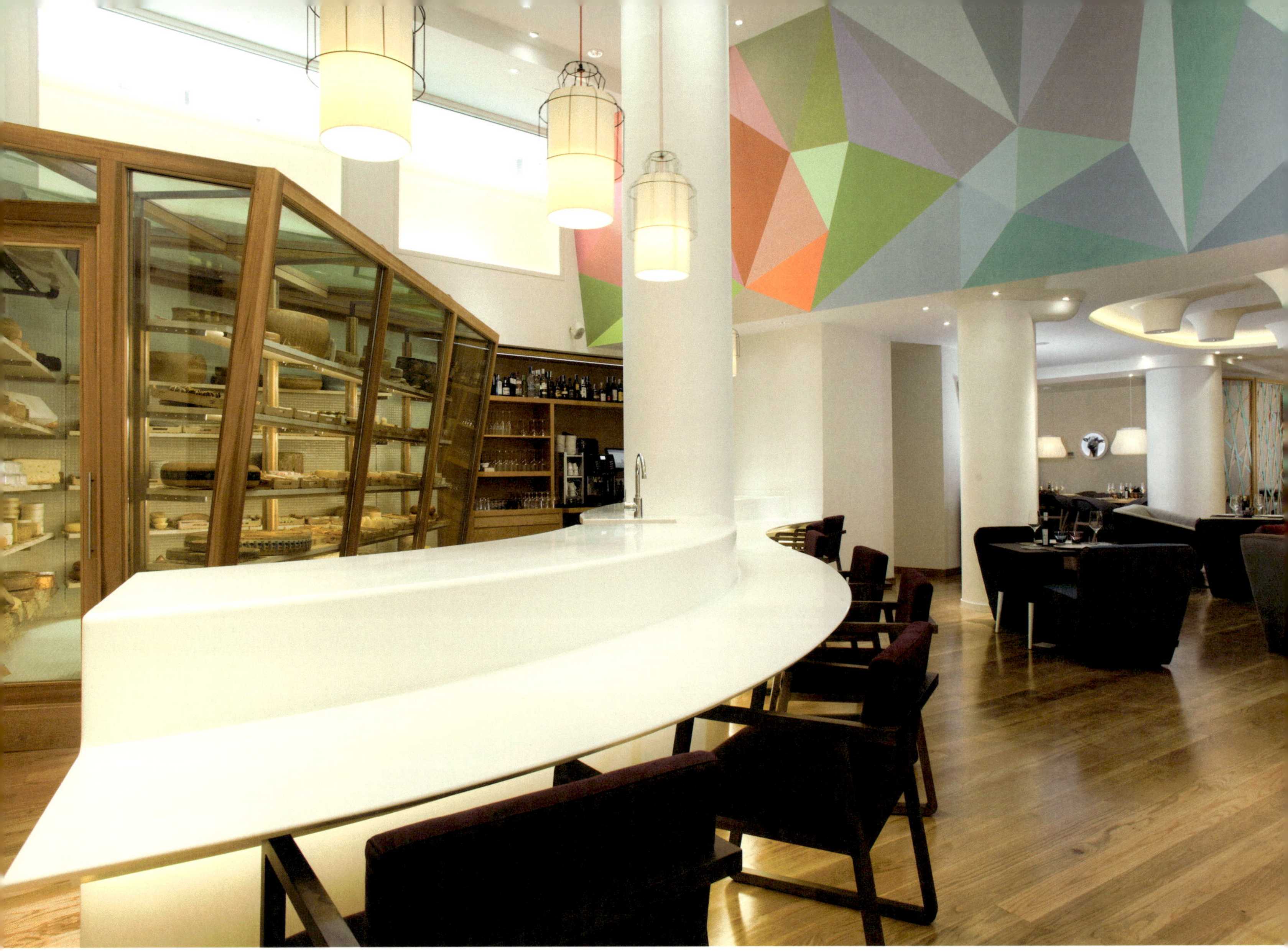

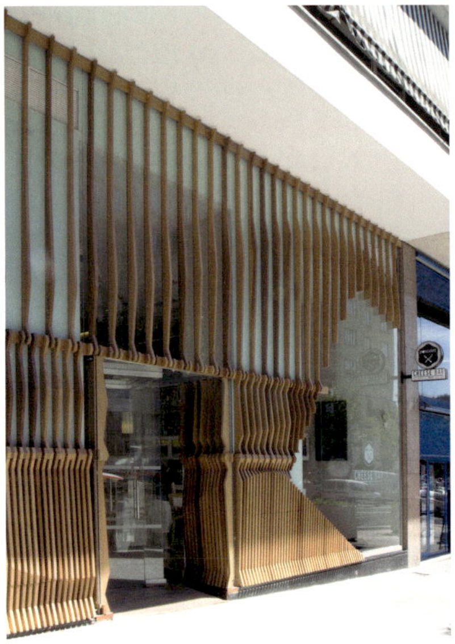

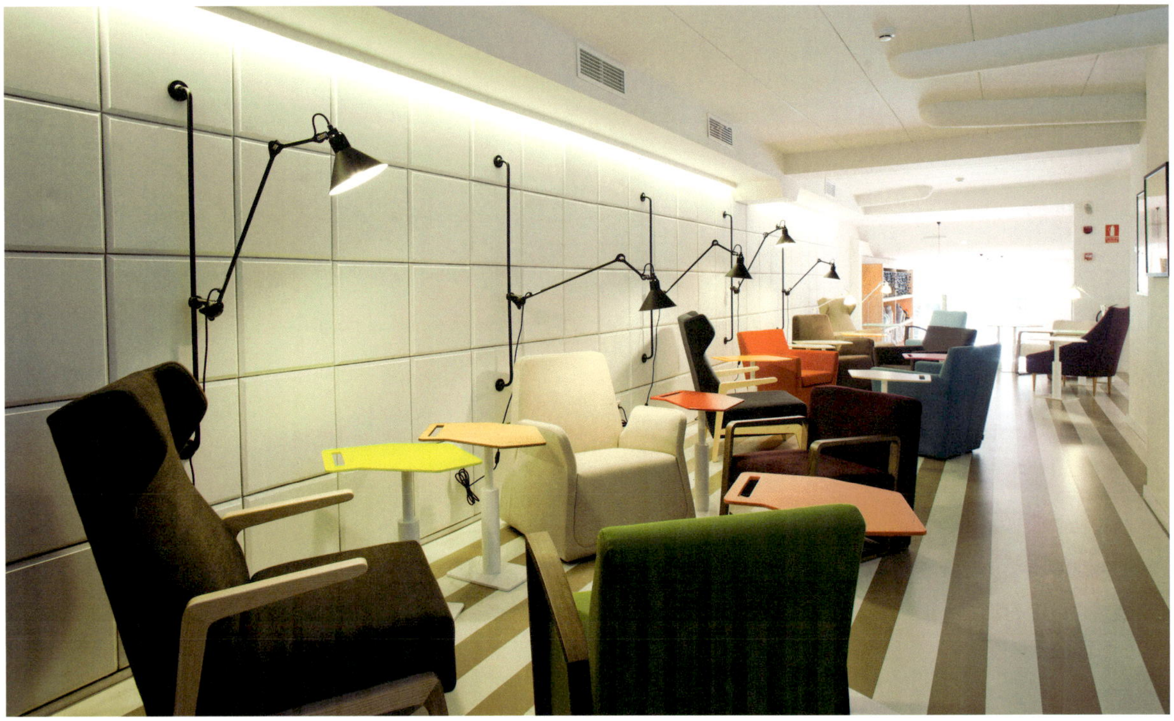

NORTHERN COMFORT

CHEESE BAR
Madrid, Spain

/ This bright, airy gastro-pub features a planet- and user-friendly design. Its façade consists of varnished cedar slats that mimic topographical forms while inside, bespoke and refined-rustic furniture made of chestnut or Spanish oak wood and veneer is upholstered with multi-patterned fabrics or lacquered white. One wall features a kaleidoscopic mural, foreground to a lush vertical garden that serves as the "lung" of the space while dampening noise and maintaining good humidity levels. Inspired by a sushi bar, the cedar-and-glass cheese cellar is the gem of the space—at least formally: shaped like an uncut diamond it seems to burst from the floor.

/ Design: Gabriel Corchero Studio
/ Client: Poncelet Alimentacion
/ Material: Wood, glas, corian
/ Type of Food/Drinks/Specialties: Cheese

AZZURRO
Zurich, Switzerland

/ The *Azzurro* restaurant is located on the light blue floor of a conference center mapped with color-coded floors and features a design scheme suggesting that azure of azures, the Mediterranean Sea. This makes the dearth of natural light in the space—the only windows are made from stained glass and look into the exhibition hall, not outward—quite unexpected. The Schweizer team recovered a sense of the outdoors, however, by using materials typical of a holiday resort in the Med: pergola-like ropes on the ceiling, bright wall tiles, and shelves ranged with items reminiscent of a traditional market while the backlit glow of a perforated wall provides the horizon.

/ Design: Andrin Schweizer Company

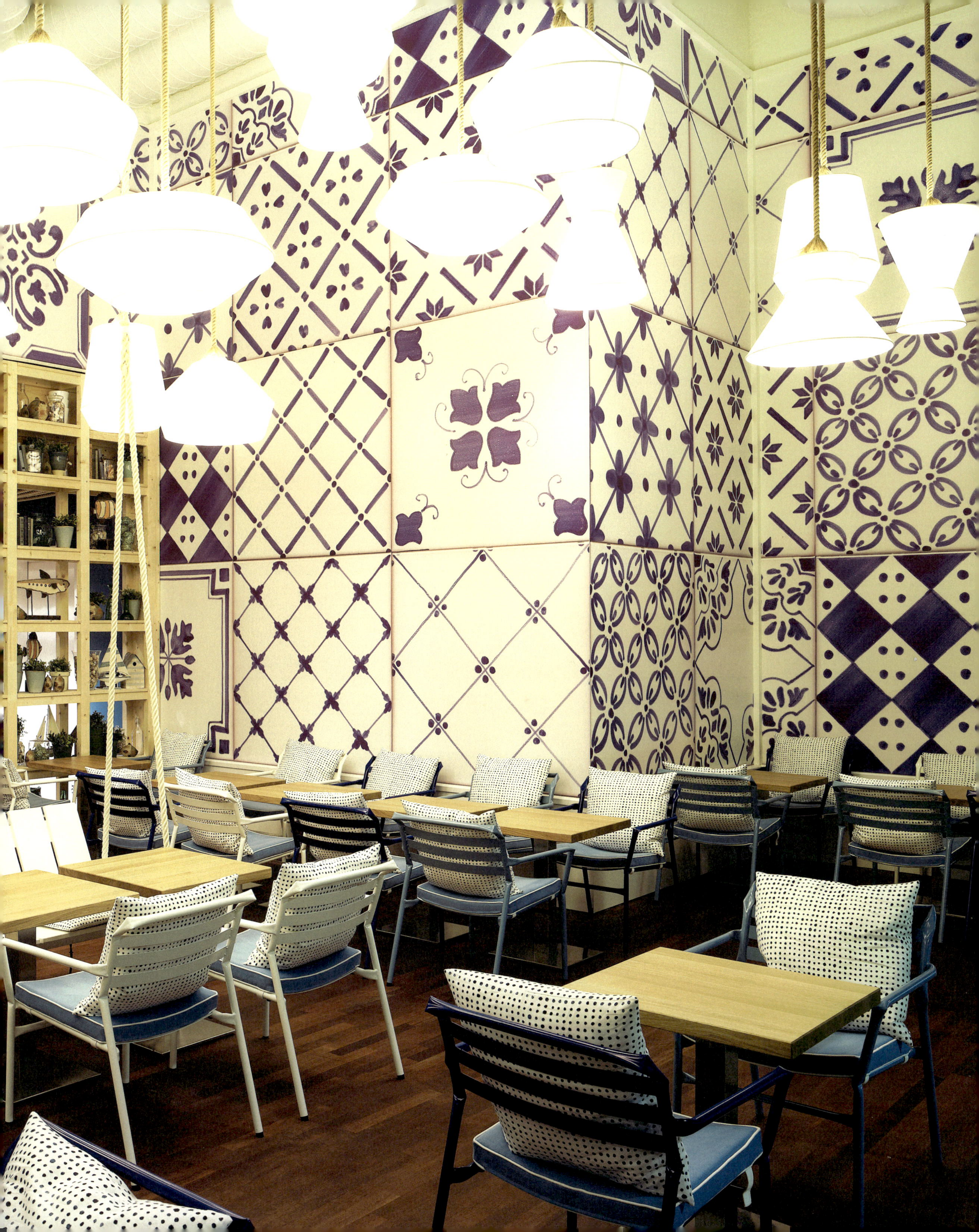

"The restaurant features a design scheme suggesting that azure of azures, the Mediterranean Sea."

NORTHERN COMFORT

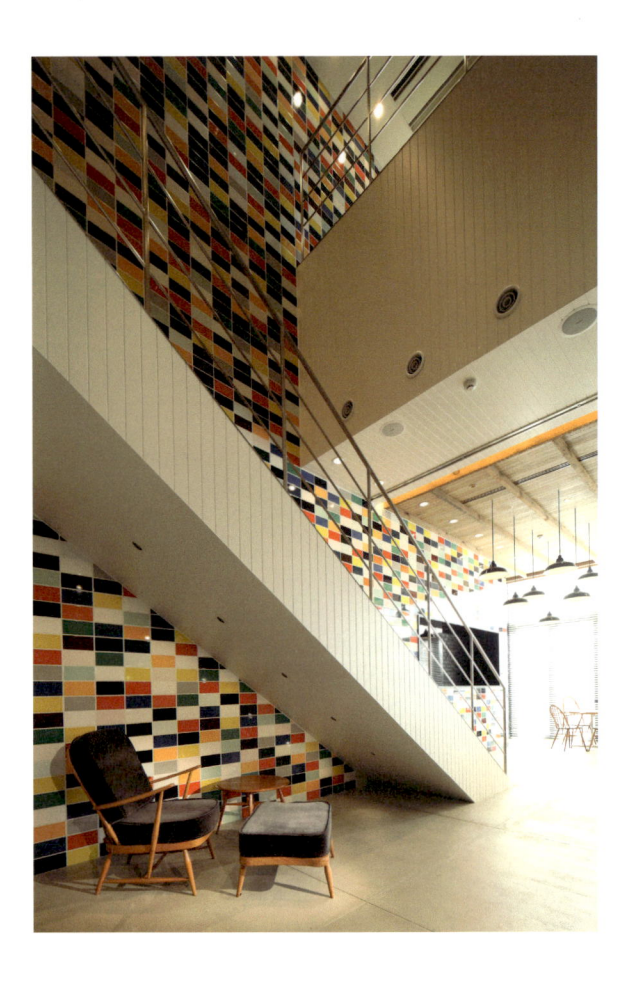

THE SOHO: THE CANTEEN
Tokyo, Japan

/ Masamichi Katayama designed this canteen in *The SOHO* hotel for daily use by the tenants of the building, both tourists and office employees. He applied the same bold, multicolor tile motif of the building's atrium to the café, lining the open kitchen with the tiles as well. Generous windows provide ocean views and plenty of natural light which is further augmented by lightly finished concrete flooring, the clean lines of blond-wood furniture, and a profusion of asymmetrically ranged pendant lights.

/ Design: Wonderwall

NORTHERN COMFORT

132 / 133

NORTHERN COMFORT

NOMA LAB
Copenhagen, Denmark

/ This two-star Michelin restaurant with a staff of innovative chefs needed an "experimentarium," a space where they could push the boundaries of Nordic cuisine. 3XN's "Innovation Unit" GXN was commissioned to design an interior—conforming to historic building codes—without anchoring any part of it to walls or floor. The team made four central multi-functional storage units, each comprising 500 individually formed wooden cubes that went from computer to fabricator to assembly without the help of carpenters. These units divide the 200 sq m room into smaller areas accommodating the Food Lab, a herb garden on wheels, staff areas, and an office space. Raw and plain, the scheme incorporated only Nordic materials. GXN's specially developed STAR lamp casts dramatic geometric shadows.

/ Design: GXN

/ Client: Restaurant NOMA

/ Material: All done in Nordic wood, for example plywood

ALEMAGOU BEACH BAR
Mykonos, Greece

/ *Alemagou* is a casual bar and restaurant on the beach. The menu revisits traditional Greek recipes and, as k-studio puts it, the interiors are likewise a reinterpretation "of beloved familiar ingredients." Inspiration was found in typical Cycladic architectural elements: whitewashed houses, dry-stone walls that get lost in the scrubby landscape, hardwearing screed floors and terraces, and natural reed-thatched roof insulation, but the familiar textures were applied to contemporary, organic forms. At the site, strong winds make the beach a surfers' sanctuary, the midday sun is scorching, and the landscape is harsh. Rather than trying to work against Nature and the elements, *Alemagou* exploits them instead.

/ Design: k-studio
/ Client: Alemagou Beach Bar
/ Type of Food/Drinks/Specialties: Contemporary Greek food and cocktails

"Rather than trying to work against Nature and the elements, Alemagou exploits them instead."

136 / 137

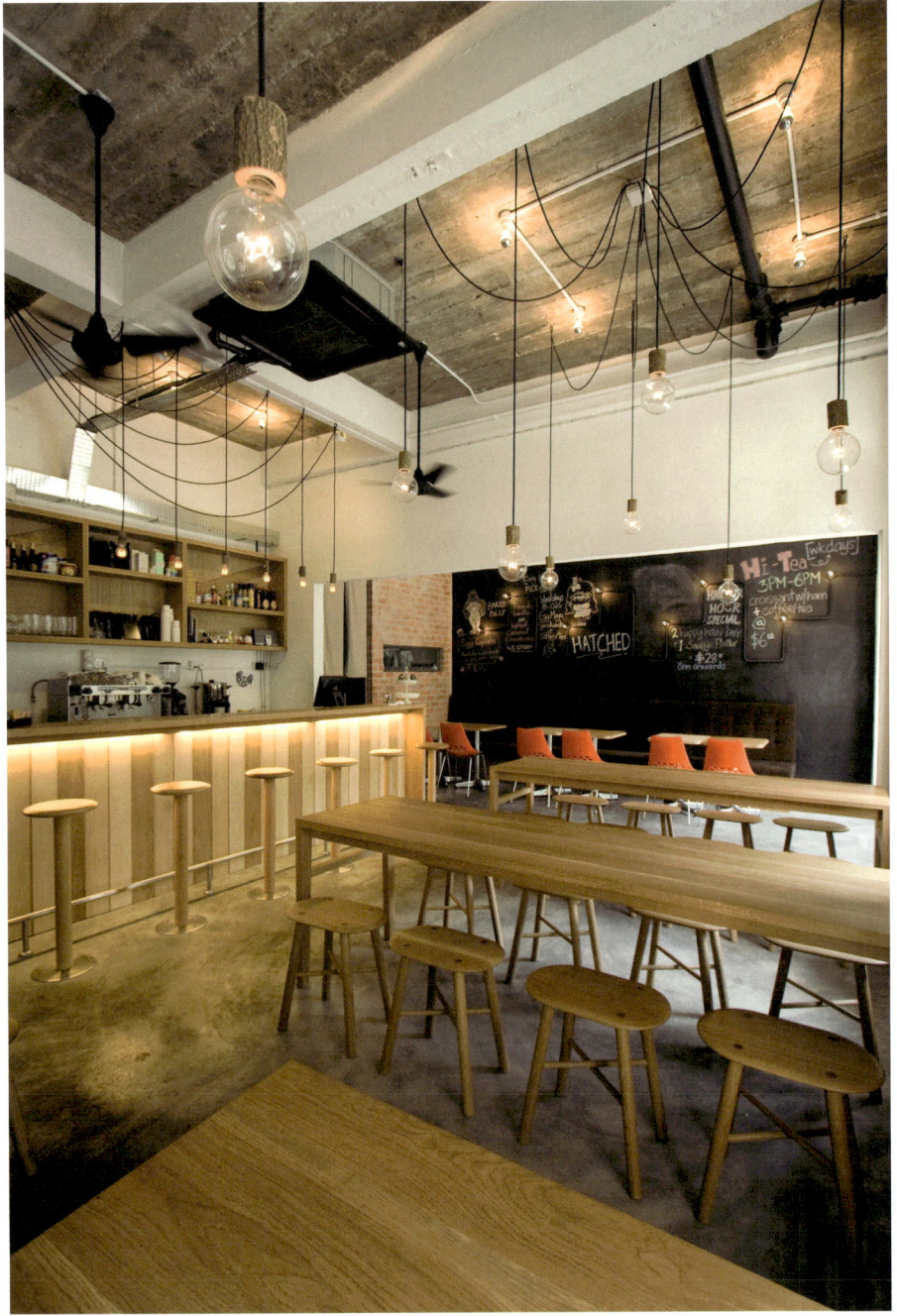

HATCHED
Singapore, Singapore

/ Conceived by a band of local designers known for their clean-lined wooden furniture, Hatched is a bruncherie, so to speak, that serves breakfast all day long. Next door to a law campus and student dorms, it serves egg-based dishes to the neighborhood crowd in a cozy but quirkily modern space, with two very different faces: in one area the walls are unevenly clad with blackboards with dishes constantly written and rewritten across them in chalk; in another, blond-wood milking stools and light bulbs hanging at various heights vaguely recall a rural farmhouse.

/ Design: Outofstock
/ Client: Gerald Tan
/ Type of Food/Drinks/Specialties: All day breakfast restaurant, specialized in egg-inspired dishes and desserts

138 / 139

NORTHERN COMFORT

BARBICAN LOUNGE
London, United Kingdom

/ SHH envisioned a restaurant and lounge that would be connected via their terraces while still remaining starkly different. The bold lounge was treated in dramatic colors, including vintage 60s tables with Murano glass tops, bespoke lighting by .PSLAB, a peacock-green banquette with red upholstered buttons, and a resin floor also poured in peacock-green, a color matching that of the Barbican lake in summer. The original hammered aggregate walls were exposed and the kitchen clad in solid timber. The 14 m black glass and mosaic bar continues through the glazing onto the terrace toward the Foodhall terrace via four of SHH's "urban tree" umbrellas, whose wooden bases house both plants and integrated seating.

/ Design: SHH

/ Client: Barbican

/ Type of Food/Drinks/Specialties:
Small plate menus, as well as gourmet bar snacks

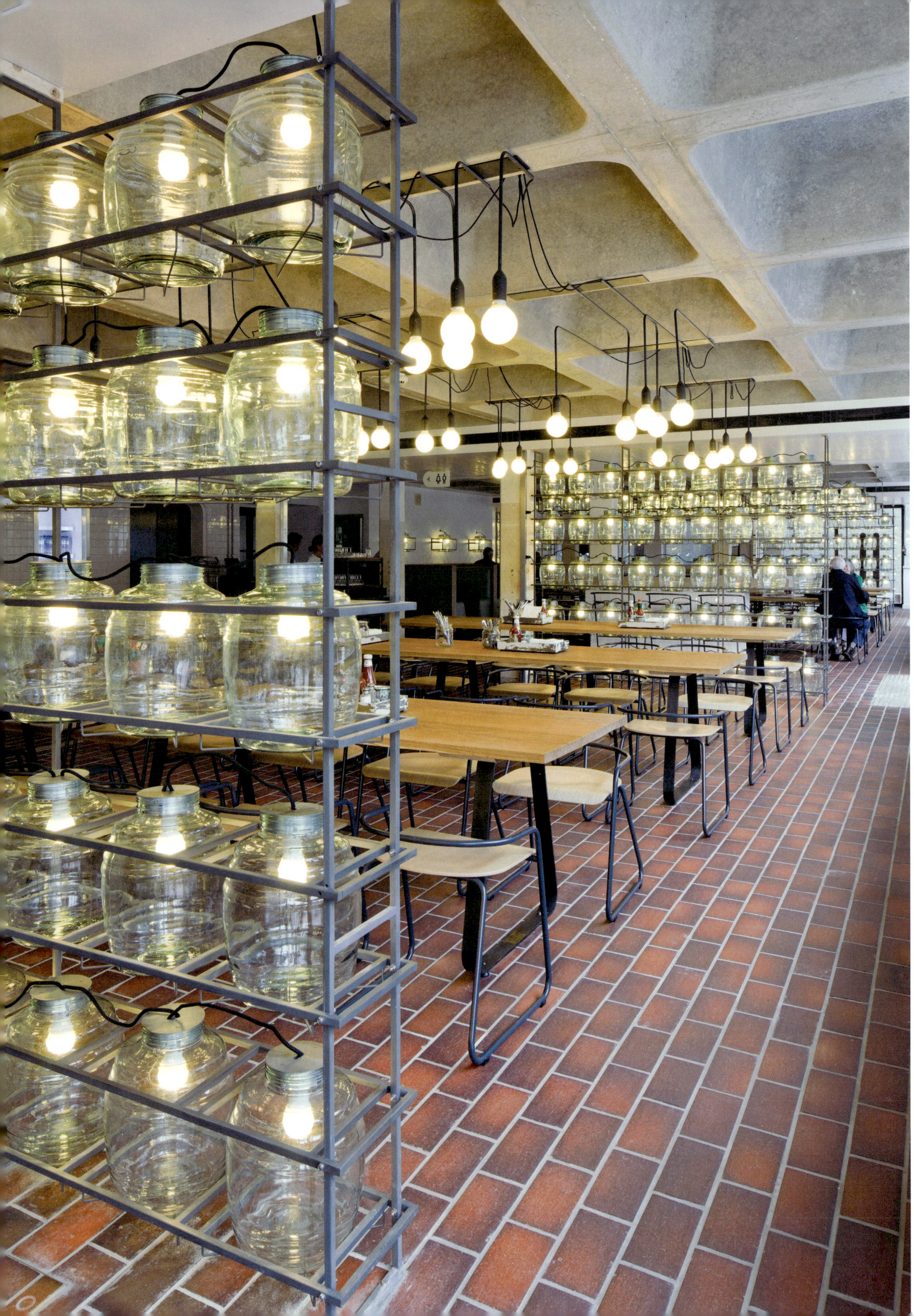

NORTHERN COMFORT

"SHH reconnected the Foodhall with external walkways and the original architecture of the Barbican using Cradley brick pavers."

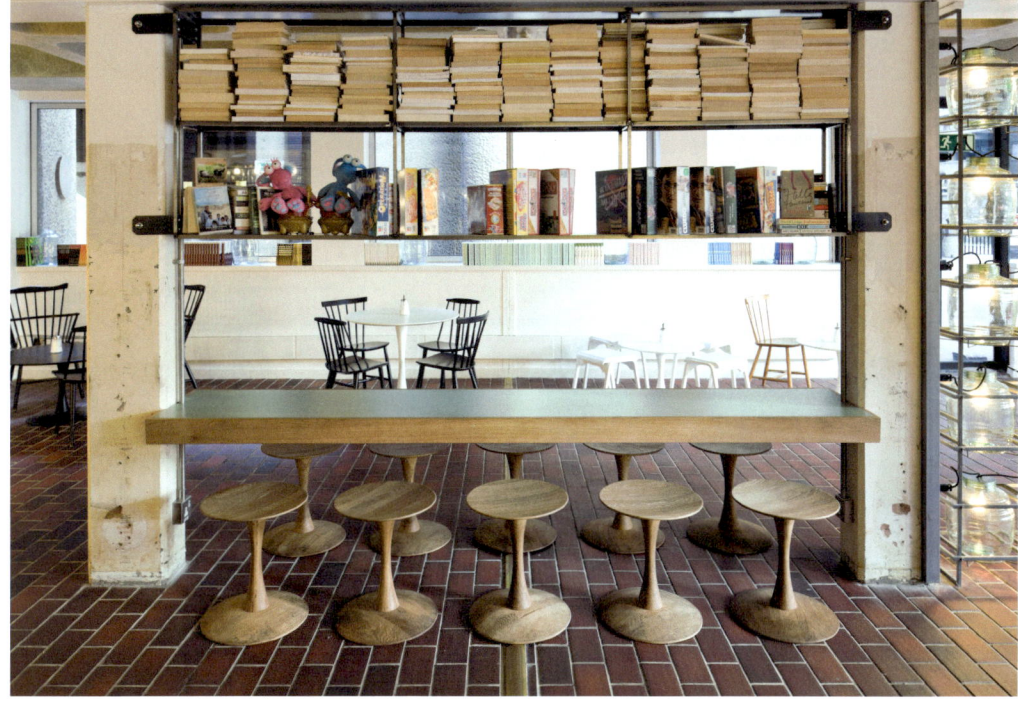

BARBICAN FOODHALL
London, United Kingdom

/ SHH reconnected the *Foodhall* with external walkways and the original architecture of the Barbican using Cradley brick pavers. Aside from a variety of bespoke furnishings, the lighting design proved a major component of the scheme. Fixtures by .PSLAB conform to the raw aesthetic of the building and respect its listed status while floor-to-ceiling shelving holds rows of olive jars containing energy-saving light bulbs. A great variety of seating was provided to suit different tastes. Quirky details include vintage Belgian army storage boxes as display shelving, miniature wooden trucks by Thorsten van Elten that transport sugar, and old metal filing drawers for cutlery and condiments.

/ Design: SSH   / Client: Barbican   / Type of Food/Drinks/Specialties: Deli style products

Zitronenhuhn en papillote mit Shiitakepilzen
und Basmatireis
Fleisch
€ 4,80
Rinderfilet in Balsamico pochiert mit
Kartoffel-Scamorza-Gratin
€ 7,80
pro Person

Knusprige Entenbrust mit gebackenem Hokkaidokürbis
und Ingwer-Orangen-Soße
€ 7,80

KOCHHAUS
Berlin and Hamburg, Germany

/ *Kochhaus* is a new retail concept that its five owners call a "walkable cookbook." For people who have little time or energy to cook healthily at home, Kochhaus provides some short-cuts on the potentially rocky road of finding recipes, sourcing ingredients, and getting it all together in the kitchen. Each of the 18 tables scattered throughout the bright, genial space holds the fresh ingredients and an illustrated how-to card for a single meal. Shoppers can find everything for one meal, scalable up or down for solo dining to dinner parties. The shop provides logistical, and perhaps moral, support by also stocking the tools for cooking and cleaning up—sponges, dish soap, even toilet paper.

/ Design: bfs design and Rejne Rittel
/ Client: Kochhaus

BEŞIKTAŞ FISH MARKET
Istanbul, Turkey

/ This market is situated on a triangular site in the neighborhood's bustling commercial district. GAD manipulated the ground surface, piercing it along its periphery to generate a hollow, porous form and an arcing concrete and steel seashell-like canopy that affords generous openings at street level without disruptive interior columns. Unlike most fish markets, both the underside and top of the shell are also used as a platform for art and performance. Inside, the space is partitioned into six display zones joined by circulation that radiates into the street and is lit by the hanging 150-watt Edison light bulbs typical of Istanbul fish markets.

/ Design: GAD

/ Client: Beşiktaş Municipality/İsmail Ünal

NORTHERN COMFORT

MAZZO AMSTERDAM
Amsterdam, Netherlands

/ *Mazzo's* building has the city's typical narrow, deep spaces cobbled together with many changes of floor and ceiling levels—vagaries that provided a natural setting for a restaurant. In the dining room, five Dear Ingo lights by MOOOI illuminate four Avedon-sized photographs that stand in for the ubiquitous portraits lining the walls of cozy Italian joints. The designers exposed steel beams and columns and linked the spaces with a single gesture, a gargantuan solid pine cupboard that runs across the entire restaurant, morphing into a staircase to the mezzanine, the back bar, and the wardrobe, and serving as storage and product display along the way.

/ Design: Concrete Architectural Associates

/ Client: IQ creative

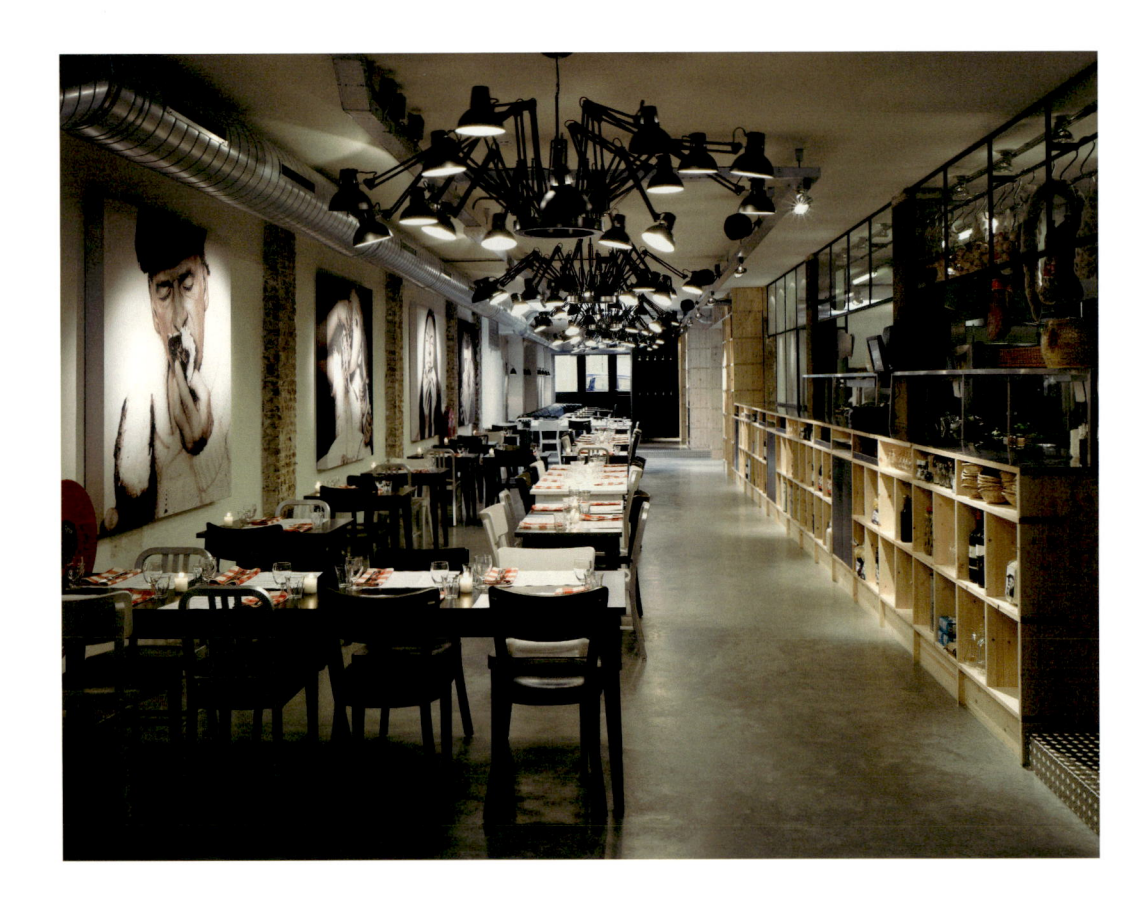

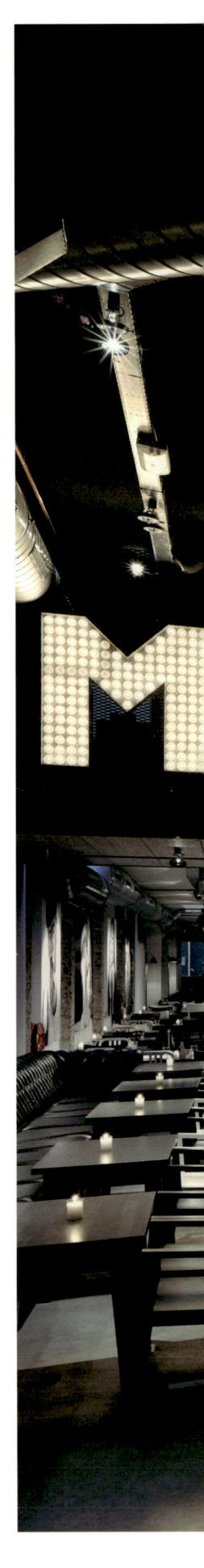

NORTHERN COMFORT

DABBOUS
London, United Kingdom

/ *Dabbous's* design took its cues from the minimal and natural presentation of the restaurant's menu. Brinkworth designed furnishings—waxed timber tables, timber and black leather chairs—that complement walls lined with burnt timber, to create a spartan, industrial atmosphere. Diverse light fixtures, including colored blown glass pieces, smooth over the otherwise uncouth surfaces. Through reeded glass panes, movements in the kitchen are visible, suggesting preparations instead of imposing them on diners. Materials expressing authenticity—steel, reeded glass, concrete, and wire mesh—define the space. Brinkworth chose a lightly wrought solution that makes the environment ever a work in process.

/ Design: Brinkworth

/ Client: Ollie Dabbous

/ Type of Food/Drinks/Specialties:
Modern European

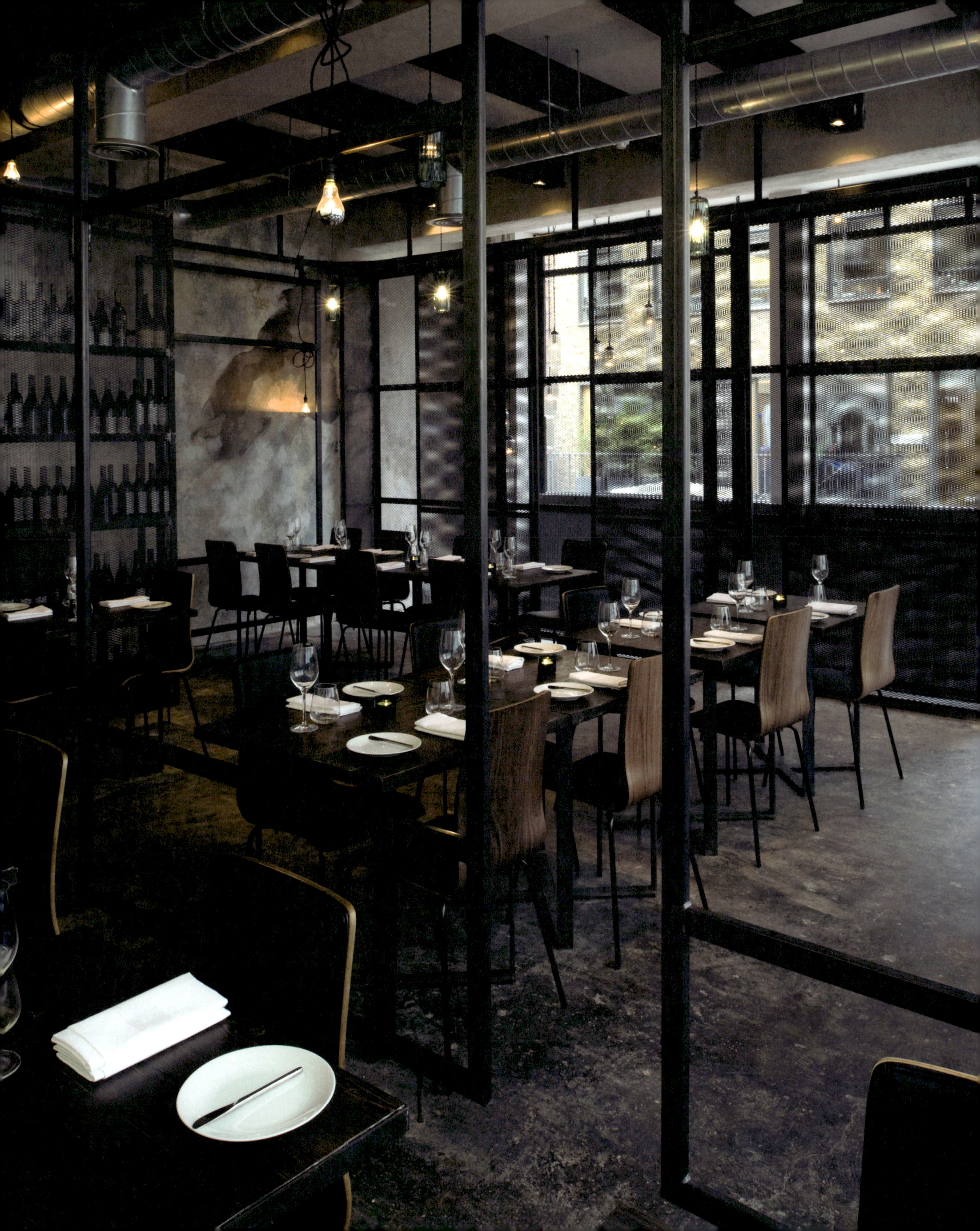

WALDEN
NYC, New York, USA

/ The name says it all at **Walden**, so called after the pond beside which transcendentalist philosopher Henry David Thoreau formed some of his most famous theories. Serving a seasonal farm-to-table menu, the restaurant needed some serious nose-to-tail interior design. Matter-Made's Jamie Gray, who both retails and commissions original furniture, took a "truth to materials" approach to the project: he outfitted the space with wood, glass, marble, brass, and copper while preserving the pressed tin ceiling of yore.

/ Design: MatterMade

/ Material: Wood, glass, marble, brass, copper

/ Type of Food/Drinks/Specialties: Seasonal menu, farm to table

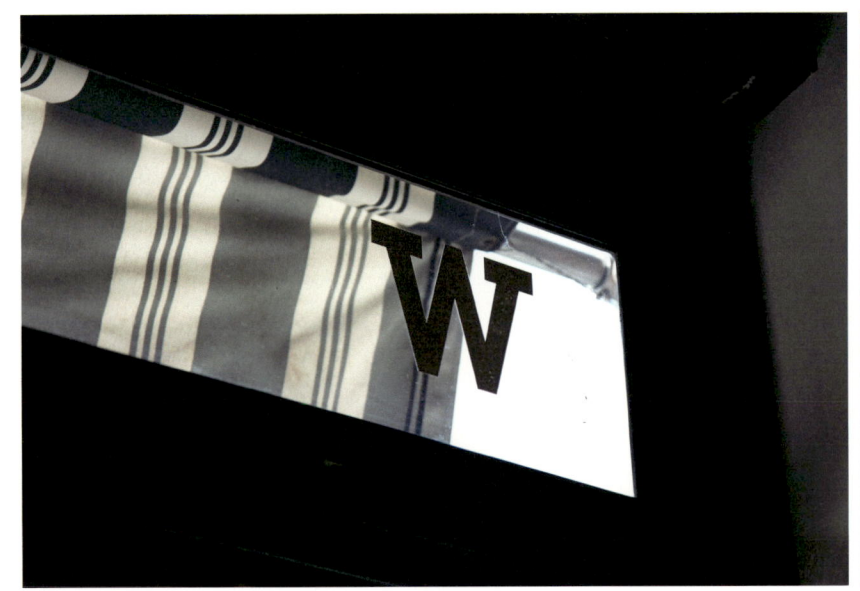

NORTHERN COMFORT

KØDBYENS FISKEBAR
Copenhagen, Denmark

/ *Fiskebar* is announced by its weighty maritime façade, a monolithic cement surface boldly marked with bright Mediterranean-blue letters. Inside, however, the design is less waterfront-industrial and more contemporary. Guests can sit on stools around a large cylindrical fish tank that is perched on a tiled circular table, declaring the freshness of the place's extensive fish and shellfish menu. The layered stone bar is downlit, emphasizing its angular surface and its representation of terra firma, allowing even landlubbers to feel at home.

NORTHERN COMFORT

/ Design: Space
/ Client: Kødbyens Fiskebar
/ Type of Food/Drinks/Specialties:
  Fish and shellfish, extended winelist, cocktails

154 / 155

MOGG & MELZER DELICATESSEN
Berlin, Germany

/ This delicatessen plucks homemade Jewish American cuisine out of old New York and fits it snugly into the hip new arts center in the former Jewish Girls' School in Berlin. Breakfast, lunch, and dinner can be taken out or eaten indoors, seated on benches made by local furniture manufacturer Tipla or on Pirkka chairs by the Finnish designer Illmari Tapiovaara. New York always had a cosmopolitan character.

/ Design: Paul Mogg, Oskar Melzer

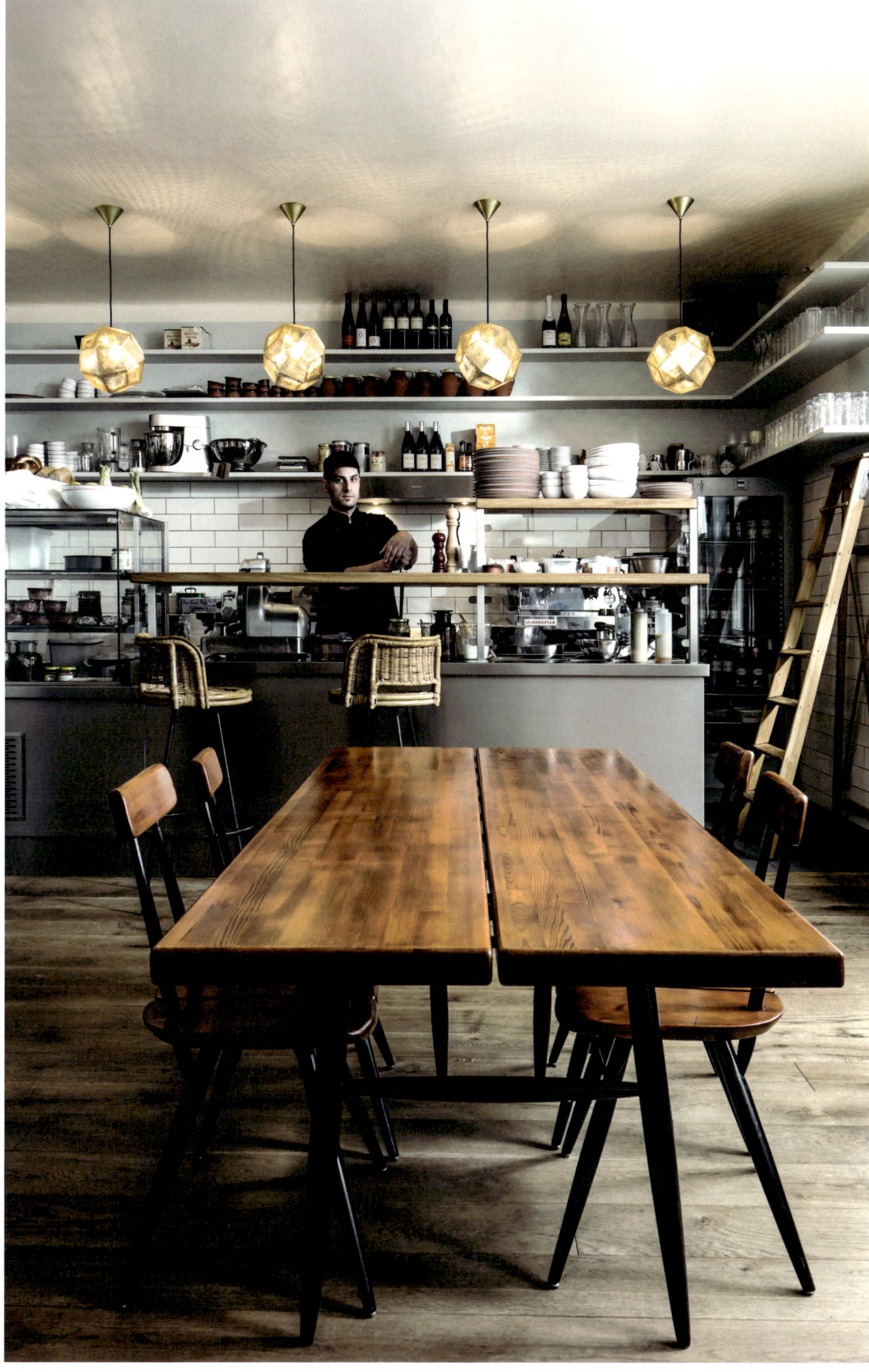

JAFFA
Tel Aviv, Israel

/ In Israel, and Jaffa in particular, where diverse culinary traditions co-exist peacefully whether people do or not, BK worked to mix this harmony with a straightforward approach to materials. Water, flour, and olive oil are the basic staples of the restaurant's cuisine; by analogy, water, cement, aggregates, and steel form the basis of BK's interior. Beyond this minimalist materials palette, however, the furnishings assume a variety as multi-culti as the local population. The team divided the space into three sections: bar, dining hall, and a kitchen that was kept open to the gaze of diners to best convey the notion of hospitality.

/ Design: Baranowitz Kronenberg Architecture

/ Client: Haim and Sigal Cohen

/ Type of Food/Drinks/Specialties: Israelian cuisine by chef Haim Cohen

NORTHERN COMFORT

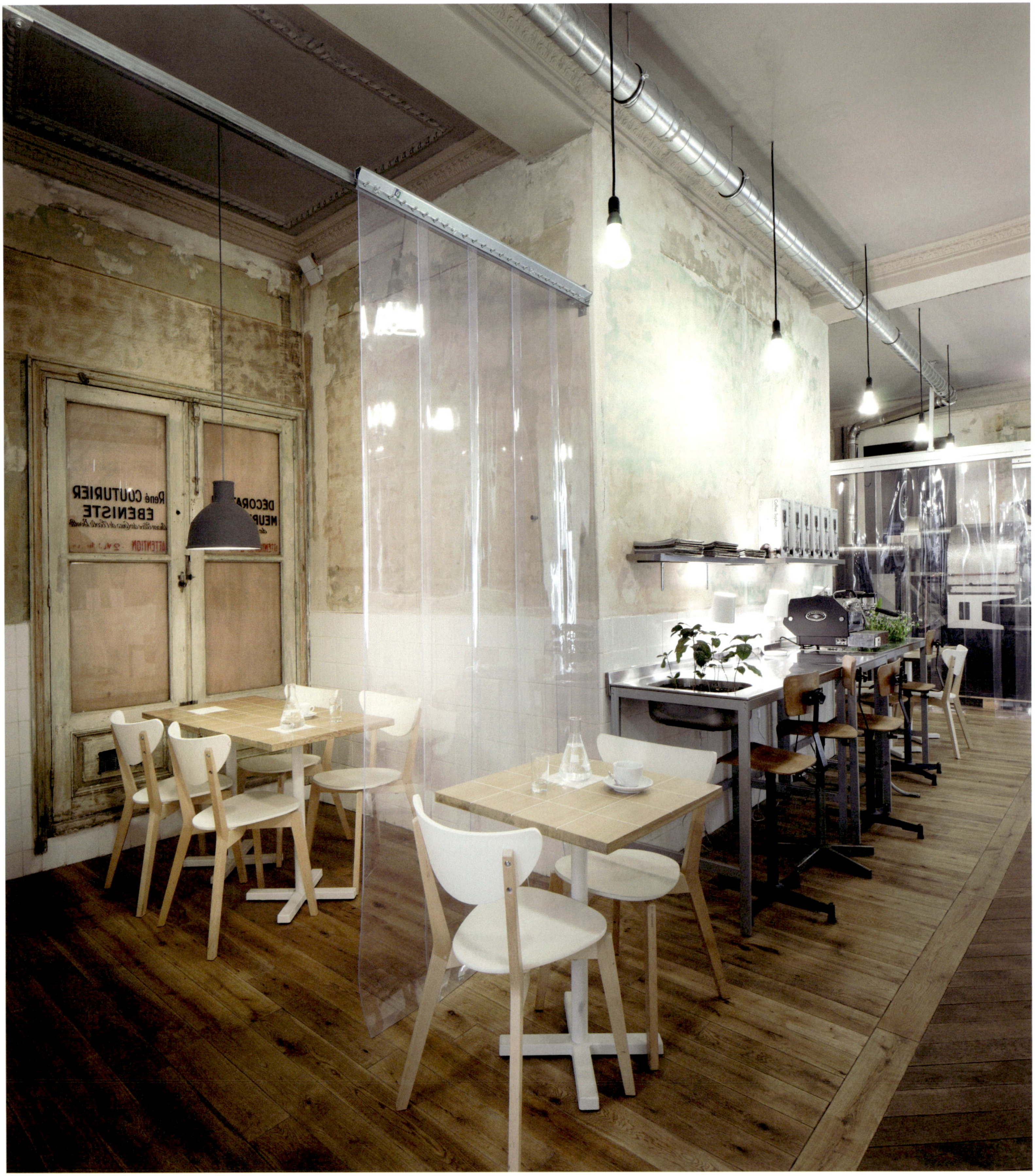

COUTUME CAFÉ
Paris, France

/ It is a space that says whatever you thought you knew, tear it out by the root and start again. The experts at this progressive roastery want their clients to rediscover coffee culture. Their blend of tradition and technique inspired the architects to tear down the walls and ceilings to reveal the anatomy of a typical Parisian interior: high ceilings, moldings, columns, an old shop door. Then they added oak flooring, square white tiles, grid lighting, stainless steel, industrial plastic curtains, and beaker-like glassware as if these elements were a white coat dressing a laboratory of caffeination.

/ Design: CUT Architectures
/ Client: Coutume café
/ Type of Food/Drinks/Specialties: Coffee

L'OBRADOR DEL MOLI
Barcelona, Spain

/ The interior of this Catalan *panaderia artesanal* lets the baking process, the bread and the pastries—made from staples like locally sourced organic flour—take center stage. The kitchen uses bread-making techniques that are in danger of extinction, along with long fermentation processes and sourdough bases. To underscore this time-honored, time-taking approach, minimalist black shelving, concrete counters, and windowed interior walls put the yeasty tones of the finished product in linen drawers and baskets and the honest ingredients that go into it on display, along with the bakers working in the open-plan kitchen.

/ Design: Sandra Tarruella Interioristas

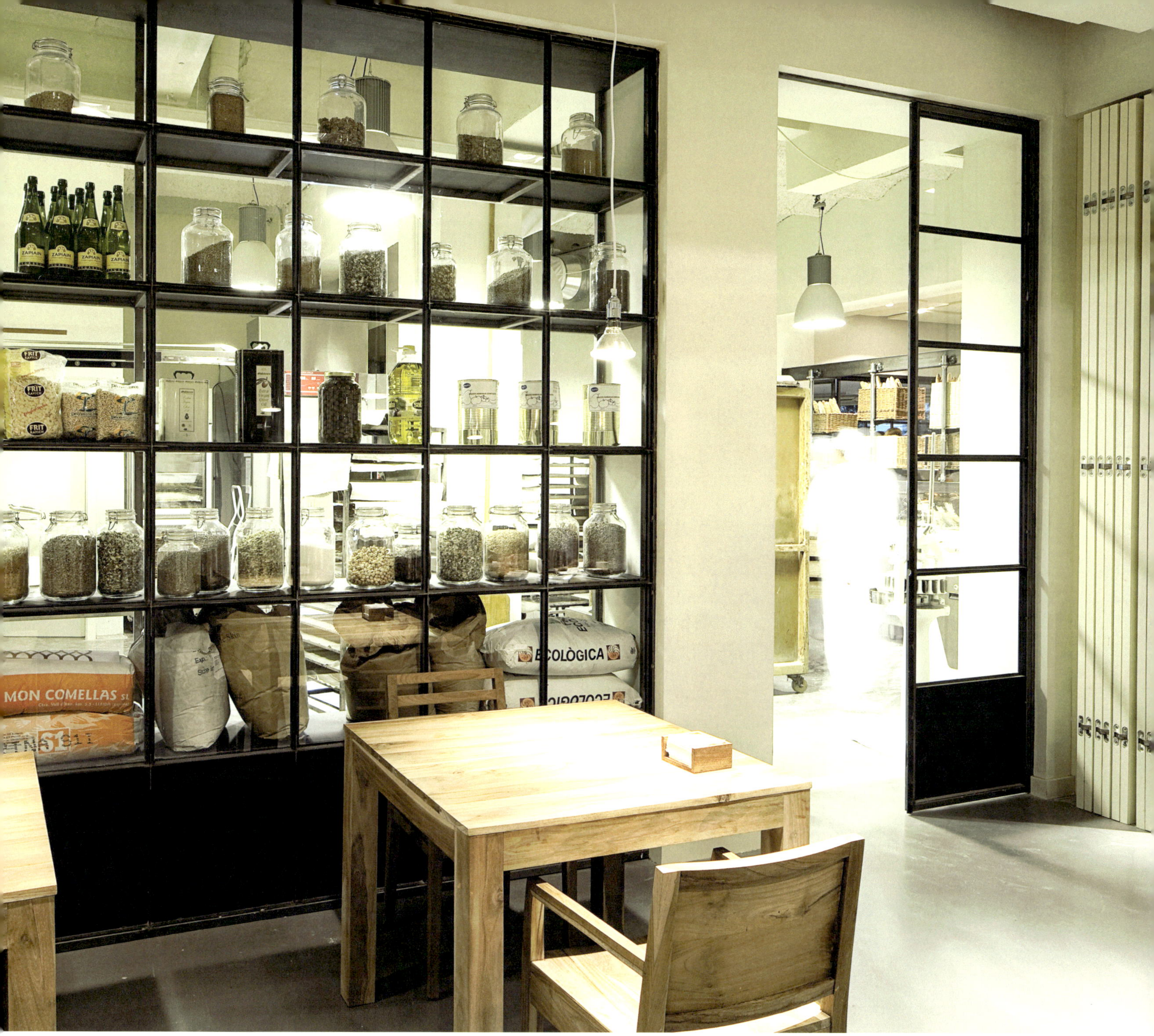
ZAPIAIN
ECOLÒGICA
MON COMELLAS SL

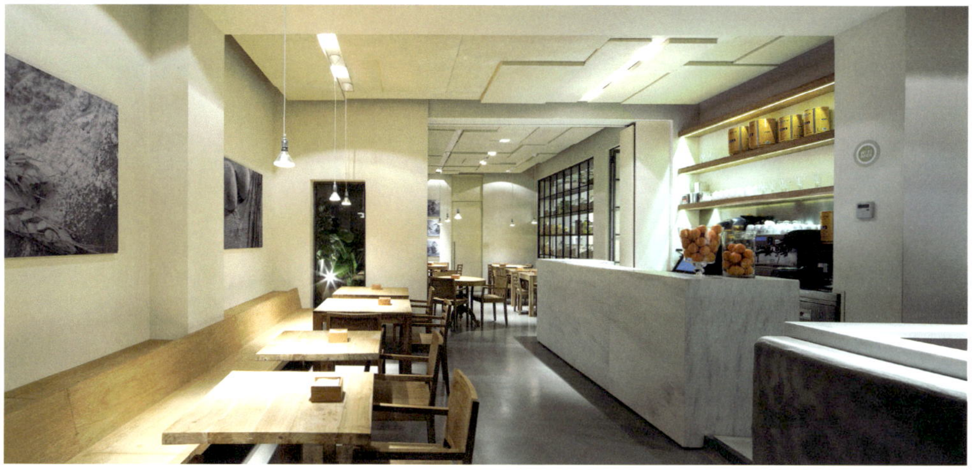

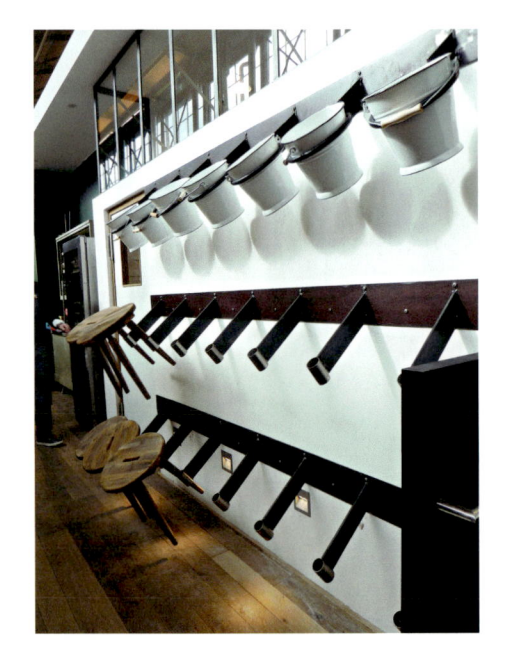

SCHRANNENHALLE
Munich, Germany

/ Oliv designed the interiors for this market pavilion including 13 vendors' stalls, a deli, and a restaurant to create a blend of retail with gastronomy. The plan opened up space for circulation which in turn ramped up the creativity of the product presentation. The idea was to let the merchandise fill the foreground while keeping the charm of the larger hall intact. To underscore the organic qualities of the products, the architects stuck to muted materials and colors. They used brushed and oiled oak and nero assoluto, oxidized steel and clean forms and lines to evoke nature and continuity.

/ Design: oliv architekten ingenieure

NORTHERN COMFORT

Alléosse
„Gaumenfreuden aus Käse"

Jede Käsefamilie von Alléosse ruht in einem eigenen Keller. In diesen Schatzkammern des Familienbetriebs wird der Käse mit ausgewählten Zutaten veredelt und in ein geschmackliches Schmuckstück verwandelt.
Die cremigen Spezialitäten von Alléosse stehen heute bei Käse-Liebhabern auf der ganzen Welt hoch im Kurs – so schätzen zum Beispiel Prinz Charles und die Queen von England den Reblochon von Alléosse, der nach Gebirgsrezept hergestellt wird.
Die Geschmacks-Bandbreite der Käse-Spezialitäten reicht von kernig-würzig, bis mild oder nussig. „Bon Appétit".

BAR LA BOHÈME (ENTRE AMIS)
Porto, Portugal

/ This redesign of a tapas and wine bar strengthened the brand's identity. Wood provided the texture, color, and form to bulk up its character and give depth and warmth to the interiors in the form of plank-lined walls and ceilings. The restaurant bristles and blinks with louver-like forms and slightly tapering vertical ribs so that the walls seem to cant slightly. Wood boards form a protective armature in some areas, but become aggressively extroverted in others: 10 planks extend from the dining room ceiling through the storefront to become an incomplete awning that broadcasts the boite's simple originality.

/ Design: AVA Architects
/ Client: Alberto Nuno Oliveira da Fonseca
/ Material: Wood, glass, and metallic structure
/ Type of Food/Drinks/Specialties: Tapas and wine

NORTHERN COMFORT

"The Pif Wine Depot features unfinished concrete walls stacked high with wine."

THE RED PIF WINE DEPOT & GARDEN
Prague, Czech Republic

/ Architects Jakub Fišer and Petra Skalická transformed a forlorn, 13 × 5 m triangle from a waste collection site that stank of urine into a garden fronting their charmingly simple design for a wine restaurant. The *Pif Wine Depot* features bottle-shaped shutters and cupboards, bright oak surfaces, and unfinished concrete walls stacked high with wine. Outside, they put up symbolic fencing made from unplaned boards, initiated the exhibition of work by local artists, and installed a statue lent by a nearby gallery, creating a tranquil, creative setting where guests can savor the wine and the atmosphere under the great crowns of maple trees.

/ Design: Aulík Fišer Architekti

CANTINA DE COMIDA MEXICANA
Mexico City, Mexico

/ In this Mexican canteen, the architects framed a rutted ceiling—that looks as if the men in hardhats will be back from lunch any time now—with finely finished light wood furnishings and polished cement floors that bring the sidewalk inside. The watercolor tones of the cement, low-budget folding chairs, and tiles are warmed by the wood and evoke not just a humble (though deftly accomplished) homemade air, but an excavation of the past—a nod to local history, a tip of the hat to what came before—that nonetheless attends to the gustatory needs of now.

/ Design: Tiliche

NORTHERN COMFORT

LA CANTINA

Palma de Mallorca, Spain

/ This Mallorcan canteen is informal and youthful without getting puerile. Tarruella is a master of simplicity in all its flavors. Here, the flavor is a blend of energy and calm, which she injects into a plain wooden box via her materials and color. Pine and birch plywood flaunt their whorls, knots and grain beside iron and micro-cement flooring. Above the communal tables, striped textiles in dynamic color combinations recall the Mediterranean seaside and beach towels: green and red, red and blue, lilac and lemon yellow. Herb gardens on carts are visible on the terrace to which the dining room opens generously via sliding doors.

/ Design: Sandra Tarruella Interioristas

WATERMOON
Sydney, Australia

/ The client wanted the offering of this restaurant, dedicated to the enjoyment of Japanese cuisine and sake, to be understood at first glance from the kerb. Facet used rice wine bottles, which are slightly larger than the typical grape wine bottle, to create a series of lanterns: the backlit bottles cast large shadows and placed behind sheer panels their translucent forms were silhouetted to create abstract colors and patterns intended to catch the eyes of passers-by. But like the restaurant's namesake, they also provide a soft, inviting glow to illuminate a dark street

/ Design: Facet Studio

/ Client: Watermoon

/ Type of Food/Drinks/Specialties: Japanese food

OMOTESANDO KOFFEE
Tokyo, Japan

/ This wood and steel coffee kiosk is tucked into swanky Omotesando, but it could be in Kyoto by tomorrow. To fit into limited square footage, *Koffee* is a boxy, stand-alone module that can be transported and "popped up" anywhere without the need to remodel. "This is exactly the same concept as our traditional tea house," says Koffee's founder, Eiichi Kunitomo. "You could say that the frame of this café works as a spiritual barrier between *shigan* (our ordinary world) and *higan* (the sacred realm)." It is a Buddhist concept that also underlies the *chashitsu* (tea house) and the tea ceremony. The moral? Enjoy a good espresso while you still can.

/ Design: 14SD

/ Material: Wood and steel

/ Type of Food/Drinks/Specialties:
Only coffee: choice of 9 coffees hot or cold; Food: one type of sweet

OMOTESANDO KOFFEE
OMOTESANDO KOFFEE

OMOTESANDO KOFFEE
www.ooo-koffee.com

"Mas adapted their 'pulpeira' to suit a more urban setting while ensuring that it is still a place to spend quality time with family and friends."

PULPEIRA VILALÚA
Madrid, Spain

/ Mas adapted their "pulpeira," a traditional Galician restaurant mainly serving octopus, to suit a more urban setting while ensuring that it is still a place to spend quality time with family and friends. The plan consists of continuous benches ranged along the walls. The architects designed the furniture for the space, using a sustainable approach that includes repurposed materials. The team equipped the entrance with a shelf-lined tunnel, which serves as a palate cleanser between the modern kerb and the more old-school, Galicia-influenced atmosphere where guests can pull up to a dining table made from a wine barrel.

/ Design: Mas Arquitectura

/ Client: Vilalua

/ Type of Food/Drinks/Specialties: Tapas bar, Galician wine, octopus

NORTHERN COMFORT

THE TASTINGS ROOM
Singapore, Singapore

/ *Tastings* bistro and wine bar is defined by a belt of black volumes that float like stage sets atop a concrete screed floor inside an old industrial warehouse. Made from black laminates cut into tiles, each crease in their bodies conforms to a function while strategically placed cut-outs reveal their internal workings, framing what the designers call "spatial appetizers." The color palette plays off the palate: wine flavors inspired the amber kitchen and the ruby wine cellar while two small rooms—one all-white, the other black—lend an Asian yin-yang balance to the European gastronomy. The architectural oppositions also underscore the eatery's mission to serve up sophistication at affordable prices.

/ Design: StudioSKLIM
/ Client: Envis Group
/ Material: Concrete screed, laminates cut into tiles, solid wood, stainless steel, solid surfaces
/ Type of Food/Drinks/Specialties: Italian/French bistro food, wine, beer

NORTHERN COMFORT

178 / 179

"Arches running the length of the interior add depth and texture while the red-and-white checked tile floor is suggestive of estate verandahs of the past."

NORTHERN COMFORT

PLANTATION COFFEE
Melbourne, Australia

/ Another successful coffeehouse designed by Adele Winteridge with interior designers Brooke Thorn and Jennifer Lowe, *Plantation*'s name has obvious links to colonial plantations in tropical zones from which the designers took their cues. Foolscap used materials like timber, stone, and copper alongside colonial forms, patterns, and handcrafted custom joinery to reflect the handmade character of the single origin coffee being served. Arches running the length of the interior add depth and texture while the red-and-white checked tile floor is suggestive of estate verandahs of the past. Finally, Foolscap included a well-considered circulation that facilitates the brand's mission not just sell its coffee, but to educate customers about it at the same time.

/ Design: Foolscap Studio and Barbara and Fellows

/ Client: Plantation

/ Type of Food/Drinks/Specialties: Coffee

VOLT
Stockholm, Sweden

/ **Volt** is an unpretentious place for fine dining. "We do not want to be in accord with regular practice or procedure. We do not succumb to a standard," the owners say. "We let the irregular speak. We have created a restaurant far from chive cross garnish, white cloths, and bowing waiters." These ambitions are articulated in the forthright details of the interior decoration—dark wood, black-painted brick, candlelit tables, a simple cozy elegance.

/ Design: reVOLT

/ Client: restaurang VOLT

NORTHERN COMFORT

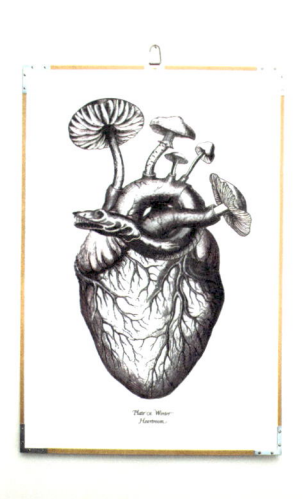

Home Sweet Home

Vinderen → 186–189

Kinfolk Dinner Series → 220–221

Surely there is no place quite like home, but there are designers out there who are making spaces that are more than friendly, more than inviting—that feel like home but, in their own inventive ways, even better: a dream of home.

HOME SWEET HOME

/ The Bakery café in the sunlit lobby of the **Hotel Daniel** →210–213 in Vienna is a space where tension falls away. It recalls urban loft-living more than maid service and is as popular with locals as with tourists. It is a space designed to feel not exclusive. At least visually, it doesn't keep anyone out: Potted plants crochet a living lace around furnishings that are a potpourri of vintage (read: comfy) and contemporary that keeps the comfy feeling cool. The domestic feeling of such environments often involves generous doses of textiles, the go-to finish for communicating comfort and security. Homely interiors like this also involve a little DIY and upcycling, both ways of bringing style and freshness to objects we already love, but with which we are so familiar we hardly acknowledge them anymore. In the case of Bakery, this comes in the form of the owner's functional found-object sculptures, which exude their own folk sensibility, combined with the welcoming or inclusive character of rustic chic: There are coffee tables made from shipping pallets and a silk couch with its legs cut away; suspended from the ceiling on ropes, it is transformed into a swing, adding a touch of the playground to the living room.

Comfort spaces, though they are sometimes designed not to look it, are actually carefully composed. Restful space, space that lets its visitors recharge, is often filled with universally beloved objects. The owners of the **KEX Hostel** →208 in Reykjavik furnished the dormitories, rooms, café, bar, and lounge with materials that they discovered and rescued during their travels around the world, creating a highly eclectic aesthetic they call "vintage industrial." It is an evocative, time and placeless style that is difficult to make convincingly coherent. At **KEX**, well-considered combinations of heterogeneous pieces make each room feel seamless and whole though nothing belongs together per se. Each room becomes a tableau of objects that we think we "recognize" and that manufacture a connection to what we think we know. In this way, comfy space becomes a home away from home, which may be what people traveling or even simply going out are ultimately looking for.

KITCHAIN →202–203 also is an efficient, space-saving home away from home. The modular, open-plan system took its cues from the flexibility, convertibility, and portability of camping equipment. Its four tables can be assembled in various configurations to provide surfaces on which to cook, eat, and socialize and their integrated grills and kitchenette units can be used in two ways: The do-it-yourself mode lets guests create their own meals and design their own evening in the process, while the I-don't-feel-like-doing-it-myself-tonight mode lets guests belly up to a domesticated chef's table to observe the kitchen in action while they enjoy a moment of inaction.

De Farine & d'Eau Fraîche →184–185

In this mode, **Kitchain** takes one step toward the supper club, a trend that peaked in major cities around the world in the last several years. The supper club is an attempt to democratize eating out, a move away from the velvet rope and hidden thresholds of the trendy speakeasy that nonetheless retains a hint of exclusivity. It is an exclusivity that has mostly to do with the cherry-picked, or at least word-of-mouth, guest lists, intended to give these deceptively informal evenings a certain frisson, to make guests feel special even while they sit around a charmingly banal backyard on candlelit picnic benches. The food remains haute couture, but the improvised space—most clubs change location for each meal—feels deliberately prêt-à-porter. This I'm-just-throwing-a-few-friends-a-little-dinner-party approach (garnished with head-chef-quality meals) places the emphasis back not merely on the chemistry and artistry of food design, but on the eating space as a place to reconnect with community. At the **Kinfolk dinner series** →220–221, for instance, meals become real-world extensions of social media: Kinfolk gathered guests at monthly dinners that traveled to a dozen cities in a dozen months, to remind them of the network that already exists around them. It is a lower-key nightlife that doesn't just promote good friendships and connections in a physically disconnected urban milieu; it also promotes creative collaboration amongst guests who are owners of studios and small businesses. Supper clubs bring nightlife back to where we once expected to find it—at the family dinner table— and turn "going out" into "staying in." Guests feel as if they don't have to go out at all—not even to return home.

Katerholzig / Katerschmaus →206–207

DE FARINE & D'EAU FRAÎCHE
Montreal, Canada

/ According to its owners, this pastry boutique, whose name means "Of Flour & Fresh Water," revolves around "love, naiveté, and escapism." In designing the space and identity, SURFACE3 sought to capture the experience of buying and eating pastries as ritual, emotion, and magical indulgence. Boxed inside striated white walls into which the lathe-turned legs of old tables half-disappear, the bakery uses rustic salvaged wood surfaces to frame black-and-white furnishings and details. Sculptural pendant lights, lightly finished wood surfaces carved with lovers' initials, and doily-framed windows evoke an enchantment as powerful as the pastries themselves.

/ Design: SURFACE3

/ Client: De farine et d'eau fraîche

"Lightly finished wood surfaces carved with lovers' initials and doily-framed windows evoke an enchantment as powerful as the pastries themselves."

"The purity of the shop's commitment to using only environmentally-friendly, renewable, and recyclable resources extends to the look of the space."

PRINCESS CHEESECAKE
Berlin, Germany

/ Elegance and a strident brightness rule the day at this patisserie and café where *Princess Cheesecakes* are crafted by hand with natural ingredients and a hearty belief in the power of the fairytale. The purity of the shop's commitment to using only environmentally-friendly, renewable, and recyclable resources extends to the look of the space with its fusion of pared-down opulence and simplicity: blond-wood benches with tufted cushions and Louis XVI armchairs with simple rectangular tables.

/ Design: brandherm + krumrey interior architecture

/ Client: Conny Suhr

/ Material: Oak whitewashed, glass, bone china, linen, steel, black granite, kashmir white

HOME SWEET HOME

VINDEREN
Oslo, Norway

/ Situated in an old pharmacy not far from the city center, Vinderen was nonetheless inspired by the countryside. The space is anchored by a large, antique wood-burning stove that Inne combined with vintage leather seating and kitchen chairs. The color scheme was limited to white, gray, and light blue to provide some modern counterpoint to the storied elements. The combination generates a space that feels casual and welcoming.

/ Design: Inne Design

/ Client: United Bakeries

/ Type of Food/Drinks/Specialties: Bakery

HOME SWEET HOME

STRAND RESTAURANT
Oslo, Norway

/ This seaside eatery hosts a bakery, foodbar, ballroom, VIP rooms, and a fine dining room. Since it first hung its shingle in the 1920s, it has seen all manner of changes to the property but the current owners wanted to revive a 1920s atmosphere while giving the interiors a modern flourish. The black-and-white interior is occasionally set off by a shade of light green that was discovered on the original walls during the initial stages of the renovation. The resulting space is intended to be inclusive of all ages, both classical and cool, with a touch of masculinity to top it off.

/ Design: Inne Design

/ Client: Masterchefs Tom Victor Gausdal, Stian Floer and Erling Sundal

/ Type of Food/Drinks/Specialties: Fine dining, à la carte, bakery

HOME SWEET HOME

United
BAKERIES
Det gode brød…
Godt, nystekt og velsmakende brød, bakt med den største nøyaktighet og med omtanke for hvert enkelt brød. Dette er bakernes stolthet og filosofi. Vårt brød er bakt etter svært gamle tradisjoner, basert på surdeigskultur, lang hevetid og inneholder kun naturlige ingredienser.

HOME SWEET HOME

MAJORSTUEN
Oslo, Norway

/ There is a sweet confusion of the modern and the old-fashioned in this Oslo bakery, the roughness of which is softened at the edges: A concrete floor and off-white wall tiles frame vintage tables and chairs and a wall of drawers that clearly did hard-time in a lawyer's office back in the day. It is a combination that invests a laid-back environment with substance, a substance that comes from the age and character of well-used objects, whose surfaces tell tales that we can almost hear.

/ Design: Inne Design
/ Client: United Bakeries
/ Type of Food/Drinks/Specialties: Bakery

ADAMSTUEN
Oslo, Norway

/ Its windows are as big as this café is small. The designers, who specialize in a sophisticated rustic aesthetic, fitted the place out with vintage furniture, an antique ceiling, and old church pews. They hung pieces from the owner's collection of antique baking tools and equipment on the wall to cultivate an old-fashioned industrial chic. The floor itself, a tapestry of parquet wood, is more than a century old and was recomposed to suit the new interior.

/ Design: Inne Design
/ Client: United Bakeries
/ Type of Food/Drinks/Specialties: Bakery

RACINE DE RHUBARBE
CAMPHRE
FUMETERRE
RACINE DE GUIMAUVE
RACINE CHIENDENT
BADIANE
RACINE DE GENTIANE
SALSEPAREIL
FLEURS DE HOUBLON
FEUILLES DE RONCES
THE NOIR
CARRAGAHEEN
FLEURS DE GUIMAUVE
QUINQUINA GRIS

SLOWPOKE ESPRESSO
Melbourne, Australia

/ The *Slowpoke Espresso* café in the popular suburb of Fitzroy serves local and organic food. To create an environment that lives up to the café's name and concept, designer Anne-Sophie Poirier upcycled various species of timber offcuts harvested from regional furniture makers to create a 12-meter wooden patchwork wall. The various grains and tones generate texture and animate the space as much as the caffeine. Blocks of wood protrude from the wall far enough to serve as shelves for condiments while recycled floorboards become tabletops. Poirier's street signage consists of a solar-powered recycled tool box. As for the business cards, they were hand-cut from disused cardboard packaging.

/ Design: Sasufi

/ Client: Slowpoke Espresso

/ Type of Food/Drinks/Specialties:
Local & Organic

HOME SWEET HOME

THE BOOK CLUB
London, United Kingdom

/ **The Book Club** is frequented morning to night by those in the creative industries looking to work or play. Its interiors feature banal materials and techniques, found and from-scratch furnishings, unexpected combinations, and reconfigurable elements that establish a series of site-specific installations or, as the designers say, "an uncommon-common environment." The adaptable frame construction they used for tables and benches was also applied to bar stools, a ping pong table, and a mobile DJ booth. In the basement, the ceiling is a mosaic of 23,000 ordinary household light bulbs while throughout conduit lighting forms constellations that descend into the room at varying heights.

/ Design: Shai Akram & Andrew Haythornthwaite

HOME SWEET HOME

"The Book Club is frequented morning to night by those in the creative industries looking to work or play."

200 / 201

HOME SWEET HOME

OTAKARA SUPPER CLUB
NYC, New York, USA

/ Sawako Okochi is moving up in the world, or at least north. The former chef de cuisine at Red Hook's Good Fork in south Brooklyn started a supper club in Fort Greene, carrying on the venerable back-to-the-things-that-matter tradition of impromptu gourmet dining. Okochi's monthly pop-up dinner dates are BYOB affairs at $100 a head in a location disclosed only to guests. Her first meal featured miso-glazed rice balls with a Negroni-style cocktail, followed by a five-course dinner of homemade tofu, crab-stuffed zucchini blossoms, and clam ceviche, among other delicacies.

/ Design: Sawako Okochi

/ Type of Food/Drinks/Specialties: Japanese, New American

KITCHAIN
Fribourg, Switzerland

/ *KITCHAIN* is a modular, open-plan kitchen system that was inspired by the flexibility of camping equipment. Its mobile units can be assembled to fit various groups and purposes, exploiting the ritual of communal cooking, eating, and lounging as a catalyst for socializing and exchanging ideas. The ready-made mode lets users observe professional chefs and taste their work, while the do-it-yourself mode allows them to prepare and serve their own meals. *KITCHAIN* was originally created for an annual performing and visual arts festival, where it will be reconfigured and used again in the years to come.

/ Design: António Louro (MOOV), Benedetta Maxia with Festival Belluard Bollwerk

HOME SWEET HOME

PROTEIN TASTE ACADEMY
London, United Kingdom

/ At this 18 Hewett Street gallery, creative agency Protein hosts evenings that bring together top creative minds to explore a high-design realm of taste and smell. The evenings include tastings guided by coffee connoisseurs and food designers that sound Michelin-worthy ("black bream ceviche, rhubarb, oxalis salt, and sorrel"). And for a nightcap? Perhaps a lowball concocted from Dalmore 15 and sloe gin sour with ginger bitters that come attached—by a fuse—to a lemon-scented balloon. When the fuse is lit, the balloon pops, providing a thrill for firecracker fans and releasing a scent that adds one more fragrant detail to a tasty night.

/ Design: Protein

HOME SWEET HOME

"Katers epitomize that wonderful Berliner phrase 'arm, aber sexy'—poor, but sexy."

KATERHOLZIG / KATERSCHMAUS
Berlin, Germany

/ Out of the ashes of a ruined soap factory, this nightclub and its sibling restaurant cater to a local creative crowd with a rough-around-the-edges street art sensibility. Dimly lit, graffiti-adorned, *Katerschmaus* serves food on the third floor. Below, at the indoor-outdoor street level bar called *KaterHolzig*, the owners screen films and host stage performances before letting their hair down for dusk-to-dawn electro, dance, and house music marathons followed by legendary "hangover feasts" to cap it all off. Word on the web is that the Katers epitomize that wonderful Berliner phrase "arm, aber sexy"—poor, but sexy.

/ Design: Mikado Stolpercrew, Hanna Rix, Pentaklon, Katerholzig

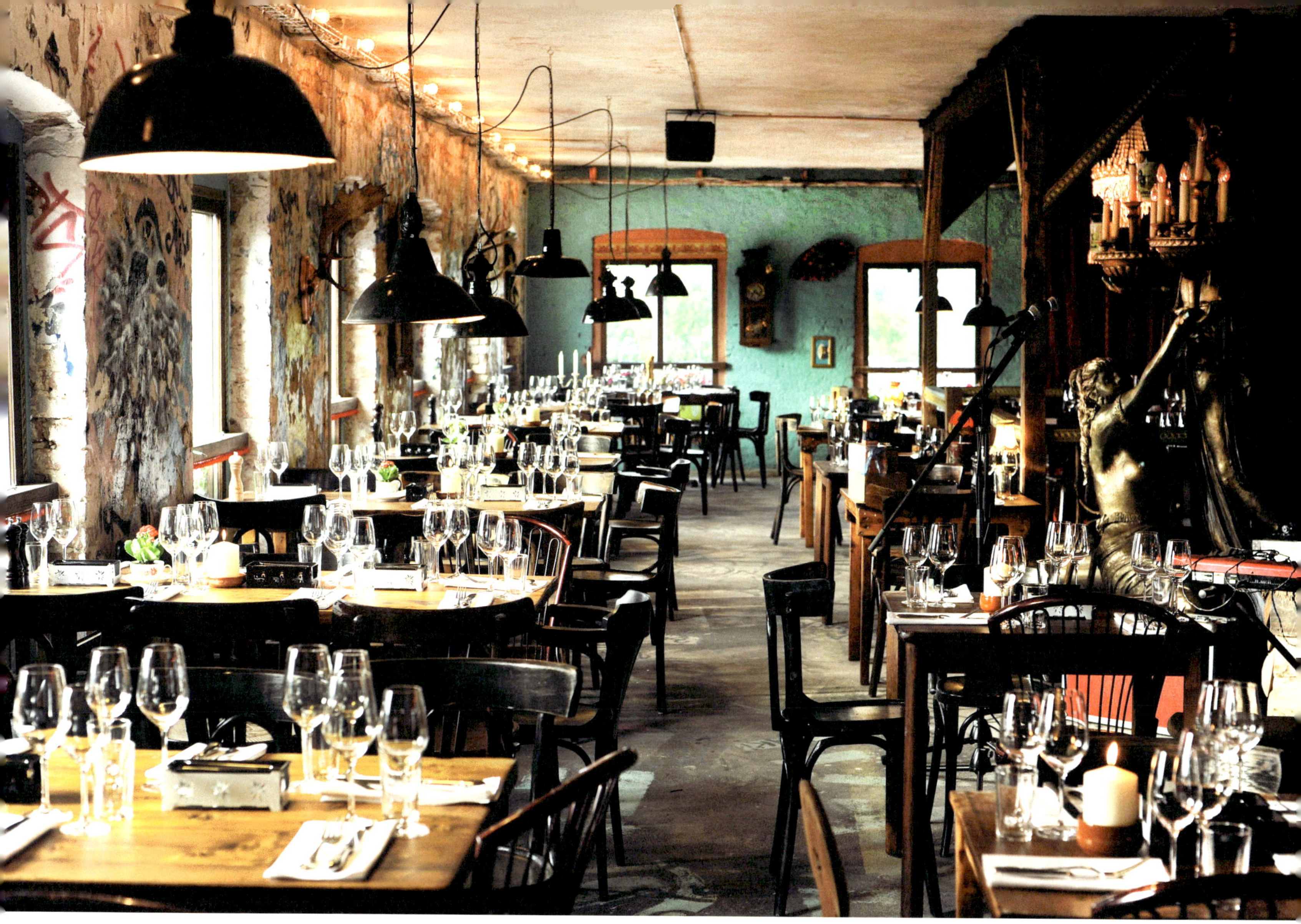

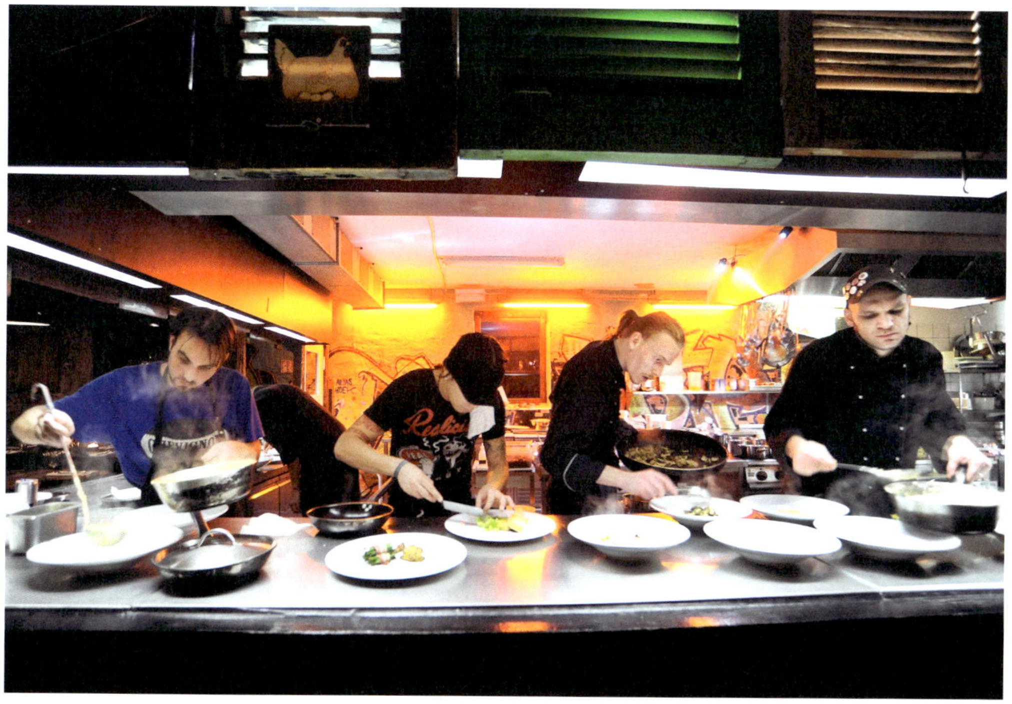

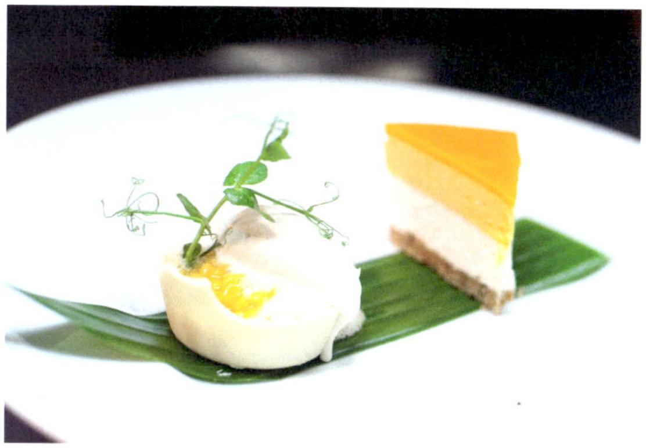

KEX HOSTEL
Reykjavík, Iceland

/ A hostel housed in an old biscuit factory in downtown Reykjavik, KEX is furnished with materials found and rescued around the world. Its owners describe it as "vintage industrial" and augmented the eclectic and modern private rooms and dorms with a café, bar, and lounge.

/ Design: Baulhús

/ Client: KEX Hostel

/ Material: Vintage and salvaged materials

/ Type of Food/Drinks/Specialties: Gastropub, local and micro breweries

HOME SWEET HOME

BRILL
Singapore, Singapore

/ *Brill* is a franchise food take-out for gourmands and gifting that exploits small shop spaces in urban settings. It caters to consumers who want to be entertained and surprised on top of being well-treated. The branding melds precision with a humble opulence, starting from the Couples-designed logo—a scalloped border with Greek fret motifs, checkers, and cross-stitch—to natural wood finishes and elegant but unfussy displays.

/ Design: Couple

/ Client: Simply Bread

/ Type of Food/Drinks/Specialties: Take-out food and food as gifts

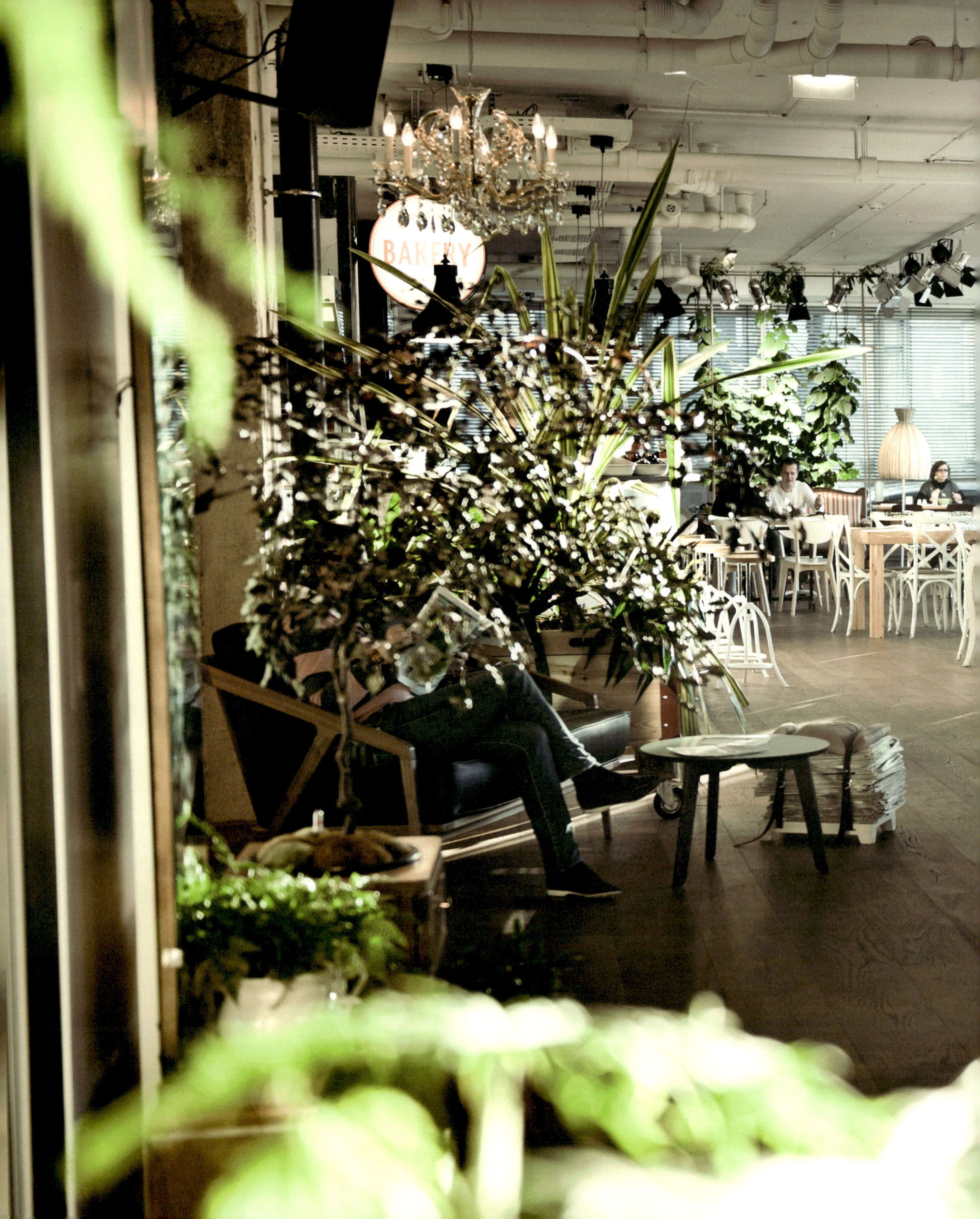
BAKERY

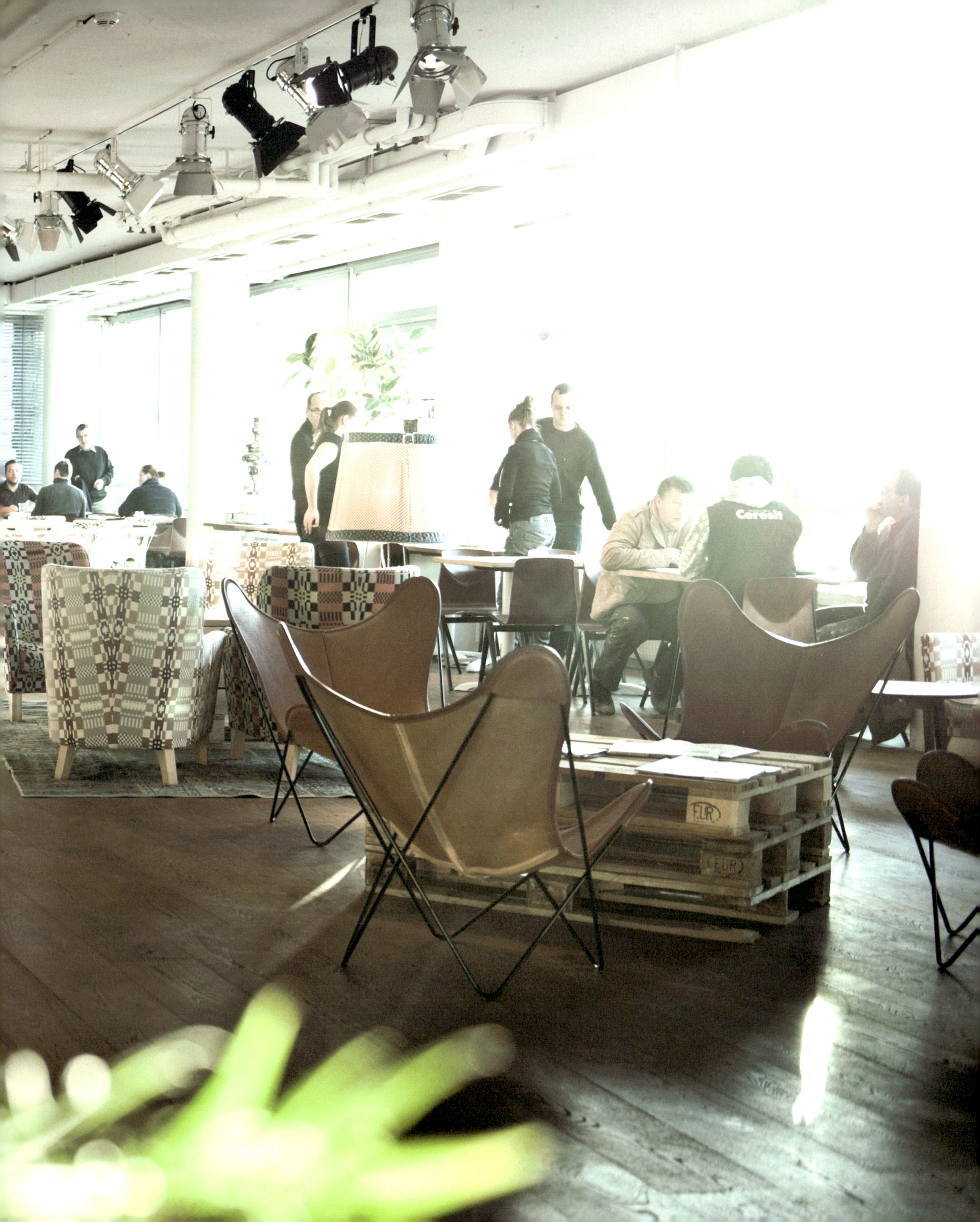
Ceresit
EUR
EUR

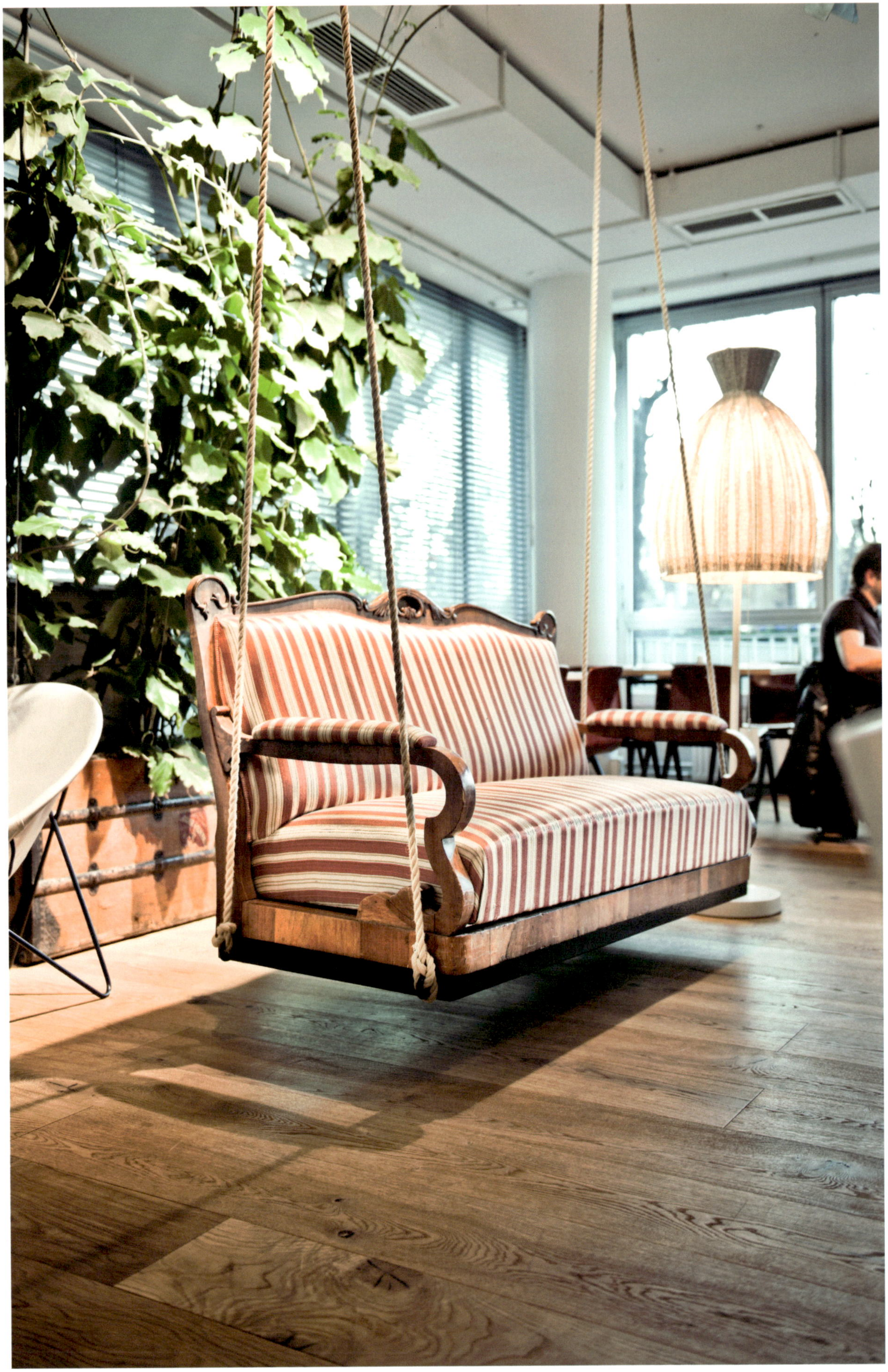

HOME SWEET HOME

HOTEL DANIEL VIENNA
Vienna, Austria

/ These days the best hotel lobby is the new neighborhood living room. The "Bakery" in this lobby is a relaxed environment more reminiscent of a loft and is as popular with locals as it is with out-of-towners. Potted greenery surrounds eclectic furnishings: original vintage furniture and contemporary pieces from emerging designers—like armchairs upholstered in knit textiles by Donna Wilson for SCP—are combined with the owner's own found-material constructions, such as coffee tables fashioned from wooden pallets and a legless silk couch swinging from the ceiling on ropes.

/ Design: Florian Weitzer (hotel owner)

/ Type of Food/Drinks/Specialties: International

MONKEY BAR FUMOIR
Zurich, Switzerland

/ Denizens of this fumoir, an addition to the *Blue Monkey* restaurant, can enjoy a Montecristo Open Master or a Cohiba Siglo in a safe haven that exists at an elegant remove from Zurich's smoking ban. Avoiding the musty-fusty tradition of smoking rooms, the designers gave the space an intimate dimness, punctuated by pinpoint spot lighting. Green walls, black-and-white photographs of film stars of yore, antiqued mirror together with an antique chandelier, Parisian wall lights, polished brass—and even modern elements like the translucent Corian bar top—exude a Prohibition-era atmosphere.

/ Design: Dyer-Smith & Frey   / Client: Kramer Gastronomie

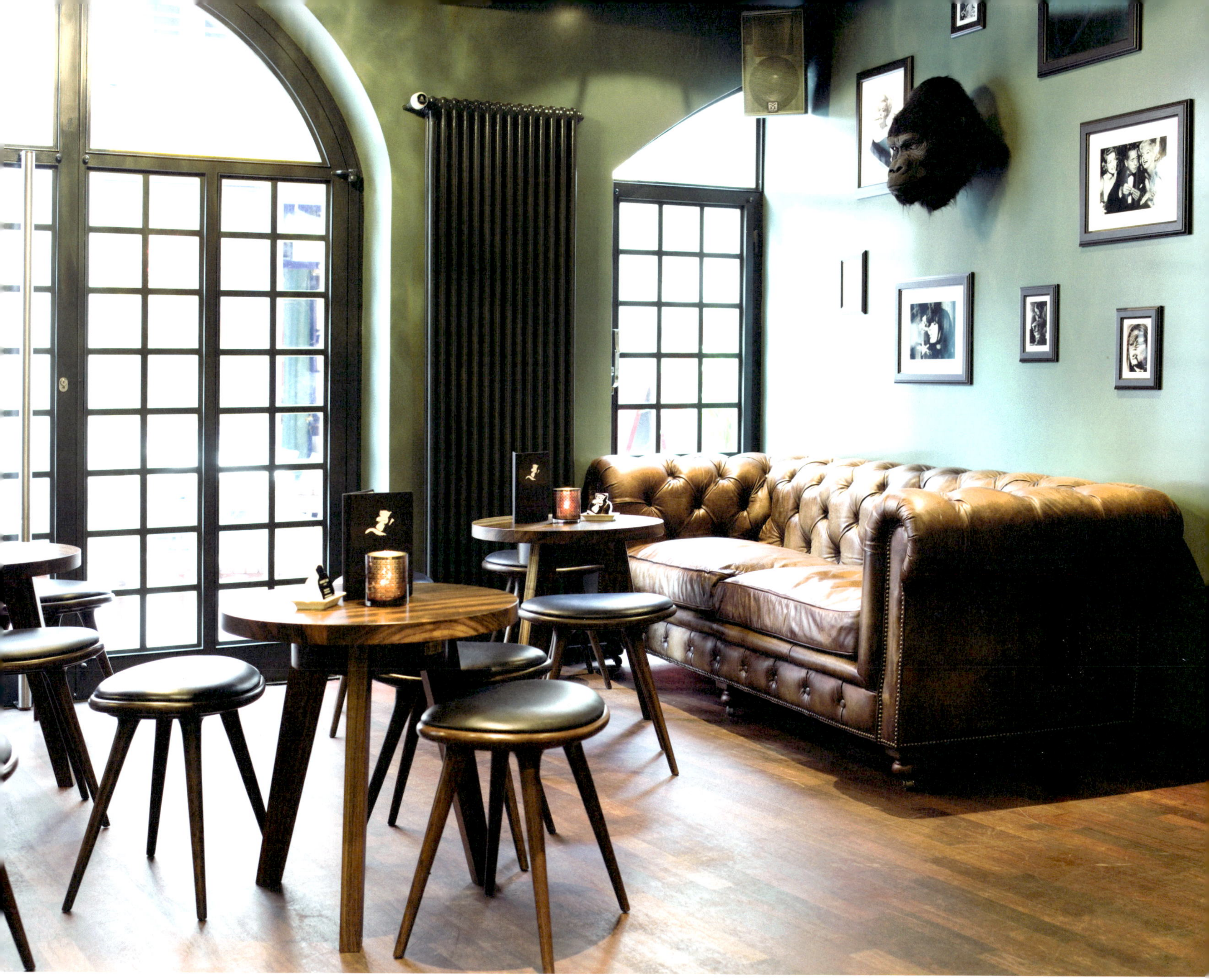

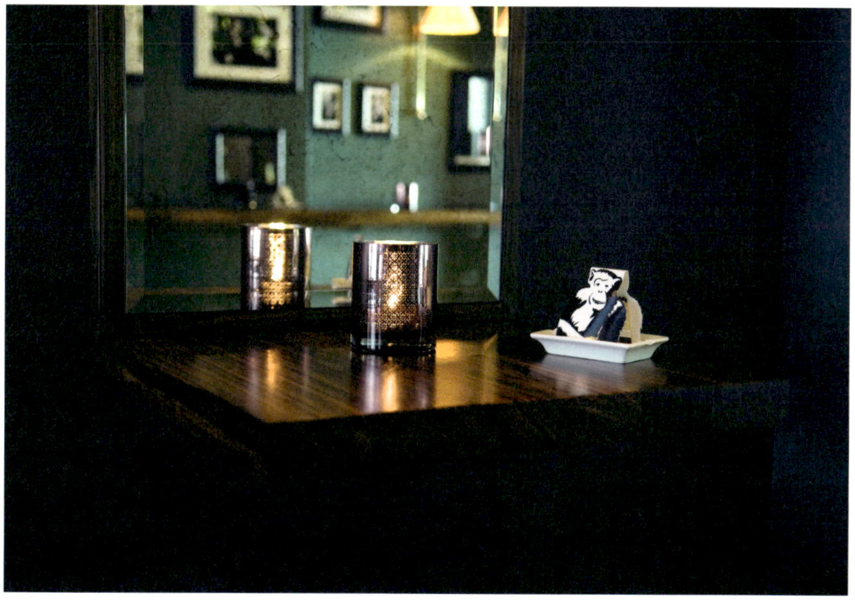

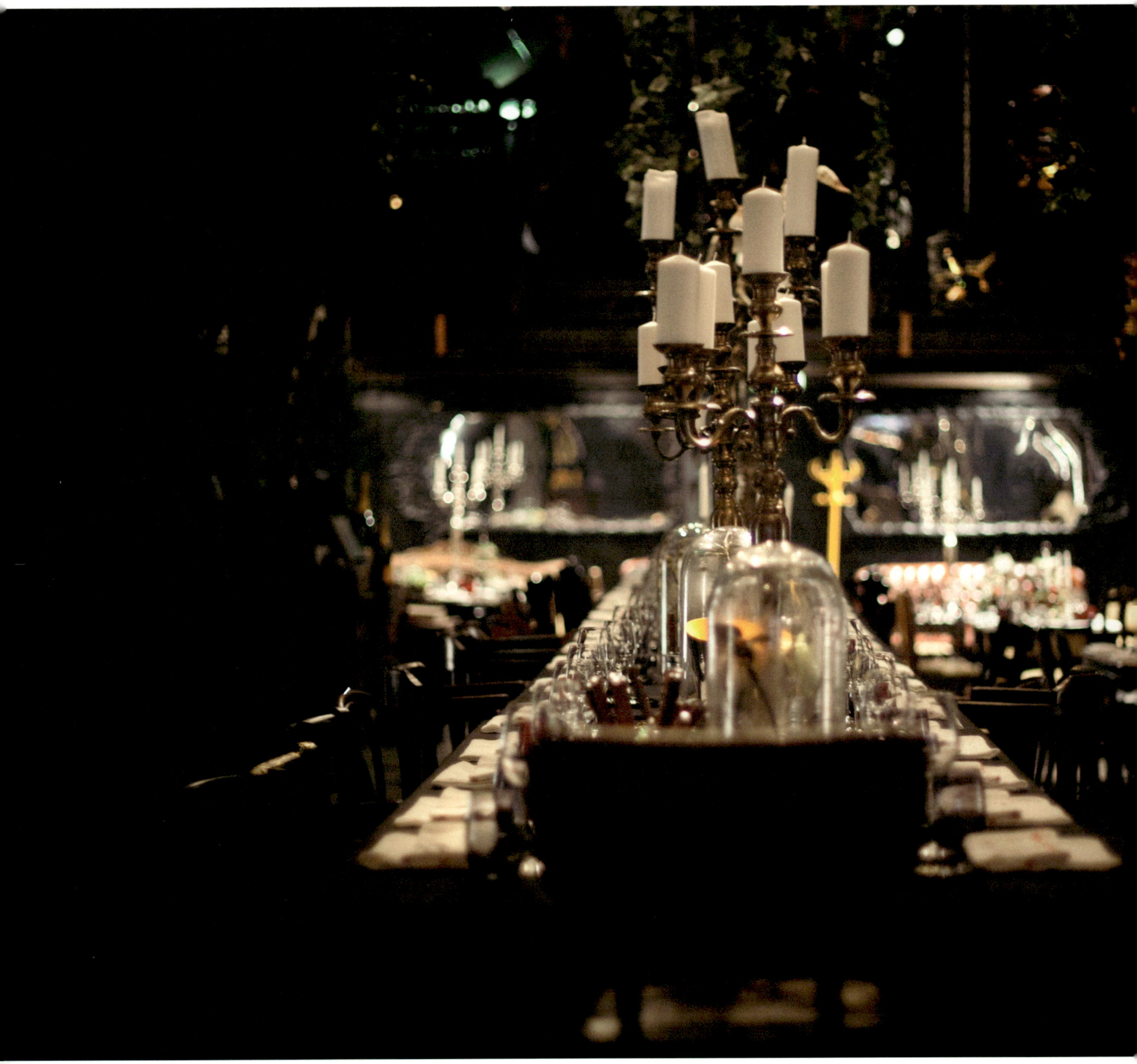

THE MINOTAUR
London, United Kingdom

/ Nearly 200-year-old caterer Kofler & Kompanie's Pret A Diner series has been popping up from Munich to Monaco since 2005, but bills itself as a dining experience, not a pop-up. Indeed, the temporary events unite art, fashion, Michelin-starred food, film, and unique interiors to create an immersive—in this case, even subterranean—social and cultural experience. For *Minotaur*, the dining room was situated in the belly of the Lazarides Galleries' labrynthine art installation. The theme slotted perfectly into the brick arches, side chambers, and long barrel vaults of the graffitied and derelict tunnels beneath Waterloo Station, which were reclaimed in 2010 by the Old Vic Theater.

/ Design: Kofler & Kompanie

RIDLEY'S
London, United Kingdom

/ This temporary eatery comprised a naked two-story scaffolding dedicated to "outdoor exhibitionist eating" set between stalls of Ridley Road Market. Visitors were invited to exchange market produce for a prepared lunch or pay £15 for dinner. The produce harvested during lunch served as the ingredients for dinner, while evening revenues were invested in the next day's lunch. Guest received a £5 shopping voucher with their dinner, encouraging them to return to the market another day. Meals prepared in the ground floor kitchen were lifted to the first floor via a mechanical table that filled a void at the center of the communal dining table above.

/ Design: The Decorators with Atelier Chan Chan

"Meals prepared in the ground floor kitchen were lifted to the first floor via a mechanical table that filled a void at the center of the communal dining table above."

KINFOLK DINNER SERIES — BROOKLYN
NYC, New York, USA

/ Food as an analog social media? The *Kinfolk dinner* series gathers people around good food to create and enrich the "community that already exists around them." The goal is also to promote collaboration amongst local artisans and small businesses, an agenda that involves 12 dinners, 12 cities, and 12 months.

/ Design: Kinfolk

/ Type of Food/Drinks/Specialties: Food by Jewels of New York

HOME SWEET HOME

Showtime

Opulent environments take myriad forms. They are not just flash-bang design or a matter of signal luxuries—bottle service, sparkling surfaces, plush textiles; some of the richest environments eschew the glitter and glare which are so obvious as to have become cheap. Today, designers make more abstract translations of our nightlife values: making sophisticated selections of material and finishes, scaling up certain details to render them larger than life, precisely framing views to the outside that can't be found elsewhere, or creating a narrative that suggests exclusivity and uniqueness of character, voice, or tone. Rarity is still a powerful lure, but interiors that provide an experience, something preferably immersive or at least imposing, fetch the highest price.

SHOWTIME

/ In *Upstairs Beresford* →254-255, we find a wealth of objects and patterns: chevrons of wide wooden planks clad the walls, yacht-like cushions hug the banquettes, abstract, painterly lightshades illuminate cushions featuring the portraits of queens. The *Monteleone Hotel* →261 sports a bar crowned with a restored carousel and seating painted with Gauguin-like jungle scenes.

Theatricality, most often a study in moods, can establish refinement in a comprehensive way. Stylt used theater, for instance, to give character to a series of richly scenographic restaurants, including one, called *Griffins* →236-241, that is modeled after a classic American steakhouse. *Griffins* is named for an imaginary couple who (invisibly) play host there and reads like a visual script as guests penetrate deeper into the restaurant's box-like rooms. The interiors are densely decorated with a mix of materials, colors, and patterns (including eccentrically mismatched seating), and a tightly edited collection of eclectic objects that, carefully arranged, tell the hosts' very particular story. Some items merely give the space a timeless upper-echelon domesticity: thick drapery, fringed lampshades, and Persian carpets accompany white tile and minimalist banquettes. Carpets and upholstery are a riot of different patterns and Stylt's quirky objects, from amethyst geodes, bits of coral, and lab beakers to antique canvases and apothecary drawers, paint a detailed portrait of the couple through the originality of their environment. It also helps that the rough-hewn industrial neighborhood that guests must pass through to arrive at the Griffins "front door" makes the interiors feel especially highbrow and well-cultivated.

Stylt used a cocktail of international allusions to cultivate a pervasive grandeur in a brasserie located inside a historically significant railway station just north of Stockholm. The space was styled to communicate the aristocratic tastes of Paris, the vibrant energy of London, and the iconic flavors of Rome—an abundance of greatness that makes the space grander than the sum of its parts.

Named after a substance that is becoming increasingly rare in the rarefied air of the stratosphere, *Ozone's* →228-233 opulence is signaled by a relentless combination of different geometric patterns: floor tiles are pentagonal, the bars are faceted, but faceted in marble. Screens behind the bars and screens that form a drop ceiling are a variant on this polygonal theme. It is a heady cocktail of materials: leather, heavily grainy woods captured under deep gloss, chrome, scaled up columns shaped like the lathe-turned legs of tables, a mash-up of furniture types, varicolored cushions, even a spectrum of multi-hued lighting.

A sense of freedom—the rules don't apply here—is a powerful way to communicate luxury: a libertine quality and exoticism provides a flip-side to patrician, conservative environments. Illicit scenarios are effective, as well: at Amsterdam *smoking club Hi/Lo* →224-227, the interiors are divided between "Heaven" and "Hell." The clutter is gone, but the fictional—even moralistic—nature of the themes creates a sense of indulgence and the exhilaration of rebellion.

A different motif filled every surface of the *Juliet Supper Club* →276-277 in Manhattan: the Arabian Nights.

Bar Fou Fou →266-267

A drop ceiling filigreed with Seljuk stars, the floor, parts of furniture and columns are slathered with an overkill of mosaic size metallic bronze tiles and shimmer against bare brick walls that are threaded with arcing black fins. Lattice-laced royal blue silk sofas are paired with chalk blue tables with exaggerated lathe-turned bases. Precisely the abundance of pattern, color, and material are the signals of abundance, an Aladdin's cave of finishes. Who cares that there are no windows?

StarEight →278-279 in China, on the other hand, conjures up a starry night with violet light falling down in clear filaments from the atrium's 10m high skylight alongside a nebula-like crystal chandelier and mirror-finish stainless steel wine racks that resemble Jacob's ladders of light.

Sumptuous materials have the power to transform interiors that are otherwise formally minimal, even astringent. The gourmet pastry shop *Poison d' Amour* →256-257 consists of hard marble, a single stone arch, and black surfaces (along with handsome but unshaded Plumen energy-saving lightbulbs), relieved only by a modest chandelier and a less modest, wall-size portrait of that historical flag-bearer of extravagance, Marie Antoinette. The starkness of the restrained surfaces actually underscores the lushness of the materials and furnishings. Opulence is sometimes best expressed in very few gestures.

Stationen Uppsala Three →234-235

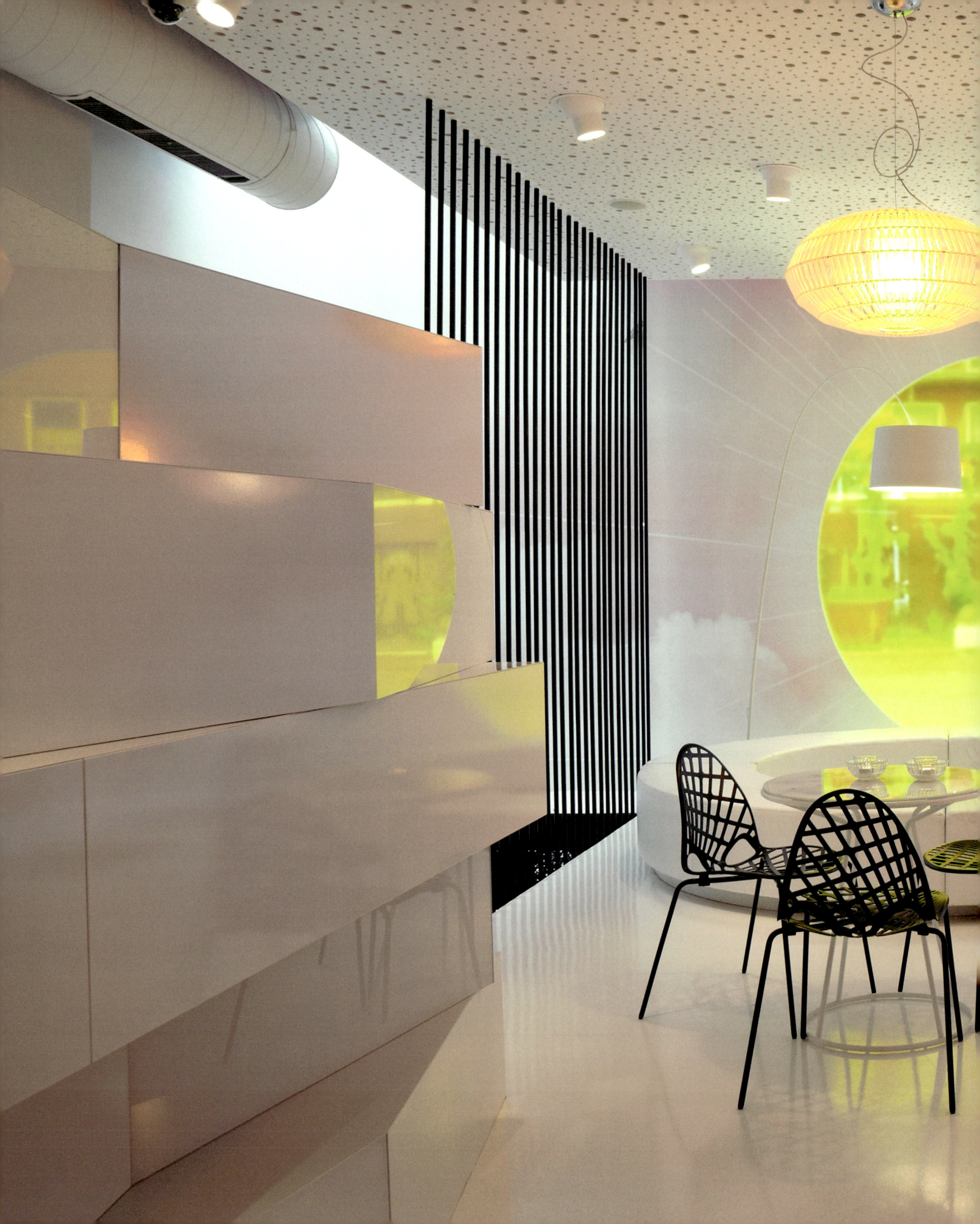

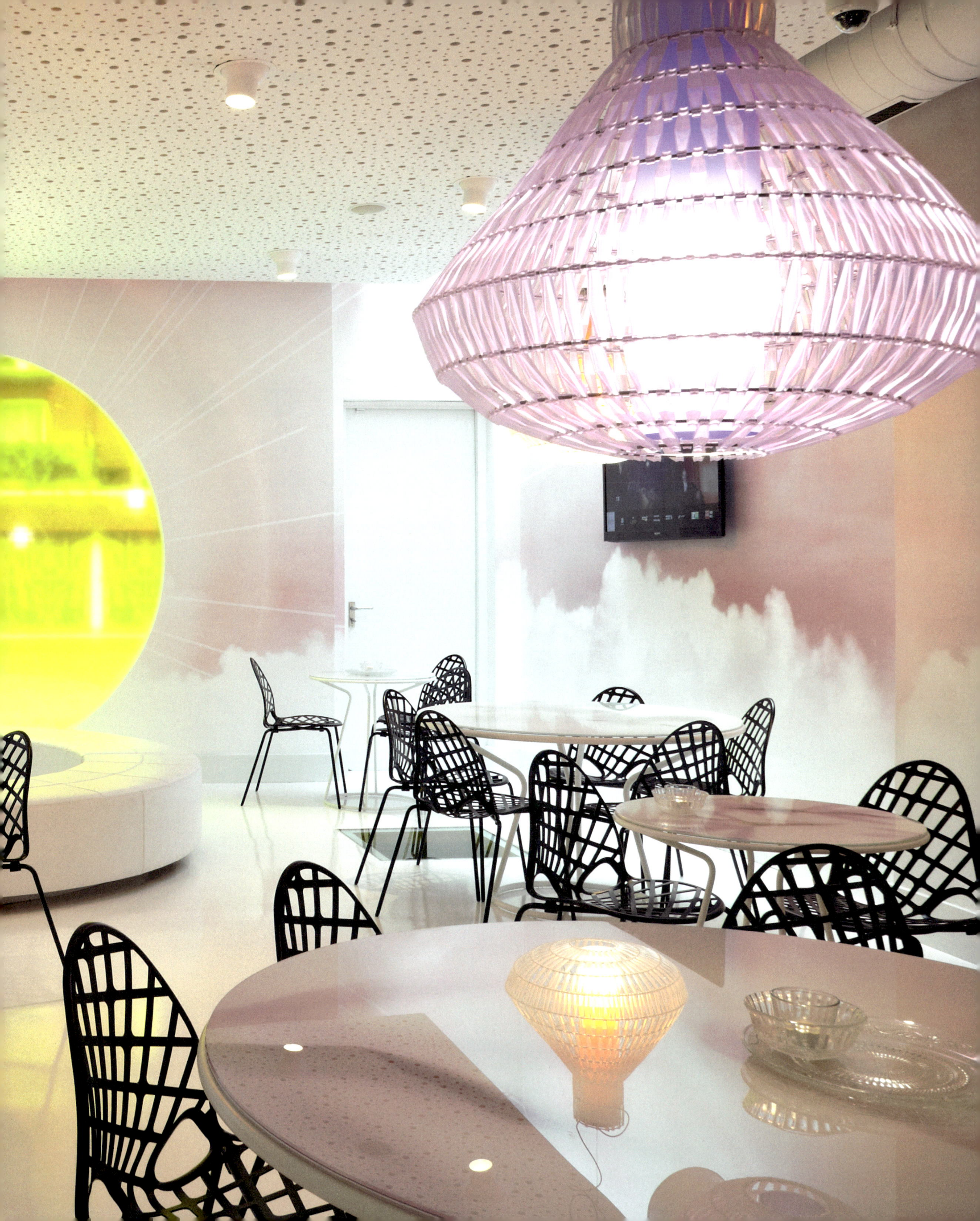

"Oppositions define this pot bar interior, a highbrow contemporary space with Eastern accents in which to smoke weed and hash."

SMOKING CLUB HI/LO
Utrecht, Netherlands

/ Oppositions—Hi/Lo, Heaven/Hell, Stoned/Sober—define this pot bar interior, a highbrow contemporary space with Eastern accents in which to smoke weed and hash. In Heaven, Vos swaddles guests in a cloudscape—bright and high-altitude with glass, steel, and leather to guard against carelessly handled burning butts and roaches. But Heaven leads to Hell, which was inspired by the opium den: a warren of dark rooms, yes, but lined with high-end design products by Moroso, Hay, and Foscarini, how bad can it be? The toilets are tucked away in a tadelakt-coated box with narrow passages, illuminated sinks, and urinals—designed by Meike van Schijndel—shaped like lipsticked mouths.

/ Design: Workshop of Wonders

/ Client: Moos Mazied

/ Material: Floors: cast flooring, Moroccan tiles, purple stained oak; Walls: printed canvas, tadelakt plastering, exploded aluminium, golden and black aluminium chain curtain; Ceilings: stucco, knauf acoustic system, structural; Stairs: coated steel, stained wood; Lighting: Foscarini, modular lighting, Diesel, Z-line, backlit exploded aluminium, LED ground spotlights and RGB strips; Furniture: Moroso, Hay, custom made reception and screen made from glass and steel, custom made leather couches, Moroccan handicrafts

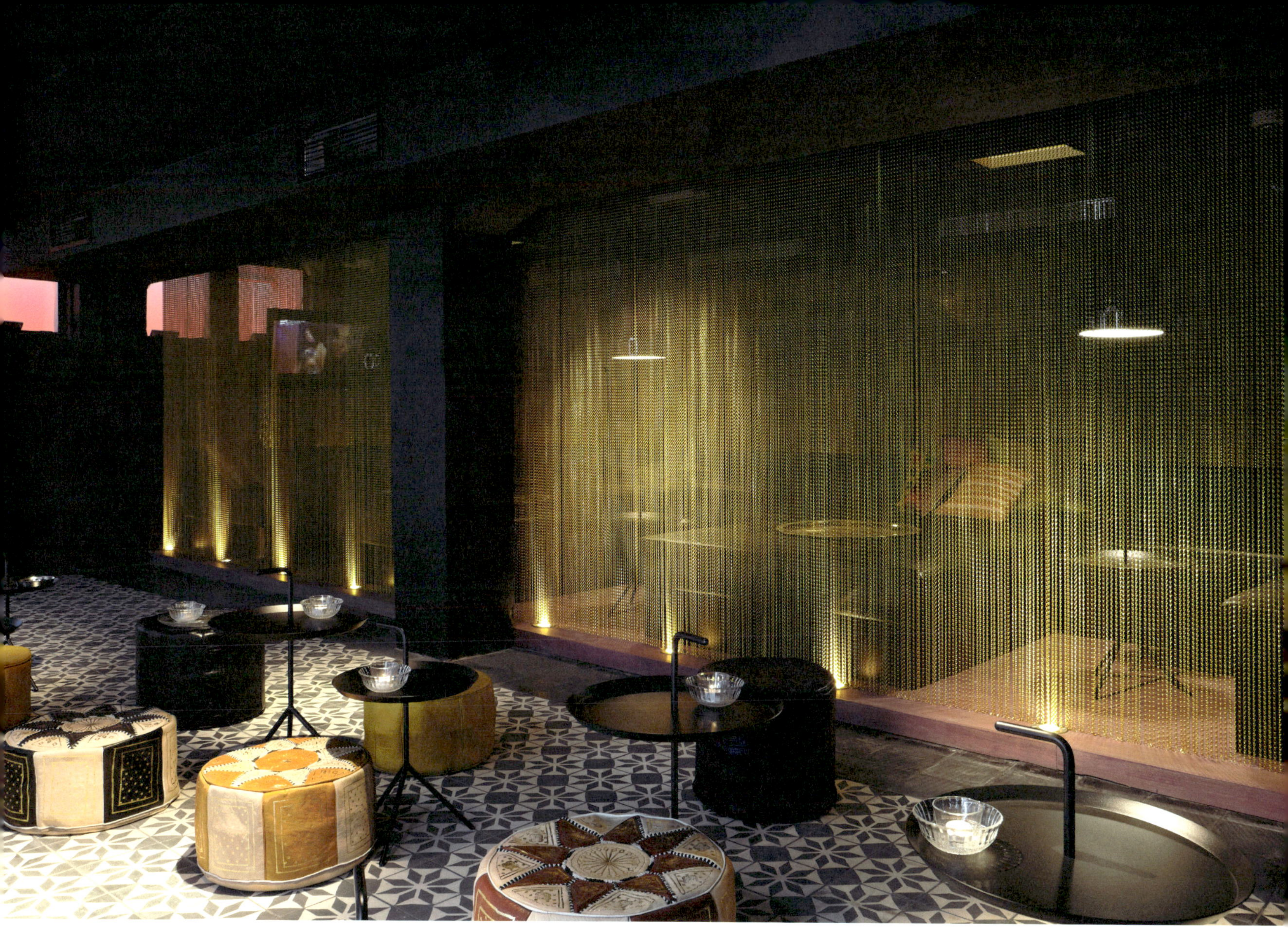

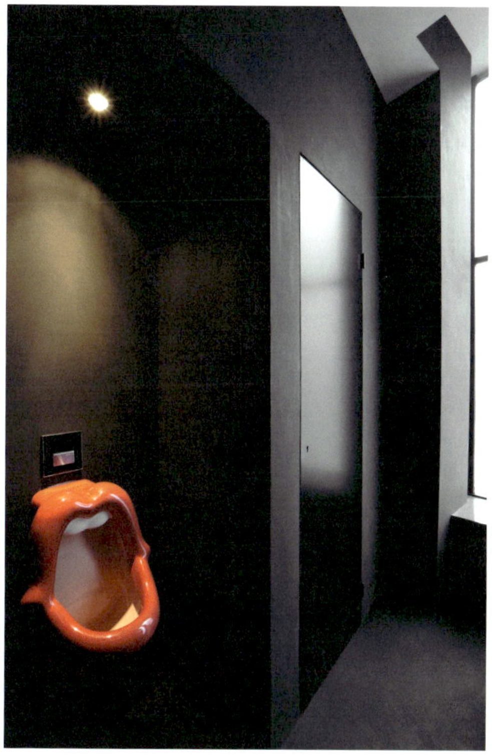

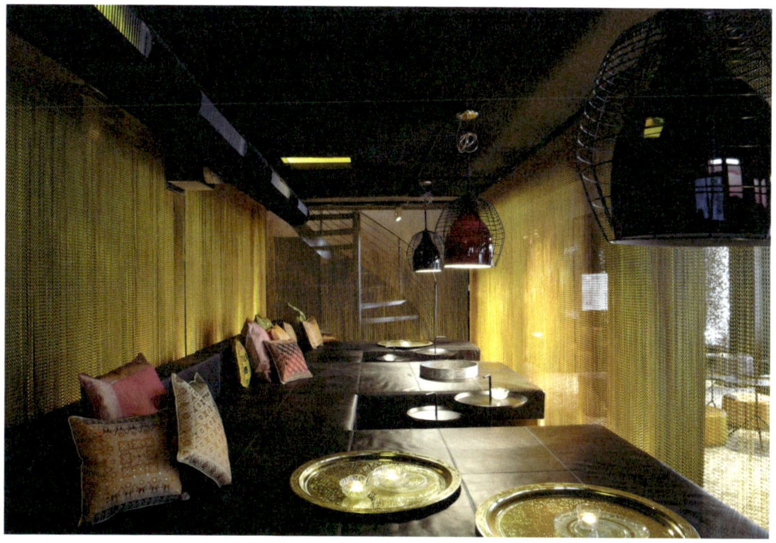

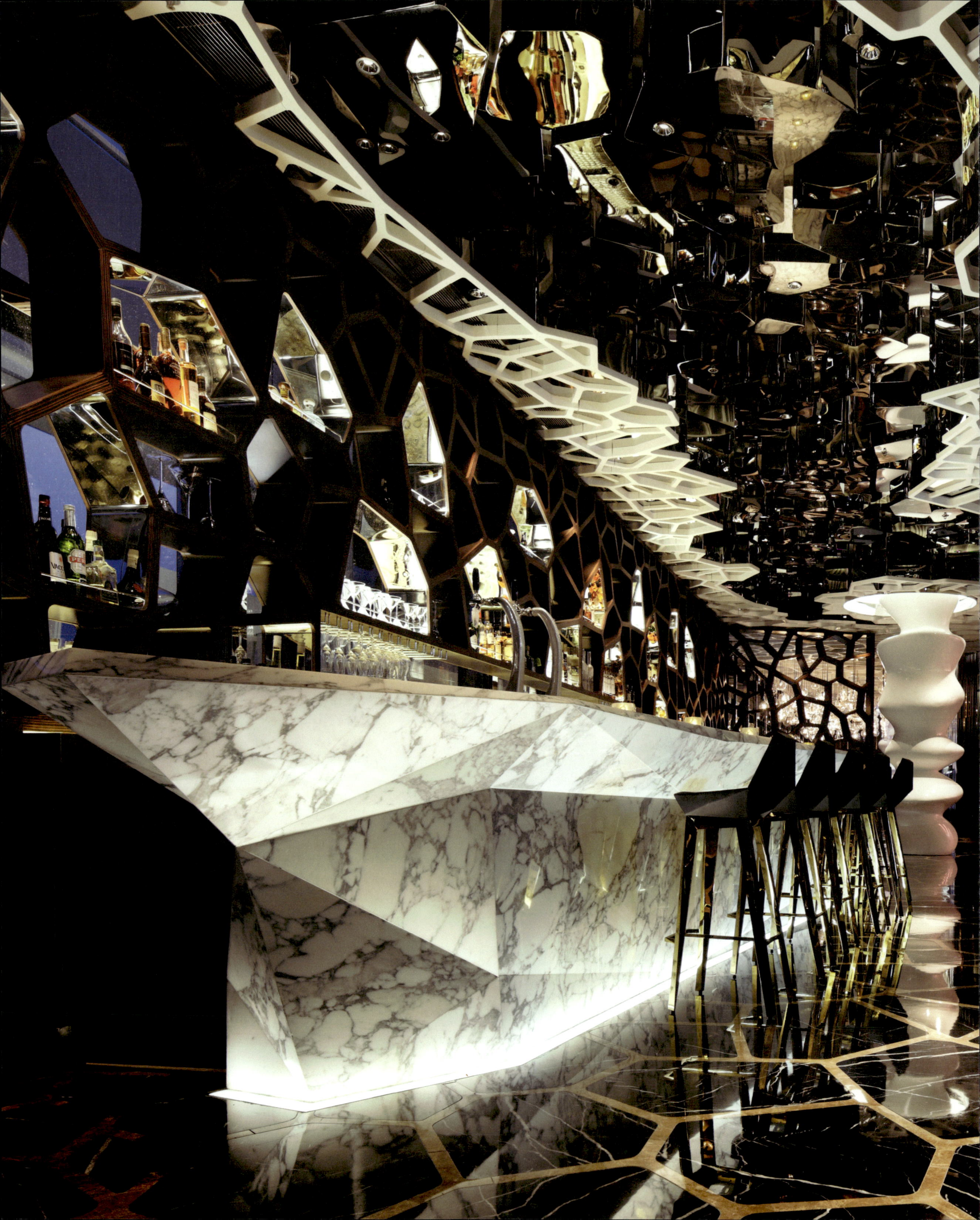

SHOWTIME

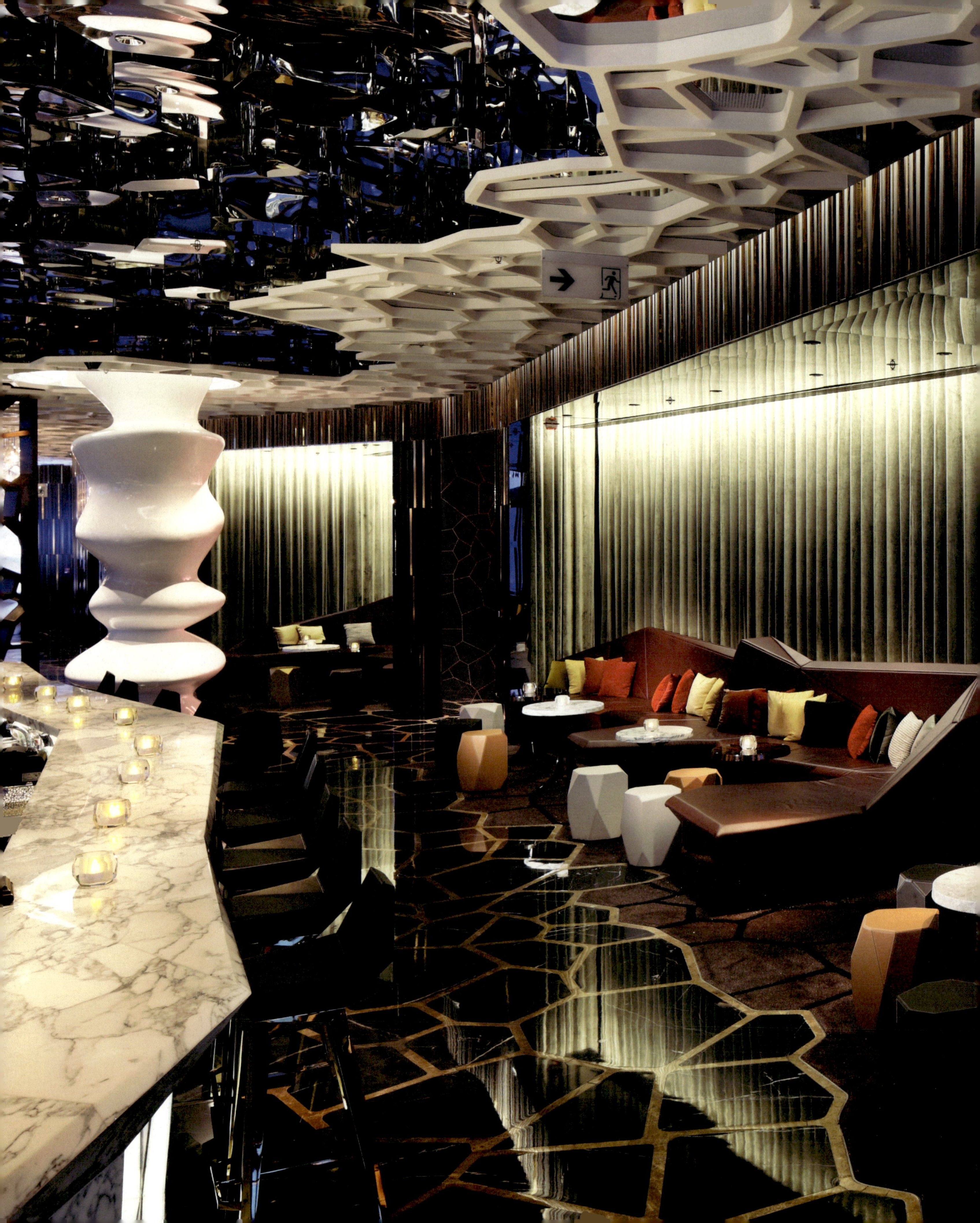

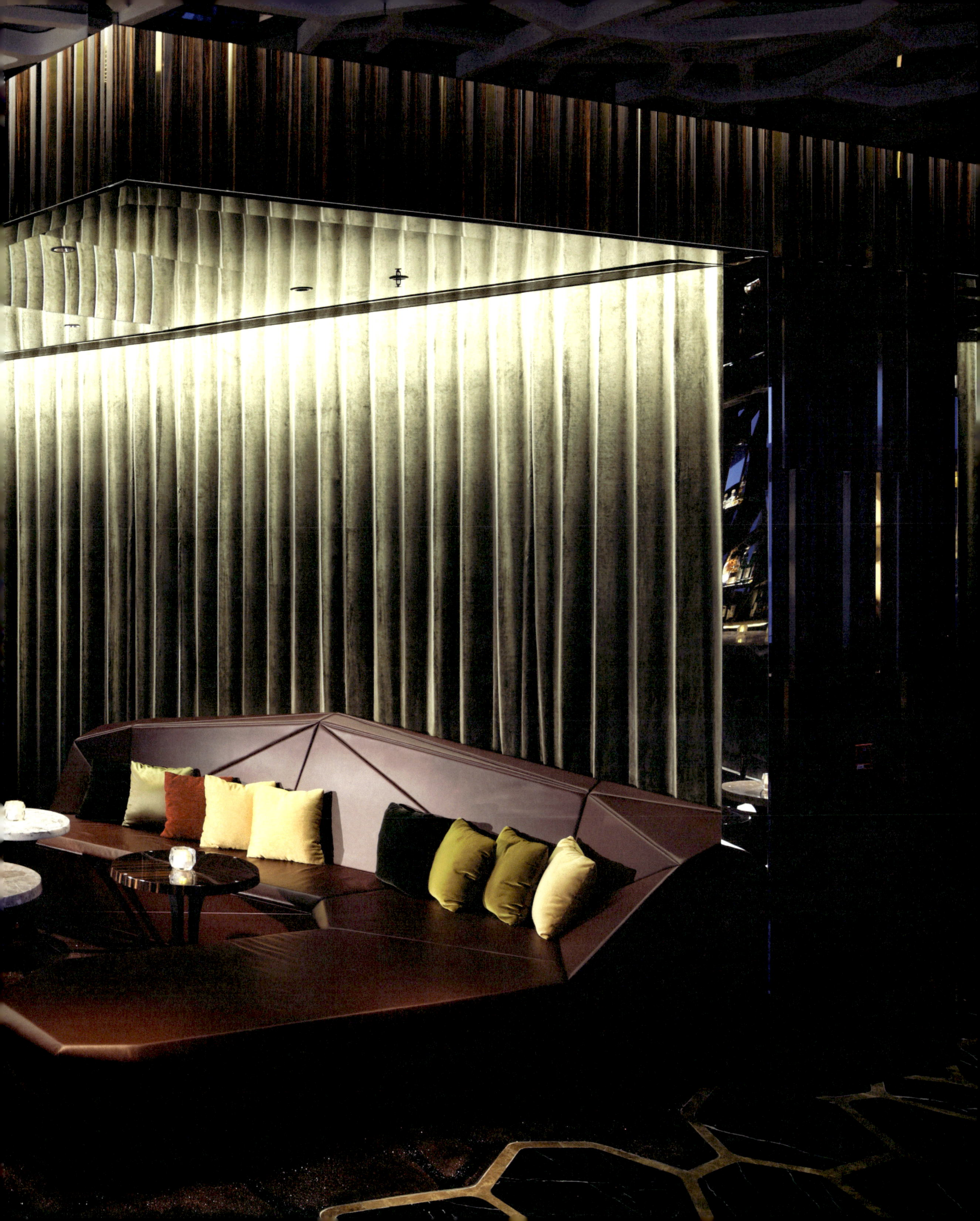

OZONE
Hong Kong, China

/ Perched atop the Kowloon Ritz-Carlton, the world's tallest hotel, *Ozone's* name is well-chosen. The nightclub takes up most of the 118th floor and its terrace, and includes a hypergraphical bar, lounge, lobby lounge, dining room, and tapas bar. The design team envisioned an "Edenic Experiment," a man-made take on nature that informs the geometric shapes that pattern the floor and turn into wall screens and the drop ceiling, the rain-like chandeliers and iceberg of a bar.

/ Design: Wonderwall

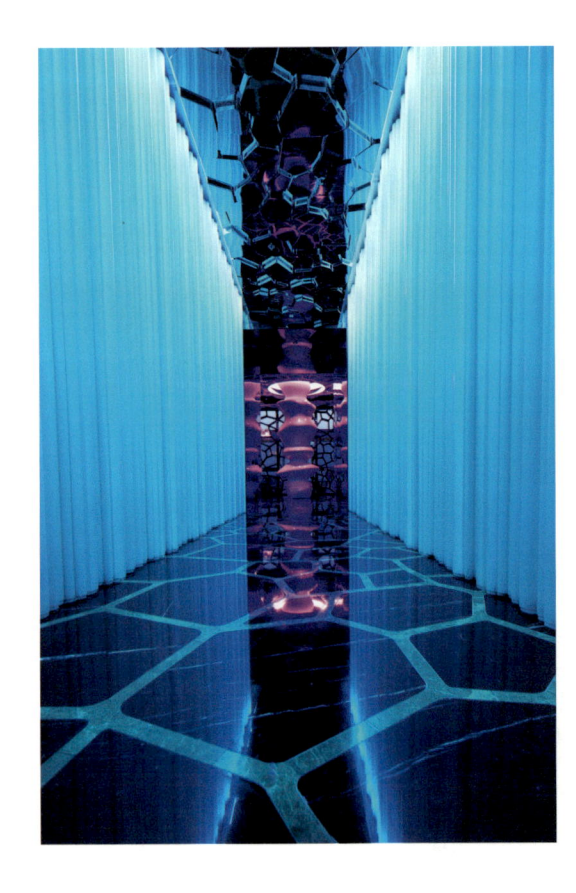

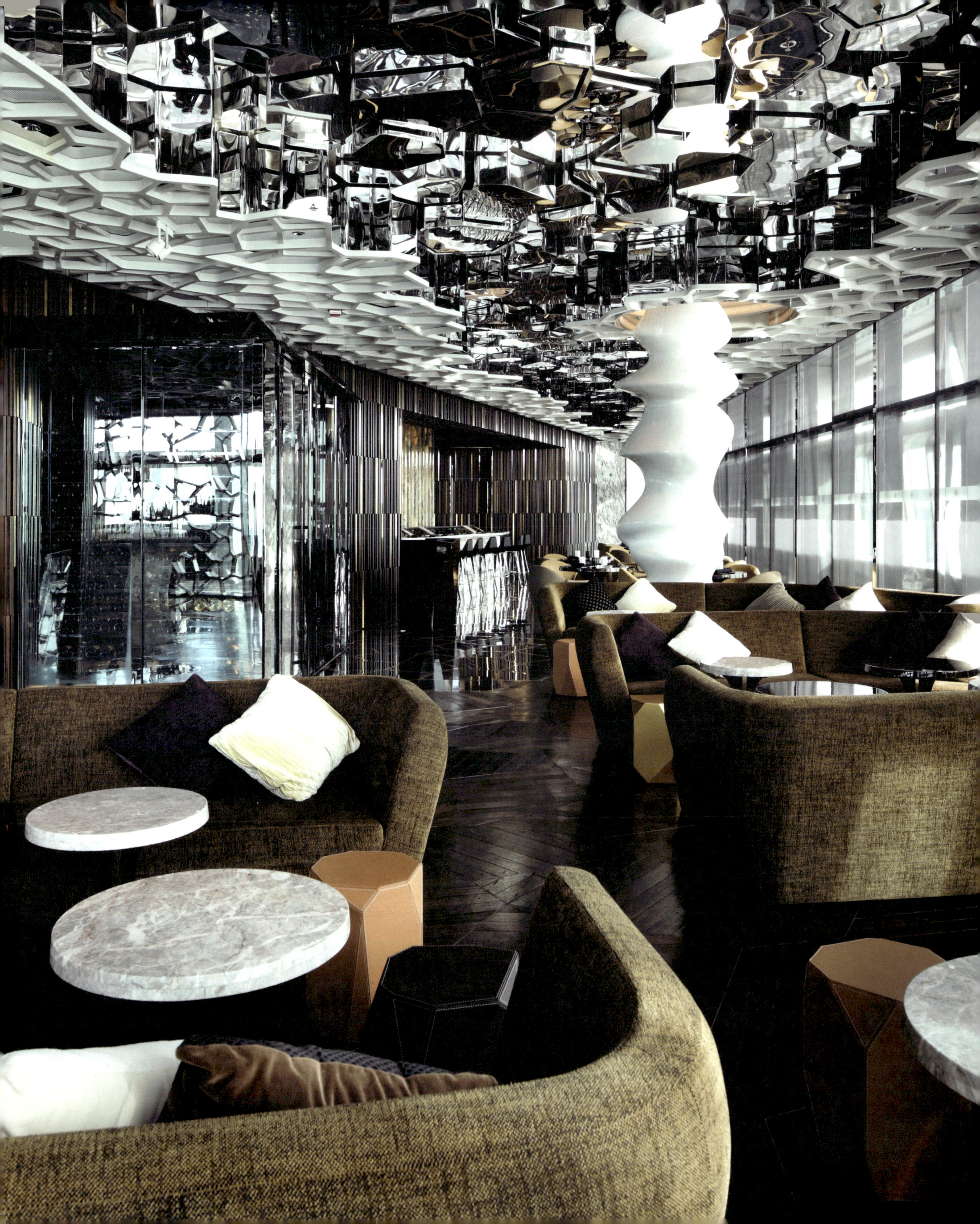

STATIONEN UPPSALA THREE
Uppsala, Sweden

/ Uppsala's railway station, just north of Stockholm, opened in 1866, finally bringing the city truly into the European fold. Architect Adolf Wilhelm Edelsvärd designed an impressive station building in the shape of a small castle. Now creative director Erik Nissen Johansen has transformed it into a day-to-night brasserie that combines Parisian style with London energy and the aromas of Rome and enables the station to play a central role in the life of the city once again. Stationen's interior design is meant to be "timeless and sustainable," and was inspired by the frequent travels of Edelsvärd who designed no less than 300 railway stations during his prolific career.

/ Design: Stylt Trampoli

/ Client: Svenssons Krogar

/ Type of Food/Drinks/Specialties: Brasserie, bar, café

SHOWTIME

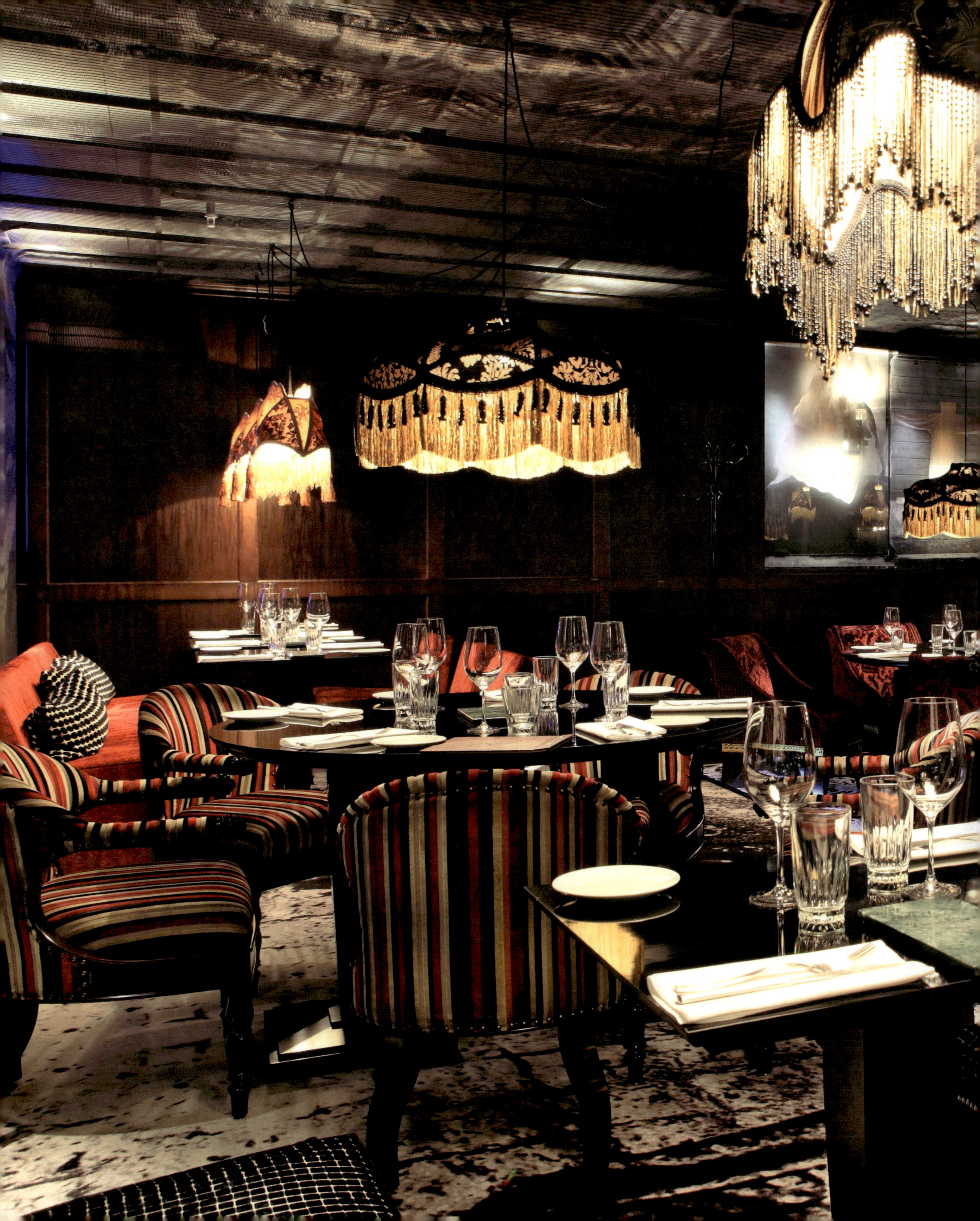

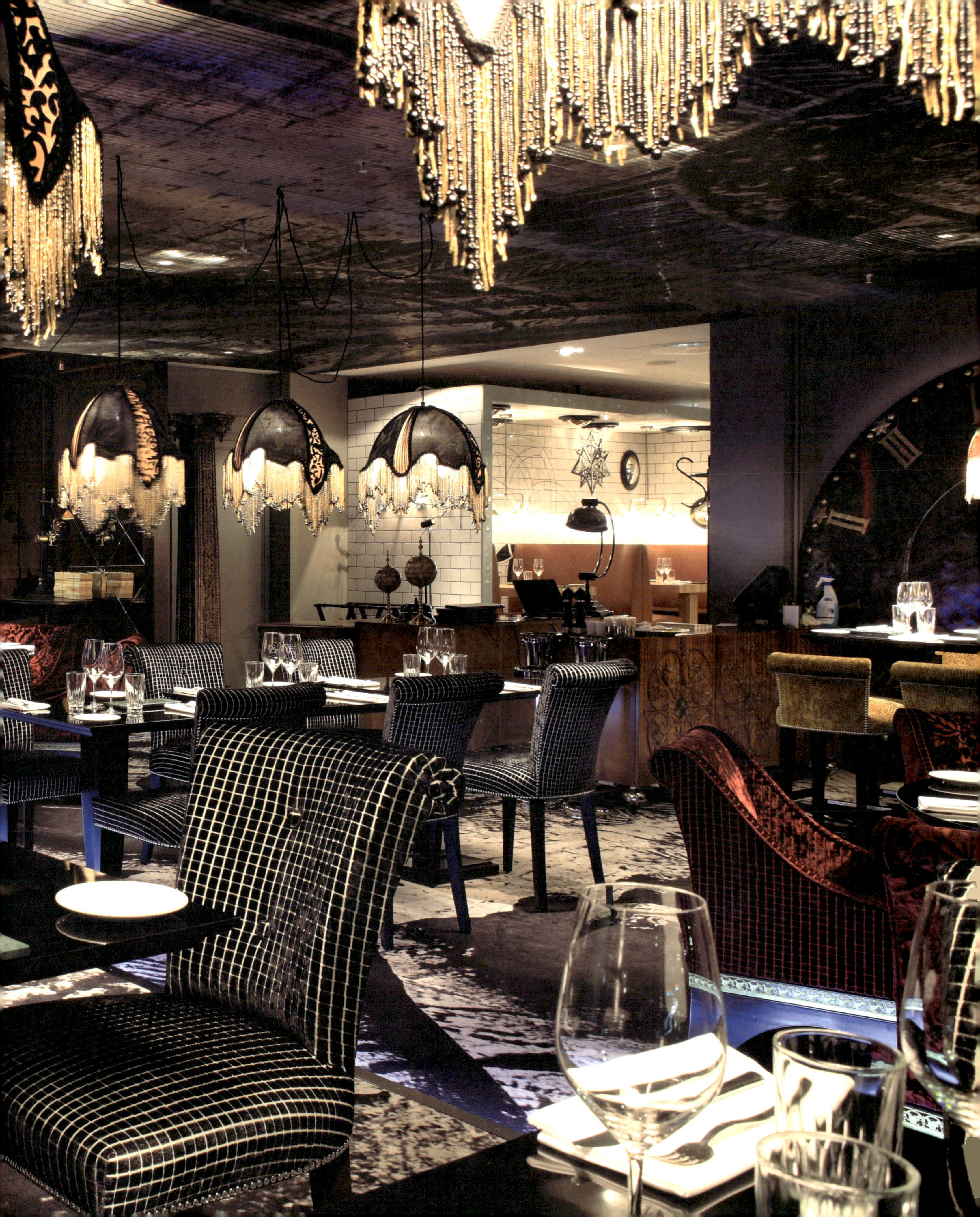

238 / 239

GRIFFINS STEAKHOUSE EXTRAORDINAIRE
Stockholm, Sweden

/ Stylt calls itself a conceptual design agency for good reason: diners at this classic American steakhouse are greeted by a space evoking the eclectic character of a pair of fictional hosts, the eponymous Griffins. Stylt's Erik Nissen Johansen, who invented the couple, remade the existing low, box-like interiors to tell a domestic story that revolves around them. A mishmash of tufted seating, thick drapery, fringed lightshades, and cushy Oriental carpets is paired with modern white tile, minimalist banquettes, and a variegated collection of interesting doo-dads. The interior elements may be considered heterogeneous, but in fact the restaurant as a whole stands in even starker contrast to the industrial neighborhood around it.

/ Design: Stylt Trampoli
/ Client: Stureplansgruppen
/ Type of Food/Drinks/Specialties: Steakhouse

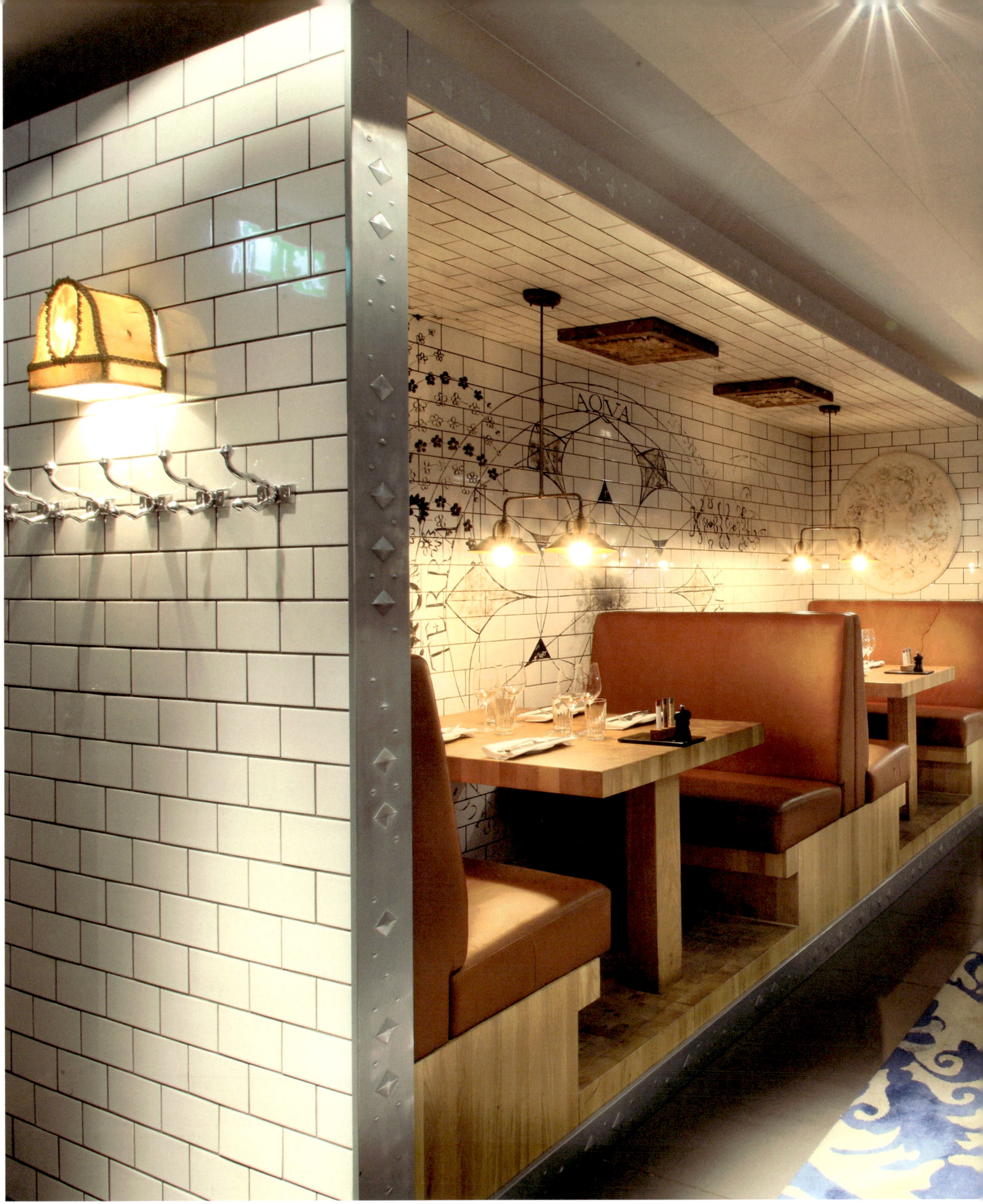
AQVA

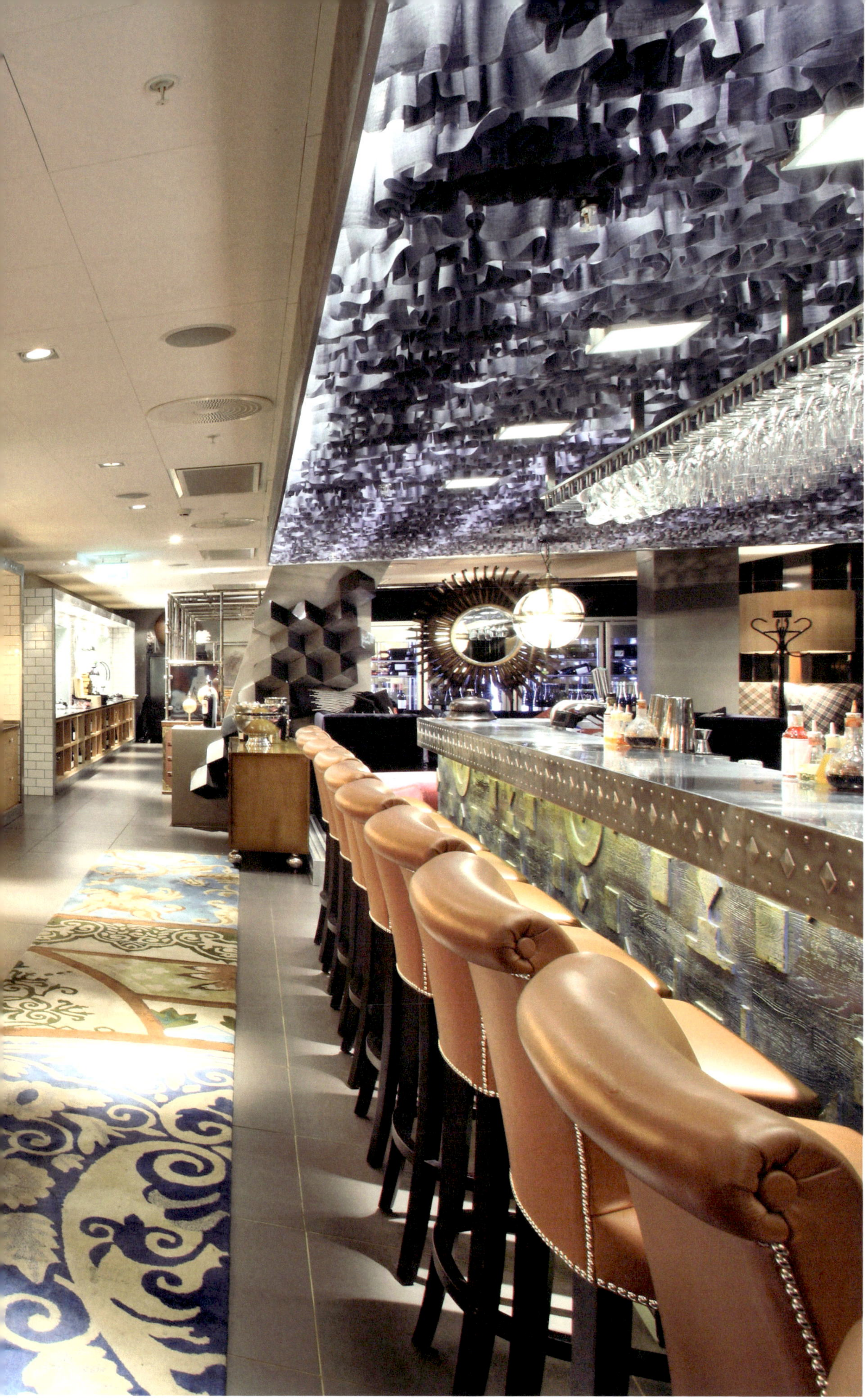

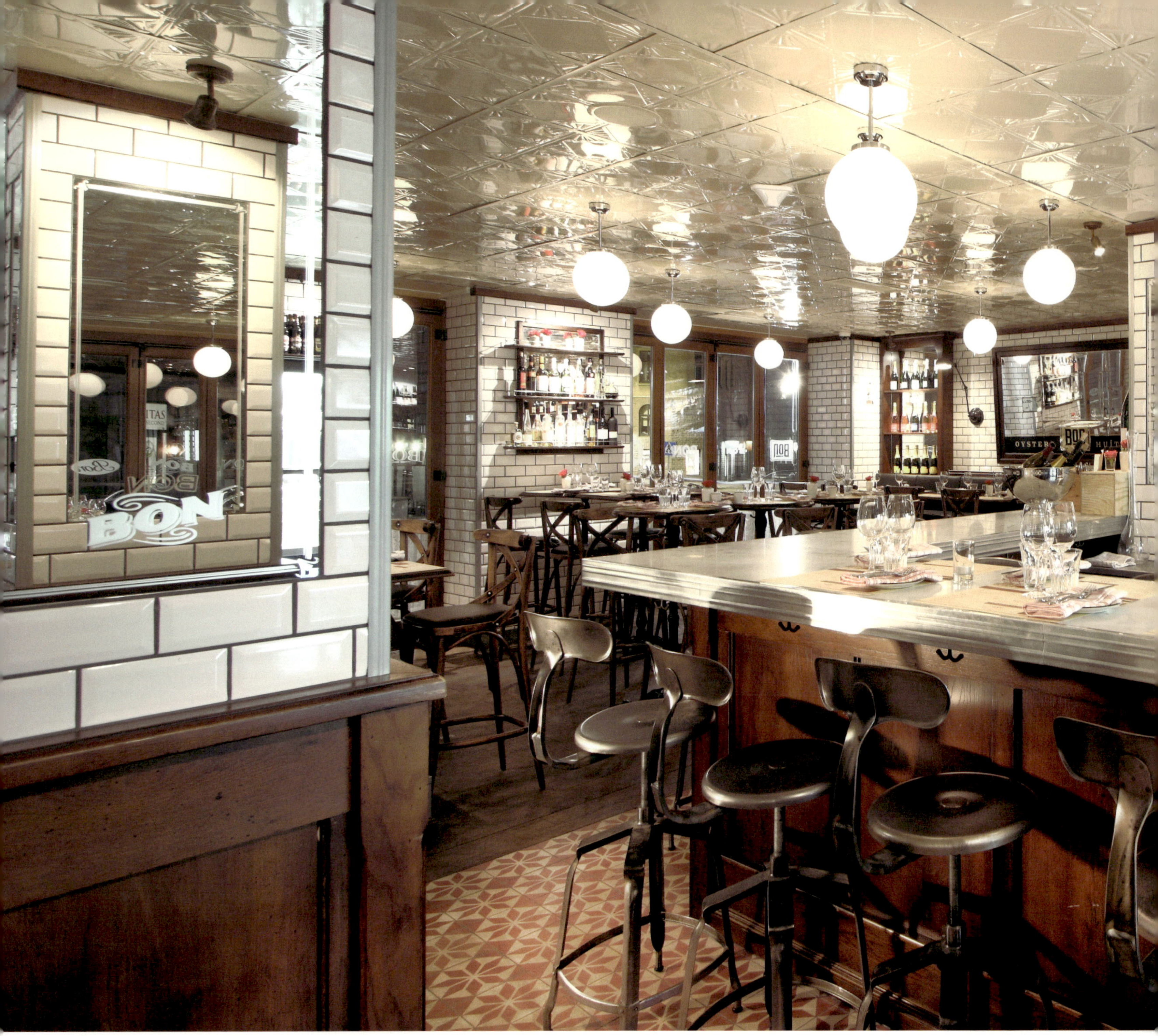
BON

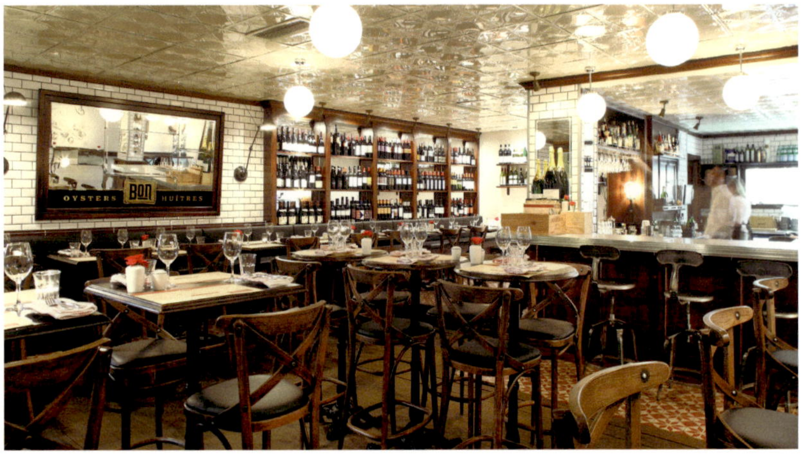
OYSTERS
BON
HUÎTRES

BON
Göteborg, Sweden

/ Once again, the designers at Stylt concocted a heady mixture of history and the brand new in the form of a French brasserie that is intended to have the character of an old hole in the wall on a side-street in Marseille or Barcelona. Johansen's team found the mosaic floor in northern Africa and the windows in a barn in southwest Sweden, but the chairs and bar stools are all newly manufactured classics from southern Europe. The large zinc and marble bar was handcrafted by carpenter Per Berndtsson while Johansen himself forged a grand mirror that lends the space an illusion of greater depth.

/ Design: Stylt Trampoli
/ Client: Kerdos
/ Type of Food/Drinks/Specialties: French brasserie

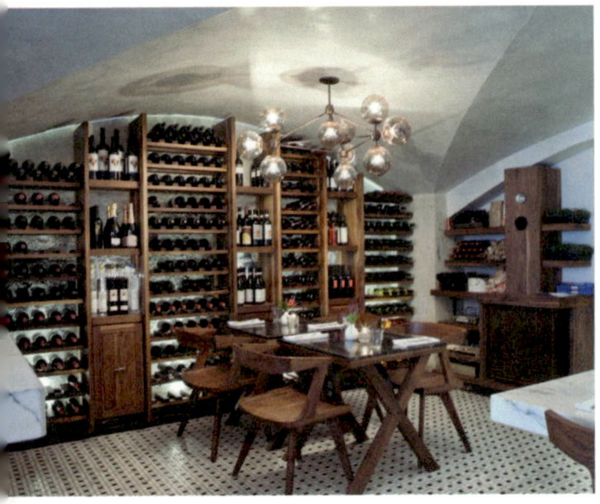

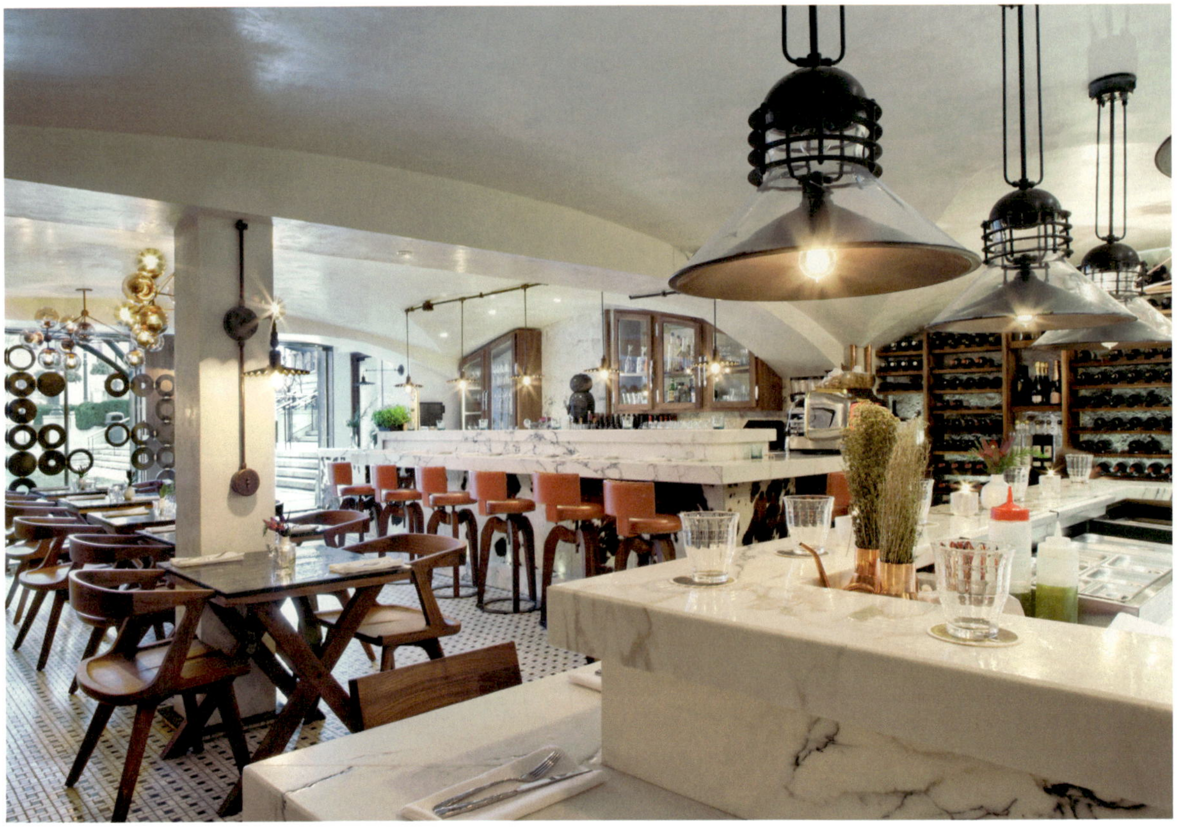

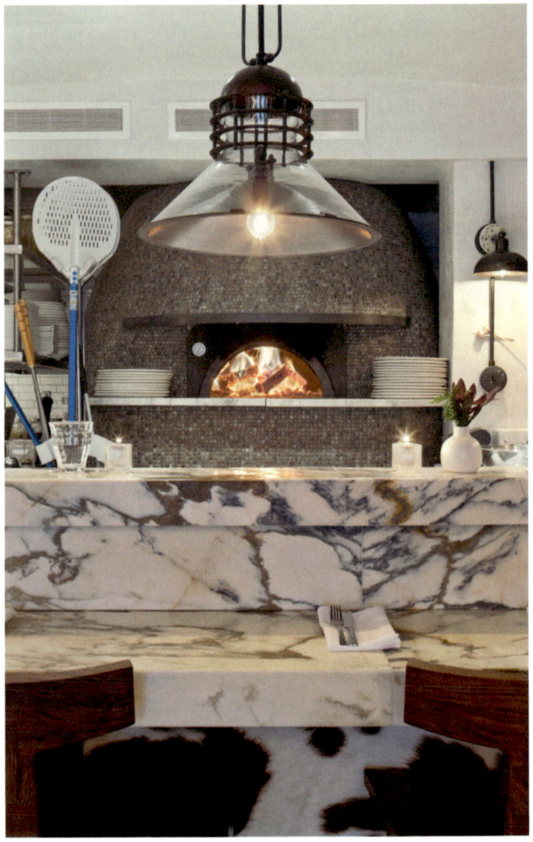

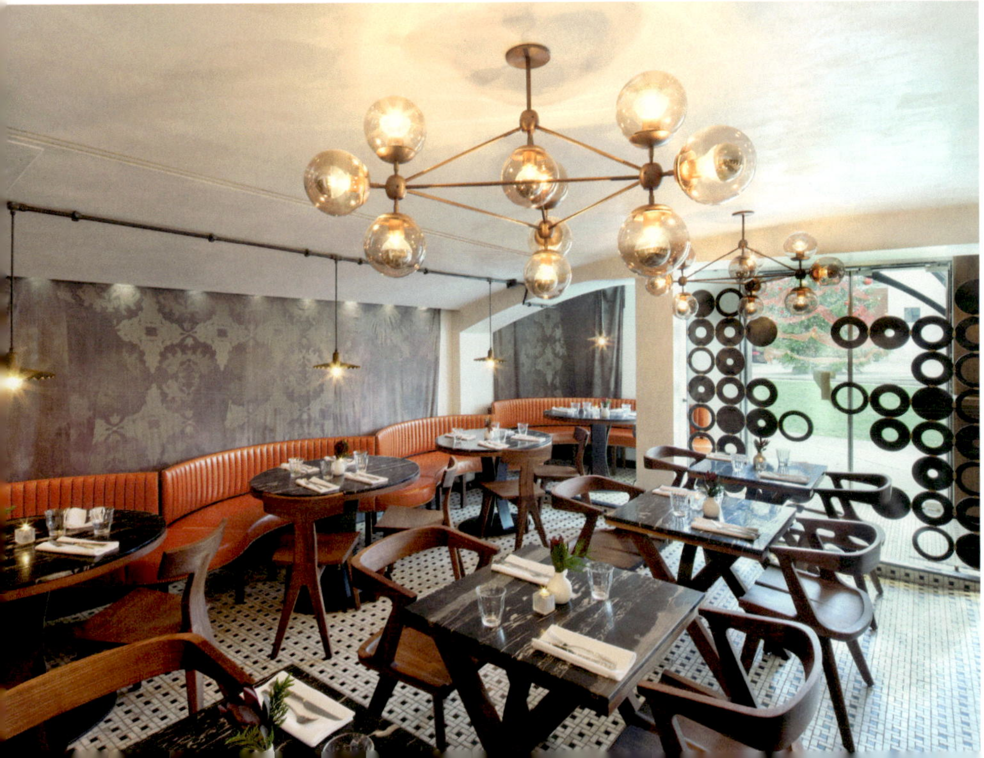

SHOWTIME

7 ENOTECA & PIZZERIA
Old Oakville, Ontario, Canada

/ Situated in a small Canadian town, this 50-seat restaurant serves Neapolitan food—though with a local and sustainable bent. The space envisioned by Brayan Stoyanov recalls an idyllic evening he spent in the Villa Lysis on the island of Capri. Tucked into the basement of the village's historic post office, it features grainy wood and glass globes, vaulted marmorino ceilings, tiled floors, richly veined marble and leather bar tops, orange leather banquettes, and weathered stone. Cameo appearances are put in by Matthew Hilton's T-back Fin dining chair and his finely crafted Colombo armchair for Portuguese label De La Espada.

/ Design: Stoyanov

/ Client: Artur Koczur

/ Type of Food/Drinks/Specialties: Neapolitan food; pizza made in wood burning oven; local and sustainable ingredients used where possible

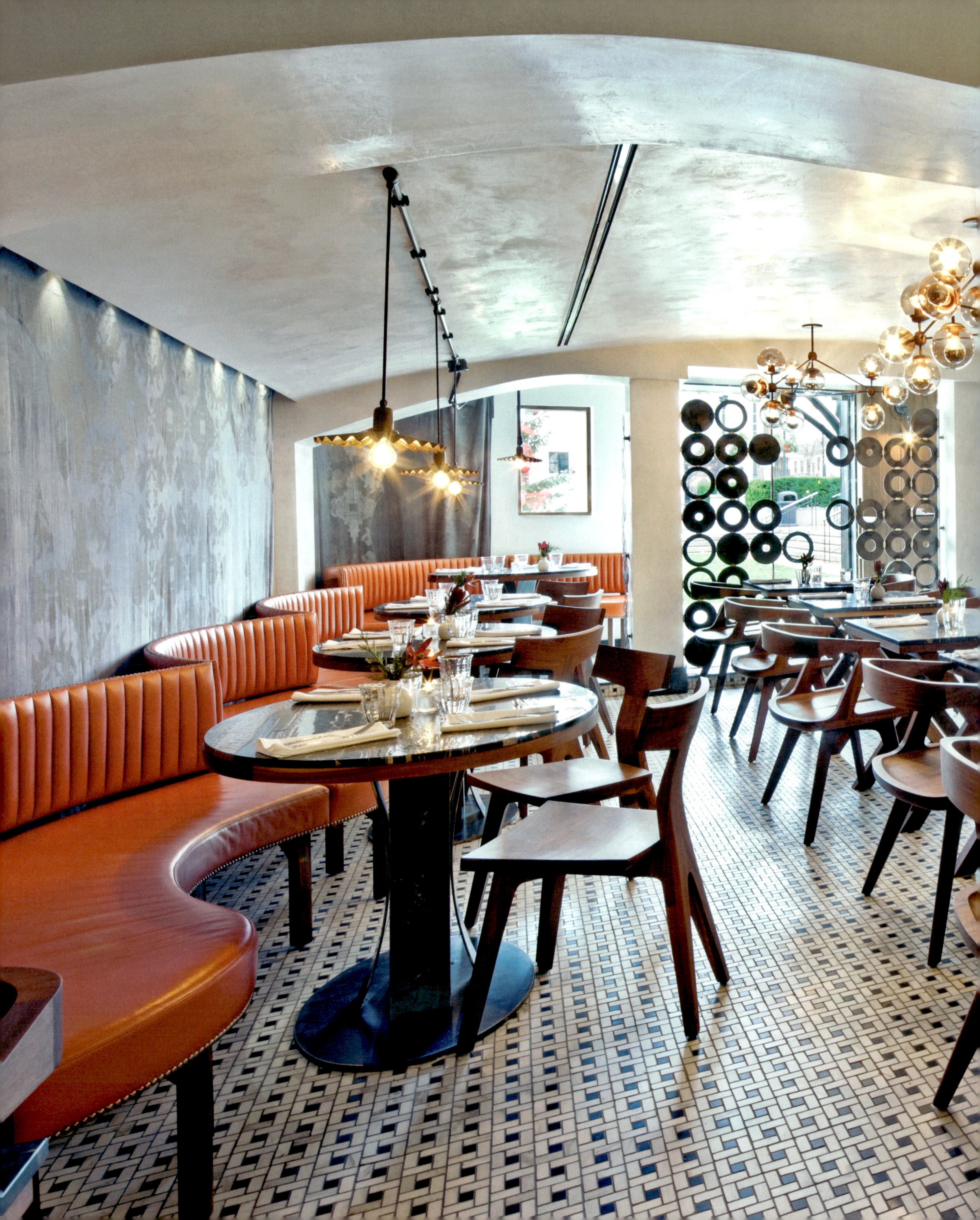

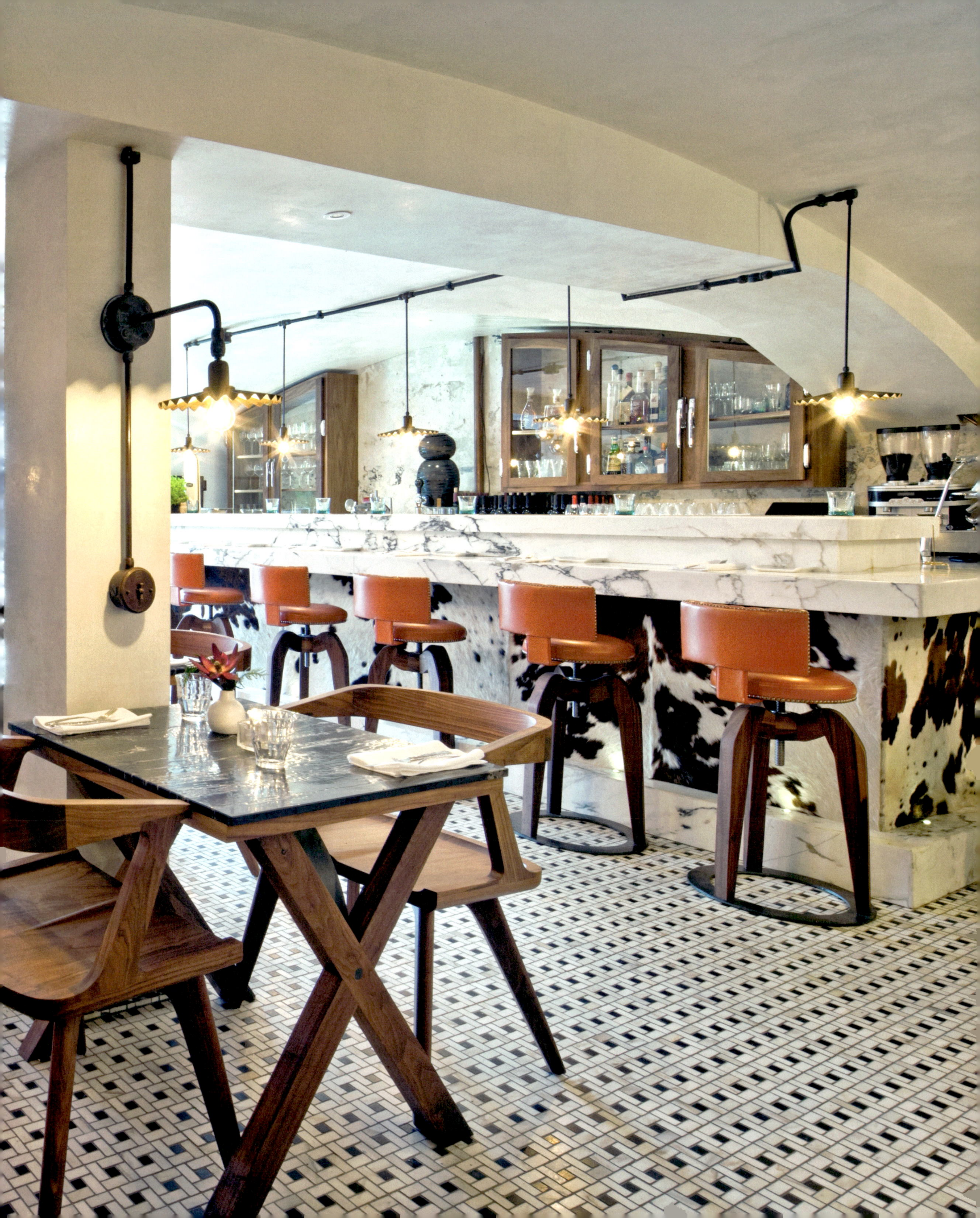

PAULY SAAL
Berlin, Germany

/ The *Pauly Saal* restaurant reaches the senses in a multitude of ways. Situated in the former Jewish Girls' School, the elegantly chandeliered interior also combines references to pastoral scenes, a bustling market, and the forest, among other eclectic inspirations. The theme that unites these disparate threads is drawn from Berlin's halcyon days of the 1920s and 30s.

/ Design: Stephan Landwehr, Boris Radczun

SHOWTIME

THE BACK ROOM
London, United Kingdom

/ Cadmium sought to design a versatile space for anything from performances to the ordinary functions of a bar while imbuing the space with a sense of recent history rediscovered. The result is a four-decade old time capsule filled with a variety of objects and furniture, arranged as if they had just been unburied. Details were closely considered: the design team scoured architectural salvage shops and then tapped a faux artist to wrap the whole thing in a nearly invisible patina of time.

/ Design: Cadmium Architects & Designers
/ Client: Hard Rock Café International

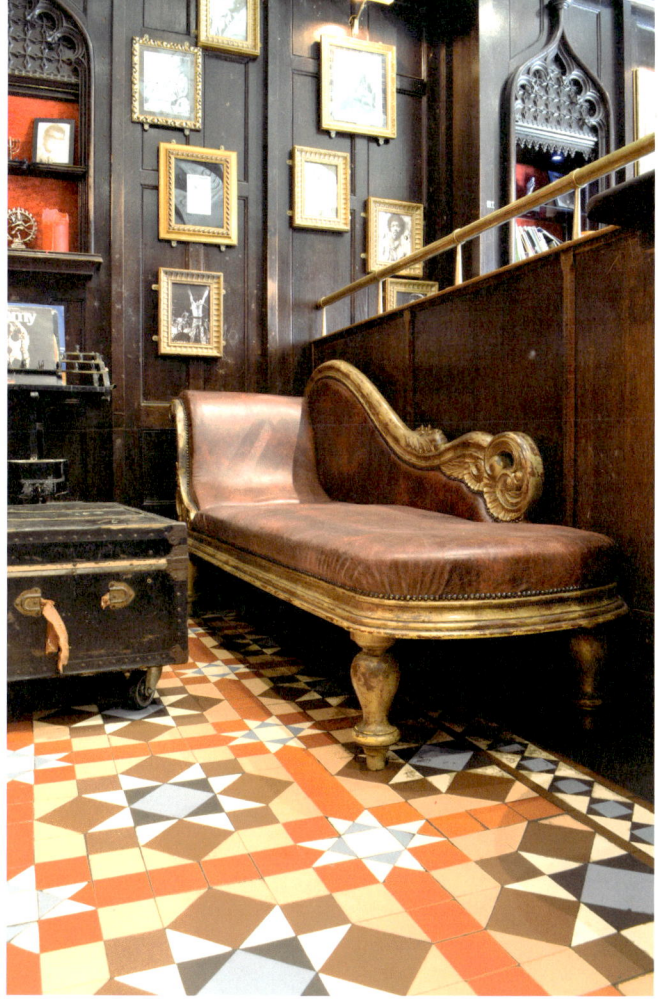

SHOWTIME

PDT (PLEASE DON'T TELL) BAR
NYC, New York, USA

/ In local nightlife parlance "Please don't tell" means, "please tell all the right people," which sums up the speakeasy style of the late aughts. The attitude is a bummer, but the interiors are not. Patrons find the "secret" entrance of *PDT* through an antique telephone booth in the back of a hot dog shop. Inside, a small room with a copper bar, bare brick walls, and wooden ceiling is inhabited by a taxidermied bear in a bowler hat and a rabbit with antlers, both of whom would be drinking the house's Corpse Reviver no. 2 (Cointreau, Lillet, lemon juice, and absinthe), if they could.

/ Design: Brian Shebairo

SHOWTIME

UPSTAIRS BERESFORD
Sydney, Australia

/ This live music venue is a mash-up of architectural eras in an art deco key that feels surprisingly contemporary. While working to synthesize these diverse aesthetics, the Phelan design team also aimed to make the spaces feel undesigned, as if each had evolved organically over time. They gave the windowless main room texture and depth by blending oversized herringbone timber panels in warm tones with bold and glossy powder-coated metals. The lighter colors strike a dominant chord that contrasts with dark finishes in heavily trafficked areas and all of it is set aglow by an orange pressed-tin ceiling décor.

/ Design: Kerry Phelan Design Office

/ Client: Justin Hemmes of Merivale

/ Type of Food/Drinks/Specialties: International live music venue and bar

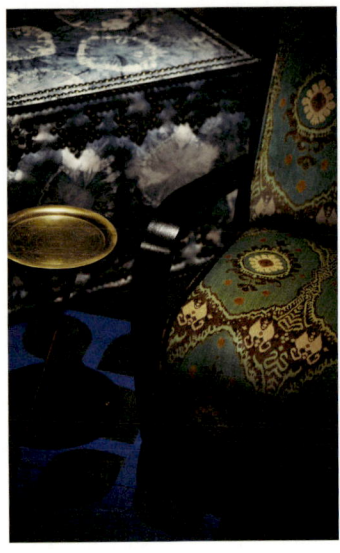

SHOWTIME

POISON D'AMOUR
Lisbon, Portugal

/ In this French gourmet pastry shop in Lisbon, the absence of color (black) and the sum of all colors (white) let the colorful pastries reign supreme. Without touching the original eighteenth-century structure, the architects painted walls, ceilings, and floors matte black, leaving only a limestone ceiling arch and counter with a ribbon of immaculate white that belts and furnishes the space. Louis XVI chairs and a dark portrait of his queen provide the décor.

Although it turns out that poor Marie Antoinette didn't actually say "Let them eat cake," she did, however, eat a great deal of cake herself, which amounts to much the same thing and makes her the best-dressed martyr a patisserie could claim.

/ Design: 71 Arquitectos and David Carqueijeiro

/ Client: Poison d`amour

SHOWTIME

STARHILL TEA SALON
Kuala Lumpur, Malaysia

/ Though Malaysia was once colonized by the tea-swilling British and tea is grown abundantly all around, the designer felt that a place serving authentic tea was nowhere to be found in the heart of Kuala Lumpur. The furniture was designed to be assembled at the site and the display column is also modular. In keeping with the high-end shopping mall setting, Design Spirits opted for a voluptuous theme, which is also reflected in the furnishings, ceiling patterns, and even the carpets. The lighting creates a simultaneously classic and contemporary look-and-feel.

/ Design: design spirits
/ Client: Autodome
/ Material: Floor: custom made carpet; Ceiling: laser cut MDF board with walnut textured sticker and pattern cut gold sticker; Waist wall: curved clear acrylic, pattern laser cut gold sticker on acrylic, lenticular sheet; Column: walnut veneer and powder coated tea cans
/ Type of Food/Drinks/Specialties: Tea salon

SHOWTIME

LA SOCIÉTÉ BISTRO
Toronto, Canada

/ Modeled after a Paris bistro but located on the high street of Canada's most cosmopolitan city instead, La Société is lavishly appointed with a majestic stained-glass ceiling and a seafood display that serves as a focal point for the bistro's plush atmosphere. But the crowning glory is undoubtedly the pewter bar top with a custom-designed and handcrafted edge profile by the metal-magic men at Bastille.

/ Design: Bastille Metal Works
/ Client: La Société Bistro
/ Material: Handcrafted pewter

THE HOTEL MONTELEONE CAROUSEL BAR
New Orleans, USA

/ This decorative, high-end bar draws on the traditions and character of New Orleans' French Quarter and the story of the Monteleone family and hotel, while updating the design to suit the zeitgeist. The redesign of the spinning bar top was conceptualized and realized by Bastille Metal Works in handcrafted pewter while the Puccini Group reimagined the classic bar décor.

/ Design: Bastille Metal Works and Puccini Group

/ Material: Handcrafted pewter

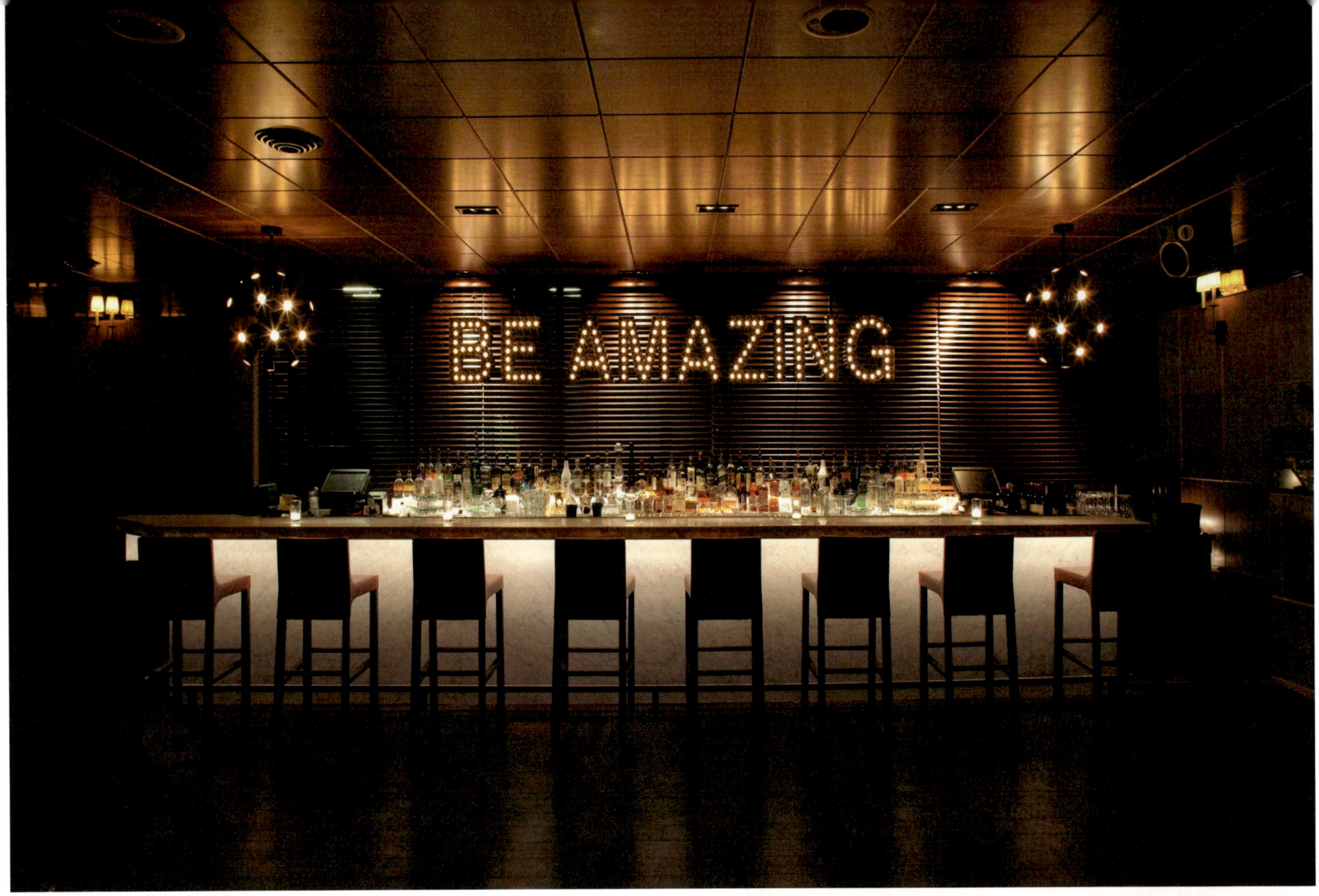
BE AMAZING

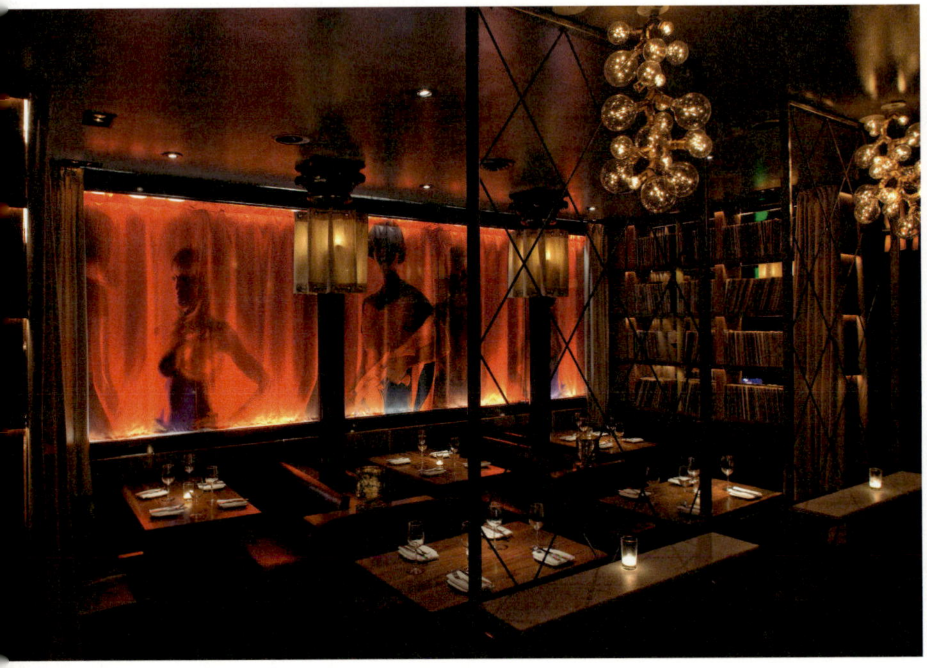

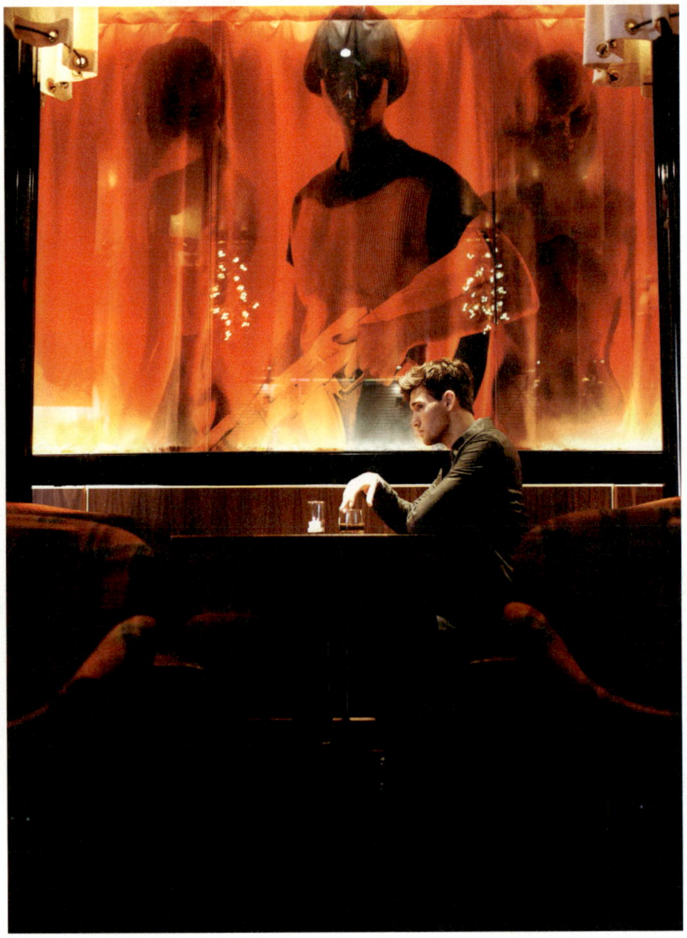

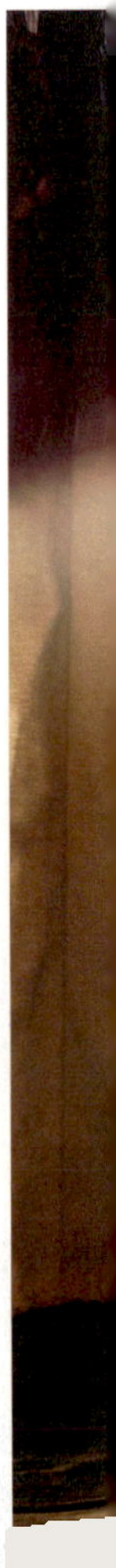

SHOWTIME

CHAMBERS EAT + DRINK
San Francisco, California, USA

/ How do you provide luxury to people who already have too much of it? The Phoenix Hotel seems to have an answer. A beating heart of low-key luxe in San Francisco's once-seedy Tenderloin district, it has acquired a reputation for hosting rock stars and celebs who want to keep a low profile. In the hotel's restaurant and lounge, luxury isn't about fan-fare and flashiness; it's about privacy, comfort, and cultured space. The interior has something of a latter-day gentleman's library, but one in which the books are replaced with vinyl. LPs that is. A music history lesson in the form of hundreds of legendary and less legendary albums.

/ Design: Mister Important Design
/ Client: Joie de Vivre Hotels

BAIXA
Porto, Portugal

/ This bar helped to reclaim an after-business-hours badland in a downtown area formerly limited to municipal buildings and office space that went catatonic at night instead of gin-and-tonic. Cruz's *Baixa* is a hybrid of the Beaux-Arts aesthetic that surrounds it and something altogether more modern. The lounge is a model of art deco—rosette-sown ceiling, wooden panels, Escher-esque floor tiles—but just as suddenly as it begins, the décor melts, Dali-like, into a deformed threshold that leads into a computer-sculpted wooden tunnel. At the other end is a dance floor inspired by Sol Lewitt but with a mirrored ceiling that's all disco ball and night fever.

/ Design: José Carlos Cruz

"Baixa is a hybrid of the Beaux-Arts aesthetic that surrounds it and something altogether more modern."

SHOWTIME

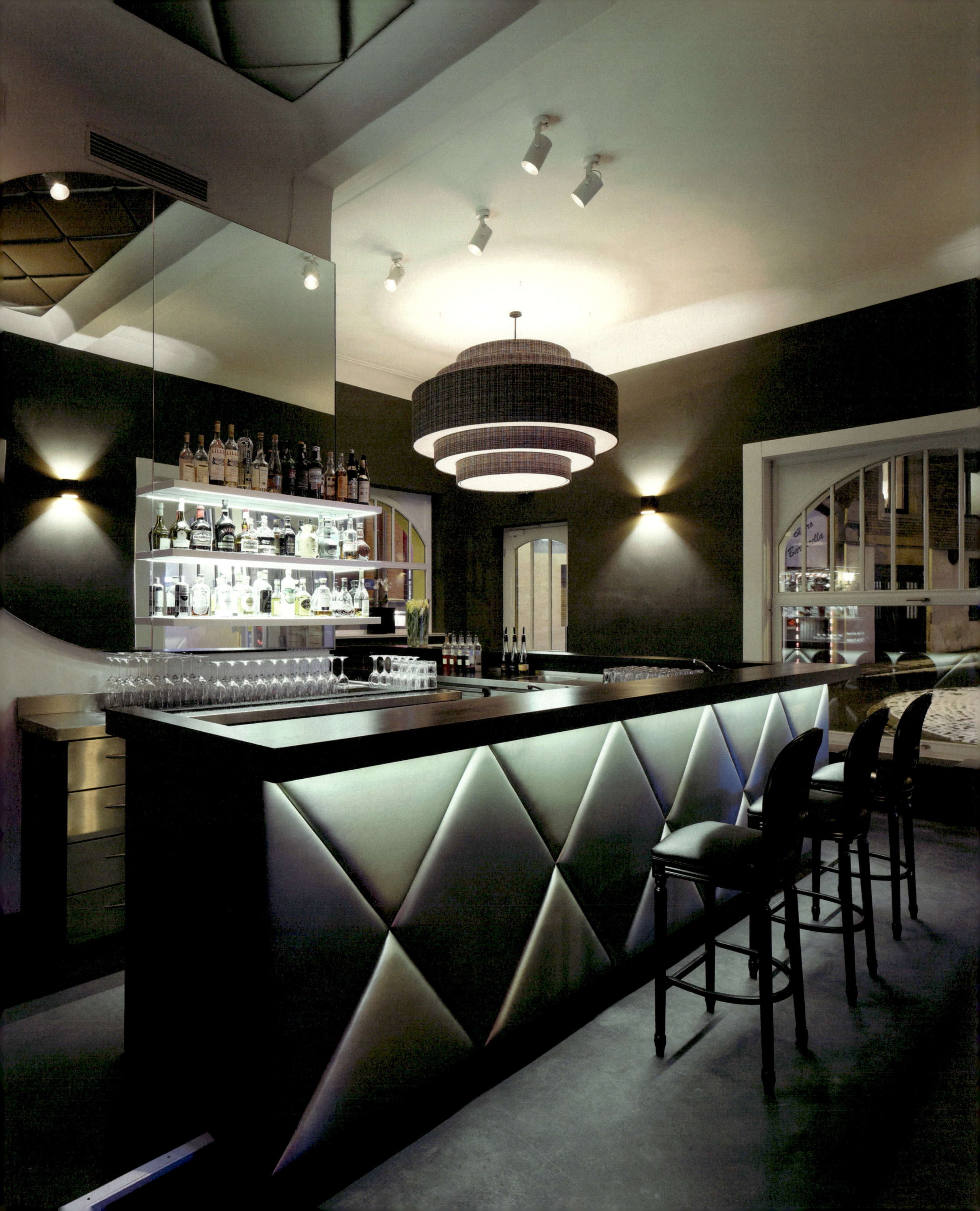

SHOWTIME

BAR FOU FOU
Stuttgart, Germany

/ Architects and builders of brand identity, IFG designed this champagne bar on the edge of Stuttgart's red light district as a cross between a boudoir and salon, inspired by the location and its history as an antiques shop. Each of the four salons has a distinct character. Upstairs, the Red Salon features thick pile carpet to contrast with the smooth cast floor of the bar, bronzed mirrors, brass lights, and hexagonal occasional tables. Downstairs, a refurbished wooden floor, jet-black furniture, and a weighty mauve curtain lead to saloon doors and the smokers' lounge with its dark-brown, crocodile leather wallpaper, Chesterfield armchairs, and open fireplace.

/ Design: Ippolito Fleitz Group – Identity Architects

/ Client: VENKO

/ Type of Food/Drinks/Specialties: Cocktails, champagne

AS APERITIVO
Ljubljana, Slovenia

/ Following the demolition of the beloved wooden garden pavilion at one of Ljubljana's best-loved Italian eateries, Zupanc designed a concrete structure that guards a century-old Caucasian wingnut tree with glass walls to draw in light and air, terrazzo and oak flooring, and brass and copper detailing. To bring the garden indoors, she used cherry-like clusters of lights from her 2009 La Femme et la Maison collection. Zupanc also used her 5 O'Clock tables for Moooi but created bespoke serving tables, restroom sinks, modular benches, mirrors, and wine cabinets for the rest.

/ Design: Nika Zupanc
/ Client: Sebastijan and Svetozar Raspopović
/ Material: Oak, brass, copper, metal, terrazzo stone floor
/ Type of Food/Drinks/Specialties: Italian, sea food, cocktails, wines

SHOWTIME

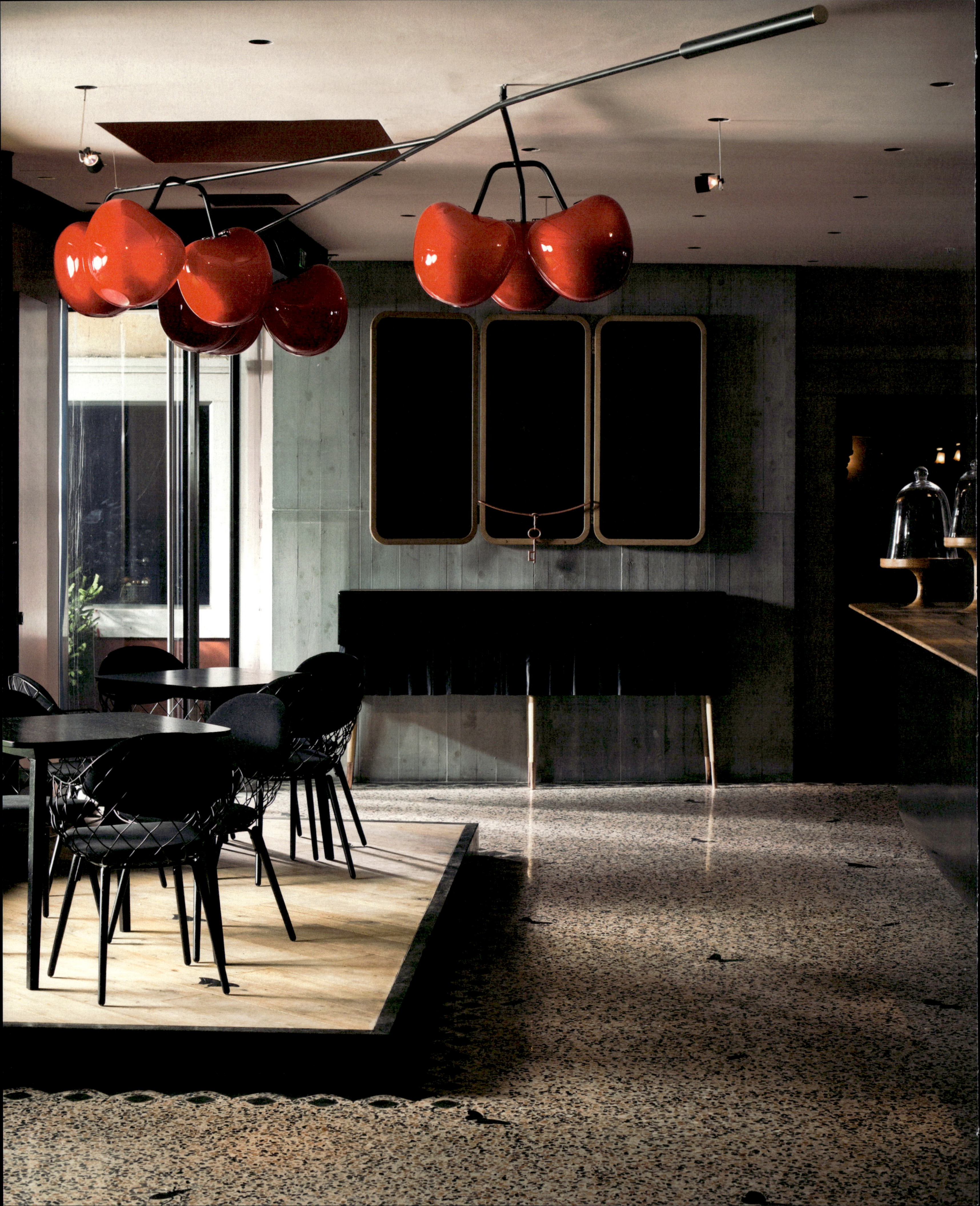

SHOWTIME

XANTHI
Sydney, Australia

/ In Westfield, *Xanthi* is a Greek restaurant that skips the trappings, and design traps, of so many Greek restaurants. Here, a vague Oriental atmosphere gives a nod to the influence of Byzantium on Greek culture. A cloud of silk forms a canopy above the room and along its perimeter with Eastern lanterns overhead and a bright scarlet Turkish carpet underfoot. Along the walls, angular benches are draped and softened with brightly dyed kilims. At the entranced embedded in the diagonally lain white tiles, small windows give guests a peek into the kitchen at the chefs hard at work.

/ Design: Luchetti Krelle

SHOWTIME

TEEQ
Kuala Lumpur, Malaysia

/ On the eighth floor roof parking of a mall, this brasserie focuses attention away from the not-so-great views around it onto the ceiling, which welcomes guests with an avant-garde installation featuring undulating waves of wooden ribs. Designer Yukichi Kawai corseted the ceiling with Nyatoh timber and created an internal wall from 6 mm glass and 2 mm mirror-polished stainless steel, gypsum board, and laminate. Finally, LED strips were mounted behind the ribs.

/ Design: design spirits

/ Client: YTL Land

/ Material: Floor: Nyatoh timber; Internal wall: glass, mirror, stainless steel mirror-polish finish, gypsum board and laminate board wood pattern

/ Type of Food/Drinks/Specialties: Brasserie

SHOWTIME

JULIET SUPPERCLUB
NYC, New York, USA

/ Flying carpets, glittering cities, wealth beyond belief: Chef Todd English's mideastern supper club is based on the Persian legend of *The Thousand and One Nights* and like its surfeit of narrative richness, the space is a trove of intrepid patterns, scales, and textures—mirrored mosaic tiles, glossy black laser-cut ribs that join walls and ceiling, Mediterranean blue lacquered tables, and diamond-fretted banquette upholstery—that survive each night because they are so cleverly composed. A "flying carpet" of golden reflective tiles drapes over the entire main room beneath a firmament of Seljuk stars and, like the tales, the shape of the sculptural ceiling ribs shifts with one's point of view.

/ Design: Antonio Di Oronzo

/ Client: Chef Todd English

/ Material: Mirrored mosaic tiles, black gloss laser-cut ribs, laser-cut ceiling with white and mirrored layers, blue lacquered tables, upholstered booth seating

SHOWTIME

STAREIGHT
WuXi, China

/ This 700 sq m steak house opened in a warehouse as part of a site revitalization project of a century-old factory compound. The design team, including Horace Pan, Alan Tse, and Ardy Tsoi, worked to preserve most of the original features while adding a mezzanine—and a glittering firmament—to the interiors: ceiling-suspended fiber optics illuminated in violet light create a "starry night" beneath the atrium's 10 m high pitched roof skylight. A full-height, mirror-finished, stainless steel wine rack and crystal chandelier highlight its verticality and volume. On the mezzanine, Panorama inserted a steel structure that serves as a semi-enclosed dining area and the starry night continues even into the washrooms, which feature a galaxy of black mirrors.

/ Design: Panorama

/ Client: Star Food Service (Suzhou)

SHOWTIME

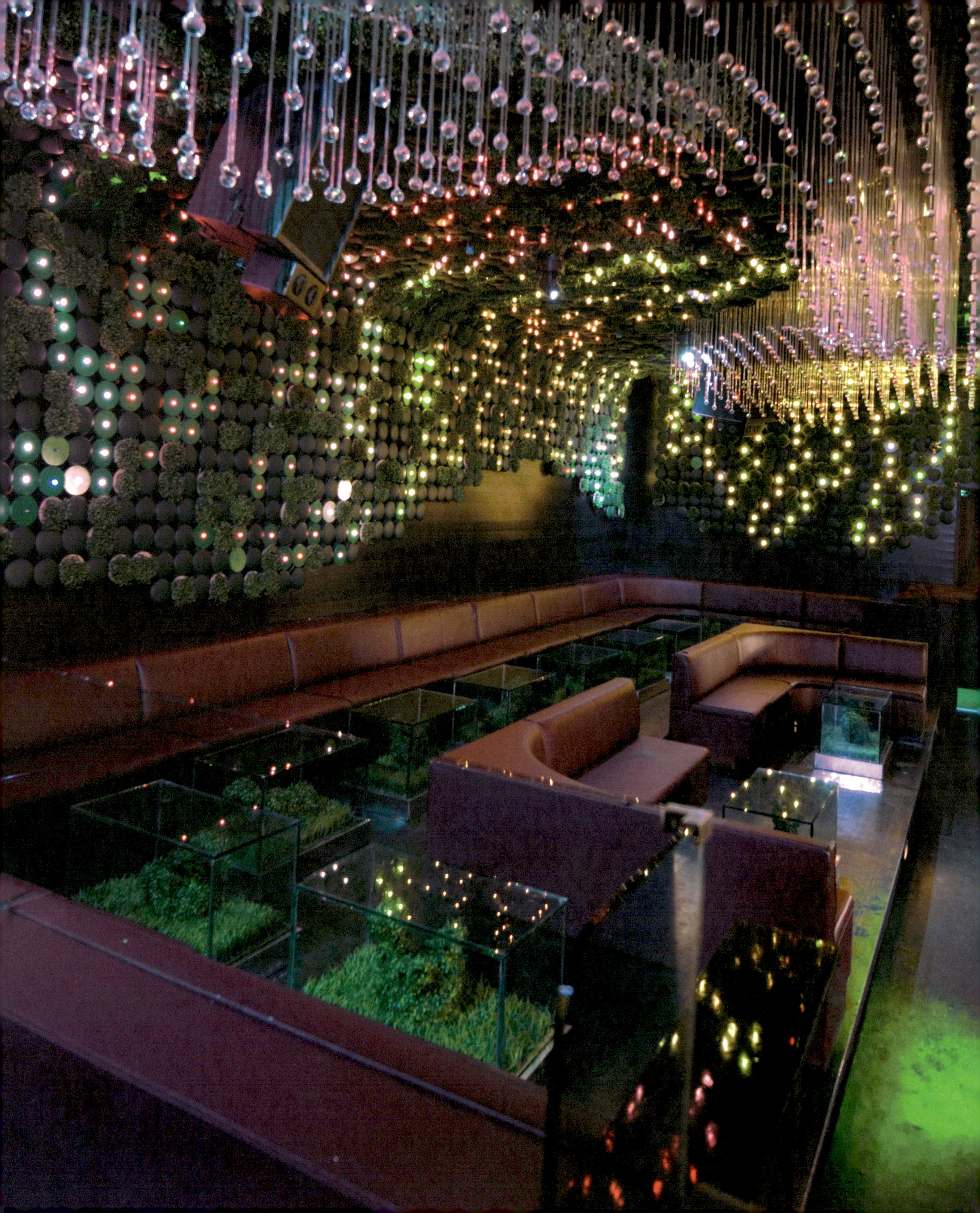

SHOWTIME

GREENHOUSE
NYC, New York, USA

/ Aptly named, this is the first nightclub in the United States to receive LEED certification for green design. Di Oronzo assembled the 370 sq m club from recycled or recyclable materials, but avoided a literal re-creation of a greenhouse. Instead, he planted a living landscape indoors: Laser-cut ribs link walls and ceiling, lined with 15 cm round panels arranged in a pattern generated by a fractal algorithm. Software runs 2500 LED lights that are sensitive to sound or video signals and an organic growth of 40 mm crystals represents a body of water on the ceiling that vibrates and glimmers in response to its environment.

/ Design: Antonio Di Oronzo
/ Client: Jon Bakhshi

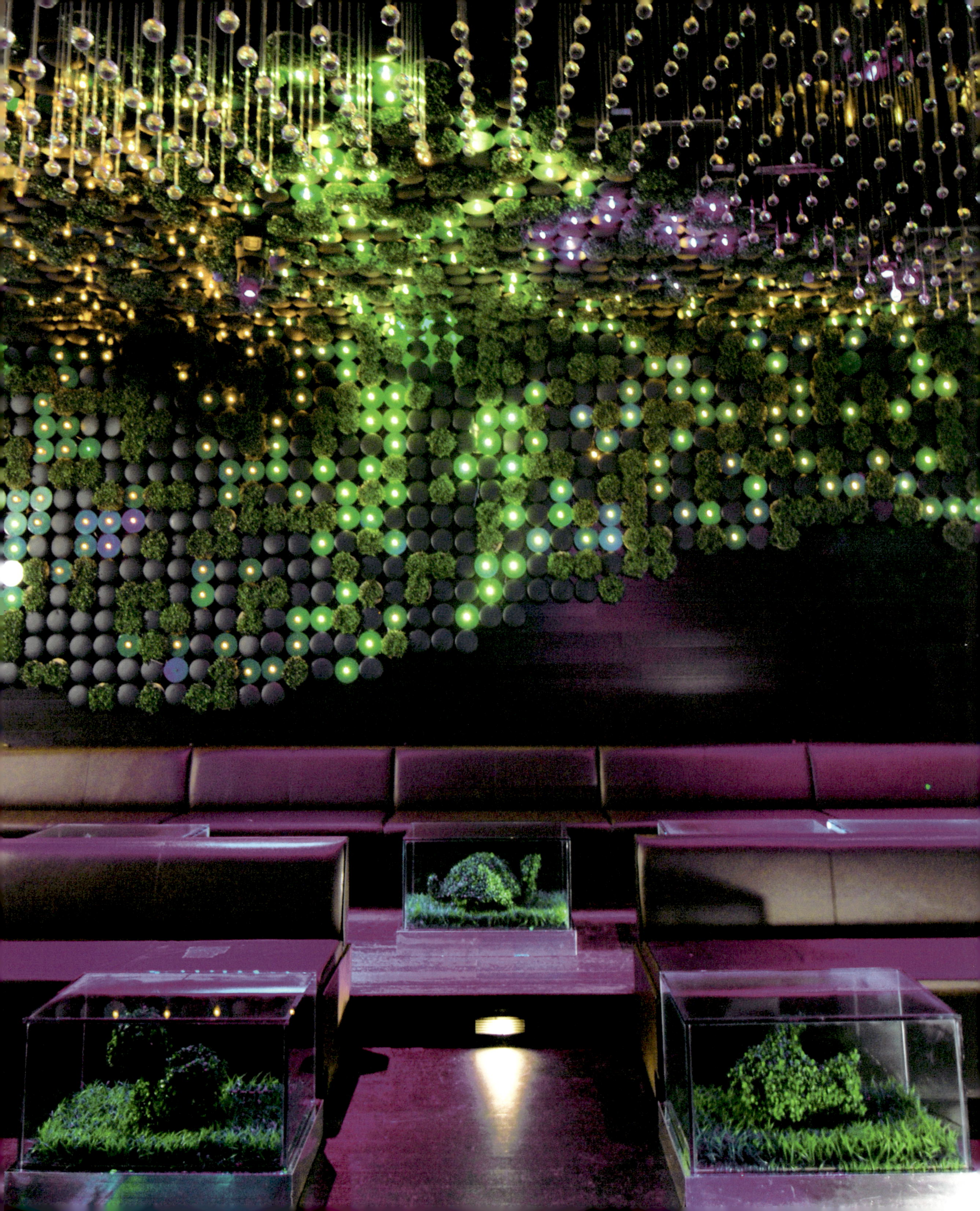

Index

0–9

14SD
www.14sd.com

OMOTESANDO KOFFEE → 172–173
/ Year: 2011
/ Photos: Shikohin-Kenkyu-sho

3GATTI China
www.3gatti.com

ZEBAR → 102–103
/ Year: 2006
/ Architect/Designer: Francesco Gatti
/ Photos: 3GATTI China

71 Arquitectos
www.71arquitectos.com

POISON D'AMOUR → 256–257
/ Year: 2011
/ Architects/Designers: 71 Arquitectos and David Carqueijeiro
/ Photos: Joao Morgado—Architectural Photography
/ Additional Credits: In cooperation with David Carqueijeiro; Coordination: Emanuel Romão; Collaboration: Paula Lemos Romão; Arnaud De Lanève; Editor: Ricardo Henriques; Measurements: Dibato; Technical Facilities: Sublimerito—Projectos e Consultadoria; Constructor: Qualiflat, lda; Catering Equipment: Sovithen, lda

A

a21studio
www.a21studio.com.vn

LAM CAFÉ → 70–71
/ Year: 2011
/ Architects/Designers: Hiệp Hòa Nguyễn, Nhơn Quí Nguyễn
/ Photos: Hiroyuki Oki

Affect Studio
www.affectstudio.com

HASHI MORI → 106–107
/ Year: 2012
/ Photos: Affect Studio

Afroditi Krassa
www.afroditi.com

DISHOOM BOMBAY CAFÉ → 30–31
/ Year: 2010
/ Photos: Sim Canetty-Clarke

Andrin Schweizer Company
www.andrinschweizer.ch

AZZURRO → 126–129
/ Year: 2011

Andy Martin Architects
www.andymartinstudio.com

CHAN → 100–101
/ Year: 2011
/ Photos: Vangelis Paterakis
/ Additional Credits: Project Team: Andy Martin, Art Waewsawangwong, Daniel Rodriguez, Tom Davies; Graphic Design: Farrow; Upholstery Design: Yulia Bakhtiozina

Antonio Di Oronzo
www.bluarch.com

GREENHOUSE → 280–281
/ Year: 2008
/ Photos: ADO

JULIET SUPPERCLUB → 276–277
/ Year: 2009
/ Photos: ADO

António Louro (MOOV)
www.moov.pt

KITCHAIN → 202–203
/ Year: 2009
/ Architects/Designers: António Louro, Benedetta Maxia
/ Photos: António Louro and Benedetta Maxia
/ Additional Credits: In cooperation with Festival Belluard Bollwerk

Atelier Chan Chan
www.atelierchanchan.com

RIDLEY'S → 218–219
/ Year: 2011
/ Photos: Dosfotos, Rachel Ferriman
/ Additional Credits: In cooperation with The Decorators; Graphic Design: Guglielmo Rossi

Aulík Fišer Architekti
www.afarch.cz

THE RED PIF WINE DEPOT & GARDEN → 166–167
/ Year: 2011
/ Photos: AI photography

AVA Architects
www.ava-architects.com

BAR LA BOHÈME (ENTRE AMIS) → 164–165
/ Year: 2011
/ Architects/Designers: Carlos and Rui Veloso
/ Photos: José Campos, Arqf.net

B

Barbara and Fellows
www.barbaraandfellows.com.au

PLANTATION COFFEE → 178–179
/ Year: 2011
/ Architects/Designers: Adele Winteridge, Brooke Thorn and Jennifer Lowe
/ Photos: Tracey Lee Hayes
/ Additional Credits: In cooperation with Foolscap Studio

Baranowitz Kronenberg Architecture
www.bkarc.com

JAFFA → 156–157
/ Year: 2011
/ Photos: Amit Geron

ZOZOBRA NOODLE BAR → 80–81
/ Year: 2011
/ Photos: Amit Geron

Bastille Metal Works
www.bastillemetalworks.com

LA SOCIÉTÉ BISTRO → 260
/ Year: August, 2011
/ Photos: Mc Images
/ Additional Credits: Bastille Metal Works worked with R&R Woodwork to create the custom bar top, while Munge and Leung worked on the design and décor.

THE HOTEL MONTELEONE CAROUSEL BAR → 261
/ Year: 2011
/ Photos: Azim Aghil
/ Additional Credits: In cooperation with the Puccini Group to assist with the overall design concept.

Baulhús
www.baulhus.com

KEX HOSTEL → 208
/ Year: 2011
/ Photos: Börkur Sigþórsson
/ Additional Credits: The Sugarpillows

Benedetta Maxia
www.kitchain.net

KITCHAIN → 202–203
/ Year: 2009
/ Architects/Designers: António Louro, Benedetta Maxia
/ Photos: António Louro and Benedetta Maxia
/ Additional Credits: In cooperation with Festival Belluard Bollwerk

bfs design
www.bfs-design.com

KOCHHAUS → 142–143
/ Year: 2011
/ Architects/Designers: Stefan Flachsbarth & Michael Schultz, Rejne Rittel
/ Photos: Annette Kisling

Blacksheep
www.blacksheepweb.com

NANDO'S ASHFORD → 10–11
/ Year: 2011
/ Architects/Designers: Tim Mutton, Ben Webb and Mark Leib
/ Photos: Ben Webb

JAMIE ITALIAN WESTFIELD → 12–13
/ Year: 2008
/ Architects/Designers: Bill McGrath and Jordan Littler
/ Photos: Gareth Gardner

UNION JACKS → 14–15
/ Year: 2012
/ Photos: Gareth Gardner

brandherm + krumrey interior architecture
www.b-k-i.de

PRINCESS CHEESECAKE → 186–187
/ Year: 2011
/ Architects/Designers: Sabine Krumrey and Melanie Leigers, Production Design by Julia Miske
/ Photos: Foto: Katy Otto
/ Additional Credits: Constructor: Andre Schowin, Objektbau Berlin

Brian Shebairo
www.pdtnyc.com

PDT (PLEASE DON'T TELL) BAR → 252–253
/ Year: 2009
/ Photos: Michael Taft

Brinkworth
www.brinkworth.co.uk

DABBOUS → 148–149
/ Year: 2012
/ Architects/Designers: Karen Byford, Kevin Brennan, Anja Haerter
/ Photos: Louise Melchior

C

CADENA+ASOC.
www.cadena-asociados.com

CIELITO QUERIDO CAFÉ → 16–17
/ Year: 2010
/ Architects/Designers: Ignacio Cadena and Hector Esrawe
/ Photos: Jaime Navarro
/ Additional Credits: In cooperation with Esrawe Studio; Branding: CADENA+ASOC. ®, Ignacio Cadena; Collaborators: Rocío Serna González; Interiorism: Esrawe Studio, Hector Esrawe; Project Direction: Jorge Bracho. Project Coordination: Joaquín Cevallos; Project Leader: Eduardo Álvarez; Collaborators: Sara Casillas, Ian Castillo, Jennifer Sacal, Roberto Escalante, Didier López, Irvin Martínez, Arturo Gasca and Cynthia Cárdenas

Cadmium Architects and Designers
www.cadmiumdesign.co.uk

THE BACK ROOM → 250–251
/ Year: 2011

Chic by Accident Studio
www.chicbyaccident.com

M. N. ROY → 62–63
/ Year: 2011
/ Architects/Designers: Ludwig Godefroy, Emmanuel Picault
/ Photos: Ramiro Chaves
/ Additional Credits: In cooperation with Ludwig Godefroy; Marco Margain, Claudio Margain, Rodrigo Madrazo, Rodrigo Diaz-Frances, Paolo Montiel, Leon Larregui

Concrete Architectural Associates
www.concreteamsterdam.nl

MAZZO AMSTERDAM → 146–147
/ Year: 2010
/ Photos: Ewout Huibers

Couple
www.couple.com.sg

BRILL → 209
/ Year: 2008
/ Architects/Designers: Zann Wan and Kelvin Lok

CUT Architectures
www.cut-architectures.com

COUTUME CAFÉ → 158–159
/ Year: 2011
/ Architects/Designers: Benjamin Clarens and Yann Martin
/ Photos: David Foessel, Luc Boegly

D

David Carqueijeiro

POISON D'AMOUR → 256–257
/ Year: 2011
/ Architects/Designers: 71 Arquitectos and David Carqueijeiro
/ Photos: Joao Morgado—Architectural Photography
/ Additional Credits: In cooperation with 71 Arquitectos; Coordination: Emanuel Romão; Collaboration: Paula Lemos Romão; Arnaud De Lanève; Editor: Ricardo Henriques; Measurements: Dibato; Technical Facilities: Sublimerito—Projectos e Consultadoria; Constructor: Qualiflat, lda; Catering Equipment: Sovithen, lda

Design Bon_O
www.designbono.com

COFFEE THE SOL → 118–119
/ Year: 2012

design spirits
www.design-spirits.com

NISEKO LOOK OUT CAFÉ → 68–69
/ Year: 2010
/ Architect/Designer: Yuhkichi Kawai
/ Photos: Toshihide Kajiwara
/ Additional Credits: Lighting Consultant: muse-D Inc. Kazuhiko Suzuki, Misuzu Yagi

STARHILL TEA SALON → 258–259
/ Year: 2011
/ Architect/Designer: Yuhkichi Kawai
/ Photos: Toshihide Kajiwara
/ Additional Credits: Lighting Consultant: muse-D Inc. Kazuhiko Suzuki, Misuzu Yagi

STS CAFÉ → 82–83
/ Year: 2011
/ Architect/Designer: Yuhkichi Kawai
/ Photos: Toshihide Kajiwara

TEEQ → 274–275
/ Year: 2009
/ Architect/Designer: Yuhkichi Kawai
/ Photos: Zainudin Ashard
/ Additional Credits: Lighting Consultant: muse-D Inc.—Kazuhiko Suzuki

Dyer-Smith & Frey
www.dyersmith-frey.com

MONKEY BAR FUMOIR → 214–215
/ Year: 2010

E

Electrolux
newsroom.electrolux.com

THE CUBE → 86–87
/ Year: 2011

Esrawe Studio
www.esrawe.com

CIELITO QUERIDO CAFÉ → 16–17
/ Year: 2010
/ Architects/Designers: Ignacio Cadena and Hector Esrawe
/ Photos: Jaime Navarro
/ Additional Credits: In cooperation with CADENA+ASOC.; Branding: CADENA+ASOC. ®, Ignacio Cadena; Collaborators: Rocío Serna González; Interiorism: Esrawe Studio, Hector Esrawe; Project Direction: Jorge Bracho. Project Coordination: Joaquín Cevallos; Project Leader: Eduardo Álvarez; Collaborators: Sara Casillas, Ian Castillo, Jennifer Sacal, Roberto Escalante, Didier López, Irvin Martínez, Arturo Gasca and Cynthia Cárdenas

LA BIPOLAR → 44–45
/ Year: 2006
/ Architects/Designers: Jorge Mdahuar, Hector Esrawe
/ Photos: Jaime Navarro
/ Additional Credits: In cooperation with Mdahuar Diseño; Team: Rodrigo Díaz; Graphics: NaCo; Coordination: Jorge Mdahuar

TORI TORI → 76–77
/ Year: 2011
/ Architects/Designers: Michel Rojkind and Gerardo Salinas, Héctor Esrawe
/ Photos: Paúl Rivera
/ Additional Credits: In cooperation with Esrawe Studio; Rojkind Arquitectos (Architecture): Michel Rojkind (Founding Partner), Gerardo Salinas (Partner); Project Team: Tere Levy, Agustín Pereyra, Raúl Araiza, Carlos Alberto Ríos, Isaac Smeke J., Enrique F. de la Barrera, Daniela Bustamante, Daniel Hernández; Esrawe Studio (Industrial design, interiorism): Héctor Esrawe (Principal in Charge); Project Team: Ricardo Casas, Basia Pineda, Ian Castillo, Karianne Rygh, Alejandra Castelao, Jorge Bracho, Rodrigo L; Franco; Design Computational Consultants Kokkugia (Roland Snooks, Robert Stuart-Smith); Construction: ZDA desarrollo + arquitectura (Yuri Zagorin); Structural Engineering: Juan Felipe Heredia; Facade Engineering: GRUPO MAS (Eduardo Flores); M.E.P; QUANTUM Diseño; Lighting Design: luz en arquitectura (Kai Diederichsen); Audio & Video Design: NTX New Technology Experience; Landscape Design: Verde 360°; Furniture: Esrawe Studio; Kitchen: San-Son; Visualization: ©Glessner Group (www.glessnergroup.com); Interior Visualization: Esrawe Studio

F

Facet Studio
www.facetstudio.com.au

WATERMOON → 171
/ Year: 2010
/ Architects/Designers: Yoshihito Kashiwagi & Olivia Shih
/ Photos: Katherine Lu

Ferroconcrete
www.fruute.com

FRÜUTE → 121
/ Year: 2011
/ Architects/Designers: Owen Gee, Priscilla Jimenez, Ann Kim, Sunjoo Park, Wendy Thai
/ Photos: Priscilla Jiminez, Vanessa Stump

Festival Belluard Bollwerk
www.belluard.ch

KITCHAIN → 202–203
/ Year: 2009
/ Architects/Designers: António Louro, Benedetta Maxia
/ Photos: António Louro and Benedetta Maxia

Florian Weitzer
www.hoteldaniel.com

HOTEL DANIEL VIENNA → 210–213
/ Year: 2011
/ Photos: Marion Luttenberger

Foolscap Studio
www.foolscapstudio.com.au

PATRICIA COFFEE → 46–47
/ Year: 2011
/ Architect/Designer: Adele Winteridge
/ Photos: Ben Glezer
/ Additional Credits: Hooks created by Nick Hacket at NMH Metalworks; Kyran Starcevich, Makery Club/Andrew Hustwaite Snatch and Knackers

PLANTATION COFFEE → 178–179
/ Year: 2011
/ Architects/Designers: Adele Winteridge, Brooke Thorn and Jennifer Lowe
/ Photos: Tracey Lee Hayes
/ Additional Credits: In cooperation with Barbara and Fellows

INDEX

G

Gabriel Corchero Studio
www.gabrielcorchero.org

CHEESE BAR → 124–125
/ Year: 2011
/ Photos: Pascuale Caprile

GAD
www.gadarchitecture.com

BEŞIKTAŞ FISH MARKET → 144–145
/ Year: 2011
/ Architect/Designer: Gokhan Avcioglu
/ Photos: Ozlem Avcioglu, Ozan Ertug, Alp Eren
/ Additional Credits: Collaborator: Beşiktaş Municipality; Project Team: Serkan Cedetas, Gozde Demir, Tahsin Inanici

gh3 Architects and Landscape Architects
www.gh3.ca

SCARPETTA → 84–85
/ Year: 2009
/ Architects/Designers: Pat Hanson, Diana Gerrard, Raymond Chow, Stephen Wells
/ Photos: Dan Couto
/ Additional Credits: libyiv Design (staging and furnishing)

Giant Design
www.giantdesign.com

NOK NOK THAI EATING HOUSE → 72–73
/ Year: 2011
/ Photos: Andrew Worssam

Golucci International Design
www.golucci.com

SPICE SPIRIT RESTAURANT → 90–91
/ Year: 2012
/ Architect/Designer: Lee Hsuheng
/ Photos: Sun Xiangyu

YAKINIKU MASTER JAPANESE RESTAURANT → 66–67
/ Year: 2011
/ Photos: Golucci International Design (Beijing)

GXN
www.3xn.dk

NOMA LAB → 132–133
/ Year: 2012
/ Photos: Adam Mørk
/ Additional Credits: Project Director: Kasper Guldager Jørgensen, Head of GXN; Project Team: Kim Herforth Nielsen, Kasper Guldager Jørgensen, André van Leth, Lila Held, Morten Norman Lund, Lars-Erik Eriksson, Pedram Seddighzadeh, Matthew Scarlett, Bjørk Christensen, Kyle Baumgardner, Elliot Mistur, Tore Banke, Simon McKenzie and Jacob Hilmer

H

Honest Entertainment
www.honestentertainment.co.uk

DISHOOM CHOWPATTY BEACH BAR → 20–21
/ Year: 2011
/ Photos: Sim Canetty-Clarke

Hou de Sousa
www.houdesousa.com

DIM SUM BAR → 64–65
/ Year: 2011
/ Photos: Hou de Sousa

I

Ina-Matt
www.ina-matt.com

RESTAURANT STOCK → 38–39
/ Year: 2011
/ Photos: Miriam Bleeker, Inga Powililleit and Ina-Matt

Inne Design
www.innedesign.no

ADAMSTUEN → 194–195
/ Year: 2009
/ Architect/Designer: Int. Architect Vigdis A. Bergh MNIL
/ Photos: Mona Gundersen

MAJORSTUEN → 192–193
/ Year: 2008
/ Architect/Designer: Int. Architect Vigdis A. Bergh MNIL
/ Photos: Mona Gundersen

STRAND RESTAURANT → 190–191
/ Year: 2010
/ Architect/Designer: Int. Architect Vigdis A. Bergh MNIL
/ Photos: Mona Gundersen
/ Additional Credits: Graphic Designer Gina Rose

VINDEREN → 188–189
/ Year: 2008
/ Architect/Designer: Int. Architect Vigdis A. Bergh MNIL
/ Photos: Mona Gundersen

Interior workshop of Sergey Makhno
www.mahno.com.ua

TWISTER → 96–97
/ Year: 2012
/ Architects/Designers: Sergey Makhno, Vasiliy Butenko

Ippolito Fleitz Group – Identity Architects
www.ifgroup.org

BAR FOU FOU → 266–267
/ Year: 2009
/ Architects/Designers: Peter Ippolito, Gunter Fleitz, Tim Lessmann, Hakan Sakarya, Yuan Peng
/ Photos: Zooey Braun

DER SPIEGEL KANTINE → 92–95
/ Year: 2011
/ Architects/Designers: Peter Ippolito, Gunter Fleitz, Tilla Goldberg, Christian Kirschenmann, Tim Lessmann, Alexander Fehre, Christine Ackermann, Roger Gasperlin, Katja Heinemann
/ Photos: Zooey Braun
/ Additional Credits: Lighting Design: Pfarré Lighting Design, Munich

HOLYFIELDS FRANKFURT → 88–89
/ Year: 2010
/ Architects/Designers: Gunter Fleitz, Peter Ippolito, Michael Bertram, Bartlomiej Pluskota, Tilla Goldberg, Tim Lessmann, Moritz Köhler, Jörg Schmitt, Joss Hänisch
/ Photos: Zooey Braun
/ Additional Credits: Lighting Design Pfarré Lighting Design, Munich

WIENERWALD CORPORATE ARCHITECTURE → 54–55
/ Year: 2010
/ Architects/Designers: Peter Ippolito, Gunter Fleitz, Moritz Köhler, Tim Lessmann, Bartlomiej Pluskota, Yuan Peng
/ Photos: Zooey Braun

J

José Carlos Cruz
www.josecarloscruz.com

BAIXA → 264–265
/ Year: 2010
/ Photos: FG+SG—Fotografia de arquitectura
/ Additional Credits: Civil engineer: A400 Francisco Bernardo; Mechanics Engineer: GET Raul Bessa

K

k-studio
www.k-studio.gr

ALEMAGOU BEACH BAR → 134–135
/ Year: 2010
/ Photos: Yiorgos Kordakis

Kerry Phelan Design Office
www.kpdo.com.au

UPSTAIRS BERESFORD → 254–255
/ Year: 2011
/ Photos: Sharyn Cairns
/ Additional Credits: In collaboration with Stylist Sibella Court

Kinfolk
www.kinfolkmag.com

KINFOLK DINNER SERIES – BROOKLYN → 220–221
/ Year: 2012
/ Photos: Alice Gao

Kofler & Kompanie
www.koflerkompanie.com

THE MINOTAUR → 216–217
/ Year: 2011

L

Lime Studio
www.limestudio.co.uk

CELLO BAR → 34–35
/ Year: 2010
/ Photos: Panos Vasiliou

Luchetti Krelle
www.luchettikrelle.com

XANTHI → 272–273
/ Year: 2011
/ Photos: Murray Fredericks

Ludwig Godefroy
www.ludwiggodefroy.com

M. N. ROY → 62–63
/ Year: 2011
/ Architects/Designers: Ludwig Godefroy, Emmanuel Picault
/ Photos: Ramiro Chaves
/ Additional Credits: In cooperation with Chic by Accident Studio; Marco Margain, Claudio Margain, Rodrigo Madrazo, Rodrigo Diaz-Frances, Paolo Montiel, Leon Larregui

M

Mas Arquitectura
www.mas.es

PULPEIRA VILALÚA → 174–175
/ Year: 2011
/ Architect/Designer: Marcos Samaniego
/ Photos: Ana Samaniego

MatterMade
www.mattermatters.com

WALDEN → 150–151
/ Year: 2011
/ Photos: Ellen Warfield

Mdahuar Diseño

LA BIPOLAR → 44–45
/ Year: 2006
/ Architects/Designers: Jorge Mdahuar with Hector Esrawe
/ Photos: Jaime Navarro
/ Additional Credits: In cooperation with Esrawe Studio; Team: Rodrigo Díaz; Graphics: NaCo; Coordination: Jorge Mdahuar

Mikado Stolpercrew, Hanna Rix, Pentaklon, Katerholzig
www.katerholzig.de

KATERHOLZIG / KATERSCHMAUS → 206–207
/ Year: 2011
/ Photos: Carolin Saage

Mister Important Design
www.misterimportant.com

CHAMBERS EAT + DRINK → 262–263
/ Year: 2011
/ Architect/Designer: Charles Doell
/ Photos: Jeff Dow, The Rhoads Photography

N

Nika Zupanc
www.nikazupanc.com

AS APERITIVO → 268–271
/ Year: 2011
/ Additional Credits: Interior designed by Nika Zupanc; Design Team: Nika Zupanc, Jurij Krpan, Spela Rogel
/ Photos: Saša Hess

Norsman Architects
www.norsmanarchitects.com

CAFFE STREETS → 108–109
/ Year: 2011
/ Architect/Designer: Brent Norsman
/ Photos: Nikola Zlatkovic

Note Design Studio
www.notedesignstudio.se

CAFÉ FOAM → 50–51
/ Year: 2010
/ Photos: Stefano Barozzi

O

Odile Decq Benoit Cornette Architectes Urbanistes
www.odbc-paris.com

PHANTOM – RESTAURANT OF THE GARNIER OPERA → 98–99
/ Year: 2011
/ Photos: ODBC, Roland Halbe
/ Additional Credits: Structure Engineering: BATISERF Ingénierie; Facade Consultants: Odile Decq / HDA—Hugh Dutton Associates; Building Services Engineering: MS Consulting; Acoustics Engineering: Studio DAP; Fire Security Engineering: SETEC; Kitchen Consultants: C2A Architectes; Project Leaders: Peter Baalman, Giuseppe Savarese, Amélie Marchiset

oliv architekten ingenieure
www.oliv-architekten.com

SCHRANNENHALLE → 162–163
/ Year: 2011
/ Photos: Edzard Probst

Orbit Design Studio
www.orbitdesignstudio.com

ALLURE → 78–79
/ Year: 2010
/ Photos: Owen Raggett

Outofstock
www.outofstockdesign.com

HATCHED → 136–137
/ Year: 2010
/ Photos: Outofstock

P

PANORAMA
www.panoramahk.com

STAREIGHT → 278–279
/ Year: 2012
/ Architects/Designers: Horace Pan (Founder, PANORAMA), Alan Tse, Ardy Tsoi
/ Photos: Ng Siu Fung

Paul Burnham Architect
www.paulburnham.com.au

CLANCY'S FISHBAR → 22–25
/ Year: 2011
/ Photos: Jody D'Arcy
/ Additional Credits: Britt Mikkelsen

Paul Mogg, Oskar Melzer
www.moggandmelzer.com

MOGG & MELZER DELICATESSEN → 154–155
/ Year: 2012
/ Photos: Steve Herud

Protein
www.proteinos.com

PROTEIN TASTE ACADEMY → 204–205
/ Year: 2012

Puccini Group
www.puccinigroup.com

THE HOTEL MONTELEONE CAROUSEL BAR → 261
/ Year: 2011
/ Photos: Azim Aghil
/ Additional Credits: In cooperation with Bastille Metal Works

R

Rani al Rajji

THE KITCHEN AT THE CIRCUS HOTEL & APARTMENTS → 18–19
/ Year: 2011
/ Additional Credits: The design concept for the Circus Apartments as a whole was from Sandra Ernst (Germany). The specific concept for the ground floor cafe and lounge "the Kitchen" was by Rani al Rajji (Lebanon).

Rashed Alfoudari

UBON → 112–113
/ Year: 2011/2012
/ Photos: Rashed Alfoudari

Reiulf Ramstad Arkitekter
www.reiulframstadarkitekter.no

TROLLWALL RESTAURANT → 58–61
/ Year: Completed 2011
/ Photos: Reiulf Ramstad Arkitekter

Rejne Rittel

KOCHHAUS → 142–143
/ Year: 2011
/ Architects/Designers: Stefan Flachsbarth & Michael Schultz, Rejne Rittel

reVOLT
www.restaurangvolt.se

VOLT → 180–181
/ Year: 2012
/ Photos: Gustav Karlsson Frost, Morgan Ekner
/ Additional Credits: Illustrations by Björn Atldax, VÅR

Robin Howie
www.robinhowie.co.uk

FOOD FOR THOUGHT → 42–43
/ Year: 2012
/ Additional Credits: Stools designed by Tom Dixon

Rojkind Arquitectos
www.rojkindarquitectos.com

TORI TORI → 76–77
/ Year: 2011
/ Architects/Designers: Michel Rojkind and Gerardo Salinas, Héctor Esrawe
/ Photos: Paúl Rivera
/ Additional Credits: In cooperation with Esrawe Studio; Rojkind Arquitectos (Architecture): Michel Rojkind (Founding Partner), Gerardo Salinas (Partner); Project Team: Tere Levy, Agustín Pereyra, Raúl Araiza, Carlos Alberto Ríos, Isaac Smeke J., Enrique F. de la Barrera, Daniela Bustamante, Daniel Hernández; Esrawe Studio (Industrial design, interiorism): Héctor Esrawe (Principal in Charge); Project Team: Ricardo Casas, Basia Pineda, Ian Castillo, Karianne Rygh, Alejandra Castelao, Jorge Bracho, Rodrigo L; Franco; Design Computational Consultants Kokkugia (Roland Snooks, Robert Stuart-Smith); Construction: ZDA desarrollo + arquitectura (Yuri Zagorin); Structural Engineering: Juan Felipe Heredia; Facade Engineering: GRUPO MAS (Eduardo Flores); M.E.P; QUANTUM Diseño; Lighting Design: luz en arquitectura (Kai Diederichsen); Audio & Video Design: NTX New Technology Experience; Landscape Design: Verde 360°; Furniture: Esrawe Studio; Kitchen: San-Son; Visualization: ©Glessner Group (www.glessnergroup.com); Interior Visualization: Esrawe Studio

S

Sandra Tarruella Interioristas
www.sandratarruella.com

L'OBRADOR DEL MOLI → 160–161
/ Year: 2010

LA CANTINA → 170
/ Year: 2011

ROCAMBOLESC → 36–37
/ Year: 2012

Saraiva + Associados
www.saraivaeassociados.com

SUSHI CAFE AVENIDA → 104–105
/ Year: 2011
/ Architect/Designer: Miguel Saraiva
/ Photos: Fernando Guerra, FG+SG

INDEX

Sasufi
www.sasufi.net

SLOWPOKE ESPRESSO
→ 196–197
/ Year: 2011
/ Architect/Designer: Anne-Sophie Poirier
/ Photos: Anne-Sophie Poirier

Sawako Okochi

OTAKARA SUPPER CLUB
→ 200–201
/ Year: 2011
/ Photos: Alice Gao

Shai Akram & Andrew Haythornthwaite
www.shaiakram.co.uk

THE BOOK CLUB → 198–199
/ Year: 2010
/ Photos: Sylvain Deleu

SHH
www.shh.co.uk

BARBICAN LOUNGE → 138–139
/ Year: 2010
/ Architect/Designer: Helen Hughes
/ Photos: Gareth Gardner
/ Additional Credits: .PSLAB—Lighting Designers

BARBICAN FOODHALL
→ 140–141
/ Year: 2010
/ Architect/Designer: Helen Hughes
/ Photos: Gareth Gardner
/ Additional Credits: .PSLAB—Lighting Design

Space
www.spacecph.dk

KØDBYENS FISKEBAR
→ 152–153
/ Year: 2009
/ Photos: Thomas Ibsen, Thomas Busk

Stephan Landwehr, Boris Radczun
www.paulysaal.com

PAULY SAAL → 248–249
/ Year: 2012
/ Photos: Stefan Korte

Stoyanov
www.delaespada.com

7 ENOTECA & PIZZERIA
→ 244–247
/ Year: 2011
/ Photos: Peter Fritz
/ Architect/Designer: Brayan Stoyanov
/ Additional Credits: Colombo Dining Armchair and Fin Dining Chair designed by Matthew Hilton and manufactured by De La Espada

Studio Greiling
www.katringreiling.com

DESIGN BAR → 40–41
/ Year: 2011
/ Photos: Katrin Greiling

Studio MODE
www.studiomode.eu

GRAFFITI CAFÉ → 116–117
/ Year: 2011
/ Photos: 3inSpirit

StudioSKLIM
www.sklim.com

THE TASTINGS ROOM
→ 176–177
/ Year: 2011
/ Photos: Jeremy San

Stylt Trampoli
www.stylt.se

STATIONEN UPPSALA THREE
→ 234–235
/ Year: 2011
/ Architect/Designer: Erik Nissen Johansen
/ Photos: Erik Nissen Johansen

GRIFFINS STEAKHOUSE EXTRAORDINAIRE → 236–241
/ Year: 2011
/ Architect/Designer: Erik Nissen Johansen
/ Photos: Erik Nissen Johansen

BON → 242–243
/ Year: 2011
/ Architect/Designer: Erik Nissen Johansen
/ Photos: Erik Nissen Johansen

SUE Architekten
www.sue-architekten.at

GMOA KELLER → 114–115
/ Year: 2011
/ Photos: Herta Hurnaus

SURFACE3
www.surface3.com

DE FARINE ET D'EAU FRAÎCHE → 184–185
/ Year: 2011
/ Photos: Vladimir Antaki, SURFACE3

T

The Decorators
www.the-decorators.net

RIDLEY'S → 218–219
/ Year: 2011
/ Photos: Dosfotos, Rachel Ferriman
/ Additional Credits: In cooperation with Atelier ChanChan; Graphic Design: Guglielmo Rossi

The Metrics
www.metricsdesigngroup.com

WHAT HAPPENS WHEN → 28–29
/ Year: 2011
/ Architects/Designers: Elle Kunnos de Voss and Emilie Baltz
/ Photos: Felix de Voss

Tiliche
www.tiliche.com

CANTINA DE COMIDA MEXICANA → 168–169
/ Year: 2011
/ Photos: Tiliche

Tobias Partners
www.delaespada.com

THE BRIDGE ROOM → 122–123
/ Year: 2011
/ Architect/Designer: Nick Tobias
/ Photos: Michele Aboud
/ Additional Credits: Deer Chair designed by Autoban and manufactured by De La Espada

Toykio
www.toykio.com

TOYKIO → 26–27
/ Year: 2011
/ Photos: Nicola Roman Walbeck

V

Von Tundra
www.vontundra.com

SIP MOBILE LODGE → 120
/ Year: 2011
/ Architects/Designers: Dan Anderson, Chris Held, Brian Pietrowski
/ Photos: Darryl James

W

Wonderwall
www.wonder-wall.com

OZONE → 228–233
/ Year: 2011

THE SOHO: THE CANTEEN → 130–131
/ Year: 2010
/ Architect/Designer: Masamichi Katayama
/ Photos: Kozo Takayama

Workshop of Wonders
www.workshopofwonders.nl

SMOKING CLUB HI/LO
→ 224–227
/ Year: 2011
/ Architect/Designer: Gerrit Vos
/ Photos: Kasia Gatkowska
/ Additional Credits: Total concept, design, art direction, project management, lighting and furnishing by Workshop of Wonders; Wall Art 'heaven' by Shop Around creative supermarket; Name, logo and visual identity by Dietwee—brand, design and communication

Y

Y.A. studio
www.ya-studio.com

FRJTZ DINING ROOM → 48–49
/ Year: 2008
/ Photos: Lucas Fladzinski
/ Additional Credits: Yakuh Askew, Kelly Waters

Yolanda Vilalta and Helena Jaumá

CAFÉ KAFKA → 32–33
/ Year: 2011

Z

Zweidrei Medienarchitektur
www.zweidrei.eu

EFA'S BOX → 74–75
/ Year: 2011
/ Architect/Designer: Dipl. Ing. Julius G. Kranefuss
/ Photos: Sittig Fahr-Becker
/ Additional Credits: Emma Billham, Claudia Herrmann, Maja Lesnik, Adrian Meredith, Clément Barbier

Zwei Interiors Architecture
www.zwei.com.au

ELEVEN INCH PIZZERIA → 52–53
/ Year: 2012
/ Photos: Michael Kai
/ Additional Credits: Logo designed by Salmon Design

Let's Go Out!

Interiors and Architecture for Restaurants and Bars

Edited by Robert Klanten, Sven Ehmann, and Sofia Borges
Text and preface by Shonquis Moreno

Layout by Jonas Herfurth and Floyd E. Schulze for Gestalten
Cover by Jonas Herfurth for Gestalten
Cover photography (top to bottom): As Aperitivo by Saša Hess, Dishoom Bombay Café by Sim Canetty-Clarke, Smoking Club Hi/Lo by Kasia Gatkowska, De Farine et d'Eau Fraîche by SURFACE3, Café Foam by Stefano Barozzi
Typefaces: Jakko by Émilie Rigaud, Romain BP by Ian Party, Neuzeit by Wilhelm Pischner

Project management by Rebekka Wangler for Gestalten
Project management assistance by Lucie Ulrich for Gestalten
Production management by Janine Milstrey for Gestalten
Proofreading by Bettina Klein
Printed by Optimal Media GmbH, Röbel
Made in Germany

Published by Gestalten, Berlin 2012
ISBN 978-3-89955-451-9

© Die Gestalten Verlag GmbH & Co. KG, Berlin 2012
All rights reserved. No part of this publication may be reproduced or transmitted in any form or by any means, electronic or mechanical, including photocopy or any storage and retrieval system, without permission in writing from the publisher.

Respect copyrights, encourage creativity!

For more information, please visit www.gestalten.com.

/ Bibliographic information published by the Deutsche Nationalbibliothek. The Deutsche Nationalbibliothek lists this publication in the Deutsche Nationalbibliografie; detailed bibliographic data are available online at http://dnb.d-nb.de.

/ None of the content in this book was published in exchange for payment by commercial parties or designers; Gestalten selected all included work based solely on its artistic merit.

/ This book was printed according to the internationally accepted ISO 14001 standards for environmental protection, which specify requirements for an environmental management system.

/ This book was printed on paper certified by the FSC®.

FSC MIX Paper from responsible sources FSC® C108521
www.fsc.org

/ Gestalten is a climate-neutral company. We collaborate with the non-profit carbon offset provider myclimate (www.myclimate.org) to neutralize the company's carbon footprint produced through our worldwide business activities by investing in projects that reduce CO_2 emissions (www.gestalten.com/myclimate).

myclimate
Protect our planet